Players of Shakespeare 5

This is the fifth volume of essays by actors with the Royal Shakespeare Company and the National Theatre on their interpretations of major Shakespearian roles. The twelve essays discuss fourteen roles in twelve different productions between 1999 and 2002. The productions covered include three plays that have not featured before in the series: *The Comedy of Errors*, *A Midsummer Night's Dream* and *Antony and Cleopatra*. The contributors are Philip Voss, Ian Hughes, Aidan McArdle, Zoë Waites, Matilda Ziegler, Alexandra Gilbreath, Antony Sher, David Tennant, Michael Pennington, Simon Russell Beale, Richard McCabe, Frances de la Tour and the late Nigel Hawthorne. The title roles in three of the major tragedies – *Hamlet*, *King Lear* and *Macbeth* – are covered and there is also an essay on Iago in *Othello*. A brief biographical note is provided for each of the contributors and an introduction places the essays in the context of the Stratford and London stages.

D1231319

792.950941 Pla

Players of Shakespeare. 5.

PRICE: $34.95 (3559/go)

Players of Shakespeare 5

edited by
Robert Smallwood

CAMBRIDGE
UNIVERSITY PRESS

PUBLISHED BY THE PRESS SYNDICATE OF THE UNIVERSITY OF CAMBRIDGE
The Pitt Building, Trumpington Street, Cambridge, United Kingdom

CAMBRIDGE UNIVERSITY PRESS
The Edinburgh Building, Cambridge, CB2 2RU, UK
40 West 20th Street, New York, NY 10011–4211, USA
477 Williamstown Road, Port Melbourne, VIC 3207, Australia
Ruiz de Alarcón 13, 28014 Madrid, Spain
Dock House, The Waterfront, Cape Town 8001, South Africa

http://www.cambridge.org

© Cambridge University Press 2003

This book is in copyright. Subject to statutory exception
and to the provisions of relevant collective licensing agreements,
no reproduction of any part may take place without
the written permission of Cambridge University Press.

First published 2003

Printed in the United Kingdom at the University Press, Cambridge

Typeface Plantin 10.25/13 pt.   *System* LATEX 2ε   [TB]

A catalogue record for this book is available from the British Library

Library of Congress cataloguing in publication data
Players of Shakespeare 5; edited by Robert Smallwood.
p.   cm.
Includes bibliographical references and index.
ISBN 0 521 81131 7
1. Shakespeare, William, 1564–1616 – Stage history – 1950–   2. Shakespeare, William,
1564–1616 – Characters.   3. Theater – England – History – 20th century.   4. Royal
Shakespeare Company.   5. Acting.   I. Title: Players of Shakespeare five.
II. Smallwood, R. L. (Robert Leo)   III. Royal Shakespeare Company.
PR3112.P557   2004   792.9'5'0941 – dc21   2003053193

ISBN 0 521 81131 7 hardback

Contents

Illustrations

Sources

2: Photograph, Hugo Glendinning; © The Royal Shakespeare
Company.

17 and 18: Photographs, Catherine Ashmore; © Catherine Ashmore.

All other illustrations: Photographer, Malcolm Davies, The Shakespeare Centre Library, Stratford-upon-Avon; © The Shakespeare Birthplace Trust.

Preface

This fifth volume in the *Players of Shakespeare* series follows the basic pattern (with which most readers will by now be familiar) of its predecessors in presenting a series of essays by actors on their preparation for, and performance of, major Shakespearian roles. The twelve essays offered here discuss fourteen performances in twelve productions that were to be seen between 1999 and 2002, all but one of them productions by the Royal Shakespeare Company. The exception is the essay on Hamlet by Simon Russell Beale, a performance given in John Caird's 2000–2001 National Theatre production. Eight of the roles are new to the *Players of Shakespeare* series, and three plays – *The Comedy of Errors*, *A Midsummer Night's Dream*, and *Antony and Cleopatra* – make their first appearance in it. The essay jointly written by Zoë Waites and Matilda Ziegler on the intimately connected roles of Viola and Olivia in *Twelfth Night* takes its cue from the joint essay in an earlier volume in the series on those other intimately connected comedy heroines, Rosalind and Celia. Of the fourteen roles dealt with in the volume, seven are (in the Folio's broad categorizations) from comedies and seven from tragedies, with a sequence of essays in the latter category on many of the major roles in Shakespearian tragedy. That the author of one of these did not live to see his essay in print is a source of profound regret for me, though it remains a great privilege to be editor of the volume that includes the late Sir Nigel Hawthorne's reflections on his last role in the theatre. Those interested in the history plays should not assume that their complete absence from this fifth volume in the series has any sinister implications: a sixth *Players of Shakespeare* collection is nearing completion and will be devoted exclusively to productions of the histories, from the RSC's Millennium 'This England' project, and later. That only four of the fourteen essayists here are women may well reflect (or even exceed) the ratio of women's to men's roles in Shakespeare's plays, but has nevertheless diverged from the editor's rather more equitable original intentions: not every invitation, sadly, produces the hoped-for essay.

The essays in the volume appear in the Folio order of plays; quotations and references are, as usual, from the New Penguin Shakespeare, the edition most likely to be issued to RSC actors in rehearsal. There is a biographical note on the writer, with emphasis on Shakespearian work, at the beginning of each essay, and at the end of the volume there is a list of credits for the twelve productions covered.

I am grateful to Susan Brock and Helen Hargest at the Shakespeare Centre Library for their patient assistance with photographs of Stratford productions and for help with many other matters archival, to Louise Ray of the National Theatre Archive for her kind assistance with photographs of the production of *Hamlet*, and to Jane Ellis of the RSC Press Office for her patience in helping to locate one of the photographs of the production of *The Tempest*. Nearly all the essays here derive from question-and-answer sessions between actors and students on the international programme of university courses jointly sponsored at the Shakespeare Centre in Stratford by the Shakespeare Birthplace Trust and the Shakespeare Institute of the University of Birmingham, for the direction of which, until my recent retirement, I was for many years responsible. I am grateful to colleagues in both organizations for their friendship and encouragement; to Victoria Cooper, of Cambridge University Press, for her continued commitment to this series, as well as for her patience with the sometimes attenuated process of bringing these collections of essays together; and, above all, to Sonja Dosanjh, RSC Company Manager in Stratford through the period covered by these essays, who arranged all of the question-and-answer sessions from which most of them derive and whose friendship and support in bridging that – I sometimes like to think – gradually narrowing gap between theatrical and academic Shakespeare has made this volume, and this series, possible.

EASTHAM, WORCESTERSHIRE

Introduction

ROBERT SMALLWOOD

'The RSC contacted various parole boards round the country and arranged for me to meet two murderers – on separate occasions – two men who'd served their time and were back in society.' Thus writes Sir Antony Sher in his essay later in this volume on a stage in the process of preparation for his performance of Macbeth – murderer, regicide, infanticide. Like all the actors whose reflexions on fourteen Shakespearian roles make up this book, Sher's task takes him on a journey to rarely trodden areas of experience at the furthest reaches of human feeling and behaviour. Few of us have killed a king, wielded magical power that allowed us to wreak vengeance on our enemies after a twelve-year wait, been instructed to kill our uncles by our fathers' ghosts, enjoyed an *alter ego* existence as the globe-circling (in forty minutes) servant and companion to the Fairy King, come face to face with an identical twin brother after half a lifetime or, while pretending to be a statue, been reunited with a husband after sixteen years of supposed death. Coming to terms with the extraordinary demands that the performance of a major Shakespearian role makes, reaching out to discover, and encompass, and communicate the extremes of experience that it explores, requires a sensitivity and breadth of imagination, a responsiveness to the nuances of poetic language, and even a level of physical fitness that are easy to take for granted as one is swept up in the process of observing and responding to a performance.

The essays that follow offer some insights into the ways in which this series of important Shakespearian performances came into being: into the balance of instinct and judgement, of artistry and technique in the creation of the role; into the rewarding (and sometimes less rewarding) aspects of developing a relationship with the audience; into the sheer hard work of preparation and rehearsal; and into the delicate issue of how the actor's conception of the character relates to the world that the director and designer have established for the production. Of their conceptions of the characters they were chosen to play, and the ways in which they were realized in performance, the essayists may speak for themselves; it is the task of this Introduction to try to characterize in general terms the productions within which their performances were to be seen.

If one considers the options in fairly broad and general terms, there are basically four main routes followed by modern Shakespeare directors in creating a world in which a play's events may seem plausibly to take place: the setting may present an historical recreation of the period of the play's composition – or, perhaps, of the period in which its events, historical or fictional, take place; it may offer the play boldly in modern dress; it may place the play in an historical period somewhere between Shakespeare's time and that of the production; or it may avoid the issue of historical period altogether, either through the evasion of period-specific images or through multi-period eclecticism and anachronism. It is immediately conspicuous that none of the productions dealt with in this volume strictly follows the first route and only *Macbeth* unequivocally follows the second, though *A Midsummer Night's Dream* comes close. The other ten productions represented here all take a version of either the third or fourth routes. Among those choosing a setting between Shakespeare's time and our own, the period most favoured by this particular group of directors (and in this they are perhaps not altogether unrepresentative of current trends) is the late nineteenth and early twentieth century: the productions of *Twelfth Night*, *The Winter's Tale*, and *Othello* dealt with in the following pages all belong very firmly in those few decades. *The Tempest* is there too, though less consistently and clearly, with *The Comedy of Errors* set a few decades later, in the world of 1930s and 1940s cinema. The remaining five productions followed the fourth route of escaping from any precise sense of specific period, *Romeo and Juliet*, *Timon of Athens*, and *Antony and Cleopatra* achieving this largely through a sort of eclecticism; *Hamlet*, though it gave a general impression of the Jacobean, by avoiding period-specific images; and Ninagawa's *King Lear*, by offering the play in a setting largely (but not exclusively or consistently) invoking an earlier era of Japanese history (and theatre), and thus presenting British audiences with the least familiar environment, perhaps, of any of the productions represented in this volume.

James MacDonald's production of *The Tempest* was created to tour, most of its venues being in towns without permanent theatres, so that it travelled, like many earlier productions in the RSC regional touring tradition, to sports halls and leisure complexes and community centres, to anywhere, indeed, suitable for the erection of its 'module' – which included everything, as those involved with these regional tours are fond of saying, from the set and the auditorium (with all its seats), to the iron and the ironing-board. In London and in Stratford, however, it played what at the time were the RSC's principal studio spaces, the Pit and the Other Place, both soon to be vacated and the Other Place closed, lamentably, as part of the devastating RSC reorganization of 2000–1, the Thatcherite version of a 'Cultural Revolution' known as 'Project Fleet'.

MacDonald's version of *The Tempest*, the last RSC Shakespeare production to be seen at the Other Place, was, then, an example of 'studio Shakespeare', that genre in which the Company has achieved some of its most notable productions of recent decades, but which, with the loss of its studio spaces, is (temporarily, one must hope) now beyond its reach. Its set was basically a white platform curving in wave-like undulations to a steep slope at the back, down which Ariel made gracefully speedy entrances and on which Trinculo and Stephano struggled in drunken clumsiness. The platform presented actors to audience in close proximity, and allowed Philip Voss's Prospero to engage spectators directly in his long narrative recollection in the play's second scene. Behind it, on a white back wall, video images were projected – of rolling, and sometimes crashing, waves, or (for the masque) of ripening corn, or (for the pursuit of Stephano and his companions at the end of Act Four) of a chase through undergrowth filmed at ground level. These projections created what many thought an eerie, dream-like background to the action (and others, of course, thought a tiresome distraction from it). A musical score of 'mouth-music', performed to nonsense syllables by six singers visible throughout the performance and acting as Ariel's attendant spirits (though dressed in the black sweaters and trousers of stage hands), provided a haunting mixture of other-worldly sounds, sometimes of ethereal beauty, sometimes of incessant, rhythmic threat, and insisted that the isle was indeed 'full of noises'. The costumes of most of the visitors to the island seemed to place the action somewhere in the late nineteenth or early twentieth century and the evening dress, complete with top-hat, which Prospero, as 'sometime Milan' (v.i.86), donned for the final scene was fairly specifically of 1900 or so; but his and Miranda's everyday island garb might have belonged to any (or none) of several decades on either side of that, while the costumes and behaviour, as well

3

as the physique, of Trinculo and Stephano alluded directly to the films of Laurel and Hardy. In this engagingly puzzling non-specific world, then, of shifting temporality, of realistic images made unreal and distant by two-dimensional video projection, and of abstract music eerily performed by physically matter-of-fact stage functionaries, Philip Voss created the performance of Prospero about which he writes in the first essay of this collection.

That little excursion to the world of film in the Stephano and Trinculo scenes of James MacDonald's touring production of *The Tempest* at the end of 2000 had been a much more extensive cinematic tour earlier in the year in Lynne Parker's production of *The Comedy of Errors* on Stratford's main stage. *Casablanca, The Road to Morocco,* the Keystone Cops, Harold Lloyd – the allusions were pervasive. The evening began with the Duke's arrival in Aegeon's cell – where the sound of dripping water echoed ominously (and melodramatically) – by a lift straight out of film-noir, and reached its farcical climax, before the arrival of the Abbess and the dénouement, with a Mack Sennett chase that involved the entire cast, street-Arab-salesman First Merchant, comic-Cossack Second Merchant, B-movie-sex-siren Courtesan, pantomime camel, and even a medieval knight in armour, Sir Walter Blount, and on occasions Falstaff too, from the *Henry IV* plays performing next door at the Swan Theatre.

Within this allusive and unreal world, the visitors from Syracuse, David Tennant as Antipholus and Ian Hughes as Dromio, established a relationship of master and servant that contrasted a touching human immediacy and interdependence with the insubstantial world of celluloid memories in which they existed. They had, one realized, been together on their eastern Mediterranean wanderings for years, these two, finding amusement in the absurdity of their little wit-combats and reassurance in their cheerful familiarity with each other to help them deal with the strangers, and the strangenesses, they encountered on their travels. Long acquaintance, too, had made them well-practised in their little stage routines – partaking of the elegant picnics, complete with check napkins, that Dromio produced from his suitcase, or acting as feed and front man for the big set piece on Nell, she of 'an ell and three quarters' (III.ii.115) – tape measure of course ready to hand to demonstrate – in breadth. As the glorious coincidences of the romance dénouement separated Dromio from his master-friend, one watched with some apprehension his only solo scene with his new companion, his twin brother, in the final moments of the play. And here, once more – and absolutely rightly for this production – the film motif took over again; for it was not with that touching final couplet that the production ended, but with a little dance between the Dromios, to the Laurel and Hardy theme tune.

Michael Boyd's 1999 production of *A Midsummer Night's Dream*, also for Stratford's main stage, in more or less modern dress, presented the court of Duke (or, it rather seemed, Dictator-Chairman) Theseus as a grey, frosty, totalitarian world, where his fiancée Hippolyta sat glowering in bitter captive resentment. Here Aidan McArdle's bespectacled and bowler-hatted Philostrate prompted polite, soulless applause at their leader's pronouncements from courtiers who stood, wrapped in great overcoats and fur hats against the cold (meteorological and spiritual), in an obedient semi-circle before the semi-circular grey walls of the set. The move to the forest began with the production's very first intimations of colour, as plastic flowers thrust their way through the floor of the stage following the mechanicals' exit after their first rehearsal, and a fur-hatted and rather clerkly lady courtier bent to pick them, Philostrate sidling up behind her as she did so; the sexual energy which transformed that moment as Philostrate and the clerkly lady stripped each other down to release Puck and the First Fairy/Peaseblossom is described in Aidan McArdle's essay.

The forest where they dwelt was an unpredictable and disturbing world of many trap-doors, through which ladders pretending to be trees would ascend and fairies with horrible hair-styles and alarmingly twitchy and disconcertingly random gestures would erupt; while from the flies swung Oberon's plastic-covered armchair-throne or a bedstead purporting to be a bank where the wild thyme blows. On the latter Titania and Bottom would later make their vertical interval exit in braying, thumping ecstasy. Presiding over this fairy kingdom was Nicholas Jones's intense and dominating Oberon, little hieroglyphic tattoos on his shaven head producing a curiously mesmerizing effect, trying in vain to control the wild and wayward Puck of Aidan McArdle, quintessentially 'rude' (as the actor calls him in his essay), rushing round with a watering-can and a wheelbarrow full of potting compost as he planted love-in-idleness, and its antidote, in the groins of his victims.

The Illyria of Lindsay Posner's 2001 *Twelfth Night*, also a Stratford main house production, was a very English place. Matilda Ziegler's Olivia was mistress of a country mansion in the years just before the First

World War, ancestral portraits on the walls (with a couple of Aubrey Beardsley prints that were presumably her own addition to the collection), grandfather clock ready to upbraid them all with the waste of time, parlour maids in black dresses and white aprons much in evidence, and a stifling sense of Edwardian mourning about the place. Malvolio became the petty-minded, domineering butler rather than the steward, and Maria his declared below-stairs enemy, the housekeeper. The social realism of it all extended even to Feste, a music-hall comedian with flappy-soled oversize boots like Little Titch, whom a tweedy and aggressively alcoholic Sir Toby had obviously brought back down to the country from one of his periodic jaunts up to London, along with a rather dandified man-about-town version of Sir Andrew.

Such was the precision of it all that one could even imagine that 'Count' Orsino might be one of the younger sons of the monarch, with his own establishment and parkland adjoining Olivia's. Like many a younger royal he had been assigned a military career, so that when Zoë Waites's Viola arrived – a very plausible distant cousin, perhaps, from another European royal family – it was as a military cadet in high-collared uniform and hair combed flat that she presented her Cesario at Olivia's gate. But although the production was firmly rooted visually in the Edwardian social world, in its exploration of the sexual tensions and ambivalences of the relationship between Olivia and Viola it was altogether modern in its approach, the energy and volatility of the emotions being explored, set against the repressive conventionality of the society in which this was happening, providing a most interesting and revealing contrast. It is of that relationship and of the issues that it raises about love, and desire, and sexuality that Zoë Waites and Matilda Ziegler write in their essay.

Meanwhile, at much the same sort of date as we were asked to imagine these Anglo-Illyrian events taking place, Antony Sher's Leontes, on the other side of Europe, was beginning to suspect that Alexandra Gilbreath's Hermione was unfaithful to him – for in Gregory Doran's production of *The Winter's Tale* for the RSC's 1999–2000 winter season at the Royal Shakespeare Theatre we were again in the world of European monarchy immediately before the First World War. This was now, however, what seemed to be a Romanov court where a priest of the Orthodox Church in ceremonial regalia would open and read the oracle declaring Hermione's innocence. The production opened with the royal family at the back of the stage acknowledging a crowd that could be heard cheering – as it were from somewhere below this kingdom's equivalent of the Buckingham Palace balcony – and with a parade downstage of the royals that was accompanied by the sound of whispering (heard only by the audience over the tannoy). This came, one realized, from inside Leontes's own head, the beginning of that process that would convince him that 'Sicilia is a so-forth' (i.ii.218). The set for the Sicilian scenes was a long, panelled state-room, the sides of which moved symbolically in for Leontes's soliloquy 'Nor night nor day no rest' (ii.iii.1 ff.) and into which a huge throne was brought for Hermione's trial, Leontes stumbling up its steps to read out the indictment against her with pitiful inarticulacy and hesitation, fumbling with notes and spectacles, while his court cringed in embarrassment. The journey to this moment of destructive, and self-destructive, madness is explored in Antony Sher's essay.

It was a central part of Sher's intention (and achievement) to make Leontes's destructiveness seem to derive from aberration rather than evil, and thus to make his final forgiveness acceptable; it was likewise central to Alexandra Gilbreath's immensely dignified portrayal of Hermione that, in spite of all her suffering, one never lost sight of her love for her husband and was prepared, therefore, to believe that she would so unhesitatingly embrace him in the reunion of the final scene. That love was evident as she put out her hand to him for support in rising from the ground where he had flung her in the scene of his first accusations (ii.i), and in the way in which she left the dock in which she stood for the trial scene, filthy and dishevelled from her incarceration, her prison dress bloody from childbirth, to walk across to his throne, her hands held out to him in eloquent appeal to his former love. Alexandra Gilbreath's essay explores some of the means she used to present so powerfully Hermione's extraordinary dignity in this scene in spite of her physical degradation, and to maintain a remarkable vocal control while nevertheless making manifest Hermione's fiercely turbulent emotions and majestic anger.

For the final scene that little prisoner's dock reappeared, now silvered with candlelight as Hermione stood, madonna-like in her statuesque stillness, prior to the moment of resurrection and of reunion with Leontes. This was played with a quiet, subdued intensity, so that our awareness of the 'wide gap of time' (v.iii.154) that had been lost, wasted away in grief and isolation, was very sharp and clear, even as we watched the first tentative beginnings of the process of restoration.

Twelve months after *The Winter's Tale*, Gregory Doran again directed Antony Sher in an RSC winter season production, this time in a version of *Macbeth* for the Swan Theatre in Stratford, moving his setting from the elegant formalities of the early twentieth-century royal palace where the romance had been set to the grimness of what seemed to be the Balkan battlefields of the century's closing decade for the tragedy. This was a harsh, dark, brutal world, all combat gear and bayonets, but one which, we learn from Antony Sher's essay, was arrived at late, after an earlier intention to present the play in a Jacobean setting. The influence on the production of Trevor Nunn's celebrated *Macbeth* at the Other Place almost a quarter of a century earlier was both declared and palpable, the design achieving in the slightly larger Swan Theatre something of its studio predecessor's brooding darkness and intensity, qualities that seem to evade productions of this play in larger spaces. The jangling harshness of the battle scenes, with Macbeth as ruthlessly conquering warlord, contrasted powerfully with the fierce introspectiveness of the central relationship, a marriage of long duration, one knew, its childlessness a constant source of pain to both partners. To remind him of their dead baby was clearly Lady Macbeth's well-tried means of emotional blackmail, though use of it to provoke regicide was no doubt a new departure.

The king to be killed was the late Joseph O'Conor's white-haired, sweet-faced old Duncan, frail, gentle, and thoroughly saintly, and the horror and brutality of his murder were vividly caught in the moment when he looked out, contented and benign, from what was apparently his bedroom window above the Swan stage before retiring for the night and Macbeth entered simultaneously below to continue the process of psyching himself up for the kill. The murder destroyed the Macbeths' marriage: Lady Macbeth winced visibly at her dismissal 'till suppertime' (III.i.43) as Macbeth began the journey towards self-loathing isolation that ends in what Antony Sher calls the 'bunker scenes' of the play's final stages – the lonely and terrible journey that he charts in his essay.

Michael Boyd's 2000 production of *Romeo and Juliet* for Stratford's main stage began, not with the Prologue but with a fight, a chair being smashed onto the stage from behind one of the curving, grey, featureless walls of the set before an actor even appeared. We then saw the first of the Capulet/Montague brawls, fought with yob brutality and including the banging of the face of one of its participants against the wall, leaving a blood-stain, centre-stage, that would remain through the evening. The mayhem was halted by the Prologue, spoken by David Tennant's Romeo (or, as his essay suggests, perhaps by his ghost), entering, as the belligerents froze, through the auditorium. At the end of the evening he would make his final exit, with Juliet, again through the auditorium, rising from the grave to do so. From the first, then, this was a production that invited our particular attention to Romeo. The set's curving grey walls, a narrow passageway between them, presented the play in the bleakest, the dourest, of environments. On the top of one of them Juliet appeared for the balcony scene, looking rather as though she were peering over a prison wall; the same space was occupied by the ghosts of Tybalt and Mercutio in the second half of the play, presiding in awful determination over the journey to catastrophe.

This was, then, never going to be one of those versions of *Romeo and Juliet* that might have been a comedy but for a few spots of bad luck along the way: a sense of doom and hopelessness hung over it from the start, along with a constant threat of violence. The dress of the young people would have allowed them to pass unnoticed on any modern city street; Prince Escalus, on the other hand, old and frail, his legs looking almost as spindly as his walking stick in the tight hose of a costume that seemed more or less Elizabethan, was a figure from the past, irrelevant in his pathetic inability to control the destructive energies of Verona. These were personified in his kinsman Mercutio, obsessively jealous of Romeo, trying, with a kind of savage possessiveness, to taunt him away from heterosexual relationships, fiercely (and prophetically) vengeful in his final curse of 'a plague a'both your houses' (III.i.99). It is of Romeo's escape from this male world of grimly bawdy humour and constantly threatened sexual violence, to the fleeting moments of doomed happiness with Juliet, and thence to the tomb and to a ghostly posterity as a legend in a love-story, that David Tennant writes.

When Michael Pennington stepped onto the main stage at Stratford as Timon in Gregory Doran's 1999 production of *Timon of Athens*, he was the first actor to do so since Paul Scofield in 1965. The production offered us a decadent, even rather sleazy, Athens, with costumes that offered little firm sense of a particular historical period – touches of Restoration dandyism here and there, rather a Dickensian look to the scene of Timon's creditors hammering at his door, a massage parlour setting for one of Timon's servant's appeals for funds, and something of a 1960s night-club atmosphere for Timon's first banquet, with a Duke

Ellington musical score, Timon's masque a high-camp drag act, and Apemantus, in sunglasses, addressing his reductive commentary into a microphone.

The transition to the second half was via a skeletal suggestion of the outline of a city, Timon's curses as he turns his back on Athens ringing in our memories through the interval as they had just been ringing so splendidly, and shockingly, round the theatre. The curiously simple structure of the second half of the play – the sequence of visitors to Timon in his self-imposed exile all, in turn, sent on their way, energetically cursed – was reflected in a boldly simple set. The stage was left entirely empty right to the strikingly toplit bare brick of the back wall, with only a pit, downstage centre, that served Timon, naked now except for a loin-cloth, as cave, as digging ground in his search for sustaining roots, as accidental gold-mine, and finally as grave. From here he lambasted the whores, from here he derided Apemantus (whose day-tripper status as misanthrope was emphasized by a sun-hat, shades and a beach-towel), from here, profoundly impressively, we heard his farewell to Flavius and his epitaph. It is, as Michael Pennington writes, 'the great atmospherics of the second half' that we value in this play (and that make the actor want the part), and the production, and the performance, left no doubt of their theatrical power.

We had been waiting a long time, and through several rumours of its immanence at Stratford, for Simon Russell Beale's Hamlet, and he had given remarkable performances of two of the role's major derivatives, Konstantin in *The Seagull* and Oswald in *Ghosts*, before, in the summer of 2000, it came, in a production by John Caird, to the Lyttleton stage of the National Theatre, and thence (and back again) to a number of touring venues, national and international. The dark and subdued costumes suggested the Jacobean in a vague and unobtrusive way, though about Claudius's regal robes there was a hint of the priestly, perhaps of the Orthodox priestly, an idea that was carried further in the lamps and crucifixes and chandeliers that appeared at times from the flies. The play began in near darkness, with figures descending from candlelit niches in the semi-circular rear wall of the stage, before a vertical slit opened at the back, then a horizontal one near its top, the brilliant white light behind them forming a cross. Should one, one wondered, be thinking of the apse of a church, or even of the Last Judgement on a tympanum. Through the bottom of the cross a figure with a suitcase entered; he would turn out to be Horatio, visitor to Elsinore, entrusted at the play's end (as Simon Russell Beale's essay describes) with the role of teller of Hamlet's story.

Within the playing space the only set was a series of cabin trunks, proposing, directly enough, the notion of a journey, of transience, of passage through a space that so often seemed darkness itself, though lit with a threatening fitfulness, anxious faces caught as their words expressed, with powerful articulacy and precision, their pains and fears, griefs and struggles, enlightenments and revelations. At the end, the figures, those dead as well as those still alive in the play's story, returned to their candlelit niches before filing out, some to the left of the cross, some to its right, into the white light beyond. Was this the final judgement – or image of that horror? Had they all been dead from the start – as the musical score, ranging from single choirboy to full chorus but constantly returning to phrases from the requiem mass, seemed to propose – and was the performance re-enacting, endlessly re-enacting, in Purgatory, perhaps, this story of love and death and bereavement? One such moment of re-enactment was the reunion of Hamlet's family in the closet scene. The scene had begun with Gertrude rummaging in a trunk and finding remnants of her past – letters from Hamlet's father, her veil for her wedding to him. The ghost's appearance then produced, for a fleeting but unforgettable moment, the image of Hamlet between his father and mother, touching them both, in contact, as it were, with past and present, living and dead, and offering a piercing sense of what, for Hamlet, had been lost. For such moments one keeps going to Shakespearian theatre.

If Simon Russell Beale's Hamlet had been long awaited, so had the late Sir Nigel Hawthorne's return to the stage, and to Shakespeare. His performance as King Lear in one of the RSC's Millennium projects also fulfilled another long theatrical expectation, the first Shakespeare production in English by Yukio Ninagawa, whose earlier versions of Shakespeare in Japanese had made so profound an impression in London and at the Edinburgh Festival. On many counts, then, the production of *King Lear* was a major international theatrical event, opening in Tokyo in the autumn of 1999, then coming to London (to the Barbican), and thence, to play through the millennial new year, to Stratford. As Nigel Hawthorne's essay makes clear, the director's work was mainly devoted to producing an imposingly simple setting, an empty space in shining black, with huge double doors decorated with an emblem from the Japanese noh stage, an ancient pine tree, signifying, as the programme note told us, in its year-round greenness, 'eternal life', while the empty space in front of it represented 'the cycle of life in this world'. From time to time the great doors opened to reveal the full depth of the stage – for Lear's impressive entry in the first scene, for the heath, for the final battle. Costumes were influenced by those of the Japanese classical theatre, especially the court dresses of Goneril and Regan. The cast, however, were all English except for the fool of Hiroyuki Sanada, his isolation in ethnic and linguistic otherness giving his performance a quality of touching vulnerability and pathos. English, too, were the acting styles, so that the production never quite achieved that cross-cultural synthesis for which (over-optimistically, no doubt) one had hoped. To see this play set in the dark backward and abysm of British time (for so early modern dramatists must have thought of the earliest reigns, Lear's among them, chronicled by Holinshed) transposed to the strange territory of a Japanese theatrical tradition rather older than Shakespeare's, was, nevertheless, revealing, and Ninagawa's emblematic presentation of the storm, with rocks thudding from the flies to the stage, gave remarkable energy to Lear's instruction (III.ii.8) that Nature should spill all its germens (the very largest, it seemed, not excluded) at once.

Nigel Hawthorne writes sadly about the reception of the production in the British press. The truth of the matter, of course, is that the high international profile of the production, of its director, and in particular of its principal actor, and the publicity around the millennial status of the event, created the sort of expectations that had positively to be excelled if the production was not to be deemed a flop. The latter it certainly was not, or so it seemed to me by the time it reached Stratford. If it did not new-mint the play, it undoubtedly presented it in an unfamiliar and illuminating world and in its title role one is profoundly grateful to have seen a deeply sympathetic reading of the part by a great actor in what was to be his last stage appearance.

Where a calculated temporal vagueness in design seems to have been the aim of most of the productions of tragedies discussed in this collection, temporal precision was Michael Attenborough's goal in his production of *Othello* that opened on Stratford's main stage in the summer of 1999. The play was set, as Richard McCabe's essay points out, very exactly in the year 1911, the senate scene all winged collars and cigar-smoke, and with a globe of the Empire centre stage. The scenes on Cyprus had a strong colonial feel to them, with the soldiers in scarlet tunics and the women in muslin dresses that had a look of

Mrs Pankhurst about them – which for Zoë Waites's determined and self-confident young Desdemona seemed altogether appropriate. This was a world of very clearly marked hierarchies, Cassio all upper-class self-confidence as he remarked with patronizing contempt to McCabe's ram-rod straight NCO Iago that 'the Lieutenant is to be saved before the Ancient' (II.iii.105).

That precision of social realism in the setting seemed to require, and certainly received, as Richard McCabe's essay describes, a search for psychological realism of motivation about Iago. Only in its final moment, as Iago, led off under guard, turned to look, enigmatically, at the tragic loading of the bed, did one wonder whether there might be something beyond the human about this creature; within the play the exploration of psychotic and destructive envy and jealousy, social, professional and sexual was devastatingly recognizable in its deranged realism.

We were back to timeless eclecticism in Steven Pimlott's production of *Antony and Cleopatra*, also on Stratford's main stage in the summer of 1999. Antony wore armour of a more or less Roman kind, but most of his soldiers seemed to be dressed for mid-twentieth-century warfare. There were cocktails and cigarettes at Cleopatra's colourful 1920s court, but Octavius's grey and white world had the classical austerity of the eighteenth century about it. Dominating the set, which included a suspended sail, a broken classical pillar, and military kit of various epochs, were three huge mirrors that demanded that we regard these as people constantly on show and constantly observed, in particular by themselves.

That sense of the histrionic was reflected in the performances, above all in Frances de la Tour's remarkable portrait of Cleopatra, a woman sometimes behaving (and occasionally dressing) like a girl when girlhood has been left behind, a woman needy and desperate in her desire for Antony's love, as well as manipulative and inventive in the roles, and the performances, she creates in order to hold on to it. There is nothing simple or straightforward about this play, or about this role, as Frances de la Tour's essay makes clear, and the courage of the production, and the performance, in never allowing us to feel easy or relaxed, or to settle to a consistent tone, gave full weight to this elusive and disturbing quality. The interval exit of Antony and Cleopatra after the defeat at Actium, she clinging to his stooping back as he stumbled from the stage, her feet dragging on the floor as he half-carried, half-dragged her off in a pathetic failure of a piggy-back, encapsulated, in its pathetic, but oddly magnificent, indignity, something of the play's remarkable tonal complexity and of the helpless, ruined interdependence of its two principal characters. It was an extraordinary moment of theatre, presenting, through the imaginative art and skill of actors and director, an image of human grief and trust, love and pain, to the audience's examination, and understanding, and sympathy. It is to discover something of how such moments are conceived and achieved that this collection of essays, like its predecessors, has been brought together.

Prospero in
The Tempest

PHILIP VOSS

PHILIP VOSS is an Associate Actor of the Royal Shakespeare Company
and played Prospero in James MacDonald's 2000–1 touring production of *The Tempest* at the Pit Theatre (Barbican), at The Other Place
in Stratford, and on a national and international tour. A wide range
of earlier parts for the RSC has included Shylock, Malvolio, Ulysses,
Menenius, Peter Quince, Worcester and the Lord Chief Justice in 1 and
2 *Henry IV*, Bassanes in *The Broken Heart*, Monticelso in *The White
Devil*, and Sir Epicure Mammon in *The Alchemist*. Roles for Shared Experience include Dr Dorn in *The Seagull*, Chebutykin in *Three Sisters*,
and Kochkaryov in *Marriage*. He has also worked extensively for the
National Theatre and for the Royal Court. Among his films is *Four
Weddings and a Funeral* and he has done a considerable range of work
for television. His essay on his performance of Menenius in the RSC's
1994 production of *Coriolanus* was published in *Players of Shakespeare 4*.

(O you wonder)

The Tempest has had more labels pinned to it than any other Shakespeare
play that I have ever worked on:

'It's about colonialism – absolutely.'
'Jacobean expansionism – without a doubt.'
'It's about Shakespeare laying down his pen.'
'It's a play of mystery.'
'It's anti-Faustian.'
'White magic against black.'
'Surely it is about the oppressed gaining their freedom from the oppressors.'

Then there is Prospero:

> 'Is he Shakespeare?'
> 'Is he James the First?'
> 'Definitely Caliban is his dark inner self, Ariel the light.'

It is the first play printed in the first Folio, so I assume Heminges and Condell thought it significant. It is unusual. No one goes mad at the end or dies. There is a betrothal and forgiveness of an unsatisfactory sort. To Antonio Prospero says 'For you (most wicked Sir) whom to call brother / Would even infect my mouth' (v.i.130–1). This, preceding the line of forgiveness, doesn't make it seem wholehearted to me; and even 'I do forgive' is followed by the continuing bitterness of 'Thy rankest fault – all of them' (v.i.132). I don't believe Prospero makes that vital self-healing leap of real forgiveness. Nor is there any great event to end the play; just a lonely (old, in my case) man asking for applause.

I was offered the part in the usual way through my agent and accepted without putting down the phone – not always a wise thing to do. It was a tour, I was told: Japan, Portugal, Virginia. I met the director, James MacDonald, for lunch the following day and the details of the tour expanded to include the inner and outer reaches of the United Kingdom – and we were to play in leisure centres *in a module*. Terrific! During the meal I also learned that James intended it to be a company production, working along vaguely Stanislavskian principles. He had seen me many years before in the Shared Experience production of *Marriage* by Gogol and admired it hugely. Was a company production a threat to me, I wondered.

So I was cast and I was hooked. I have used a particular hybrid version of Stanislavsky since discovering the process with Mike Alfreds in 1980. Often I use the system in a secretive sort of way, but with this director maybe I would be able to discuss motives and objectives openly – which, in the event, proved to be the case.

I read the play – four times. When writing about Menenius in *Players of Shakespeare 4* I set out the procedure in fullish detail, and that is the course I embarked on with Prospero – and pretty quickly, for I realized that the opening duologue with my daughter, Miranda, was incredibly difficult. I made my four lists: facts about Prospero; what other people said about me; what I said about myself; and what I said about other people; then the conclusions. I soon learnt the scene with Miranda – out of fright at its complexity. As a rule I would never start to learn anything until at least a couple of weeks into rehearsal. We had six weeks to rehearse, which is too short for my liking. At that time I thought I would be playing a strict disciplinarian, bookish and aloof. I had seen Gielgud at Drury Lane in the mid 1950s – no module for him.

The list of words and phrases I jotted down at that time include 'absolute power', 'control freak', 'bully' and 'loving father' – but the last with a question mark. His objective in the play is to get his dukedom back and to go home. His pulse is controlled; his physical centre is the mind. His animal ranged from a golden eagle (I think I had the voluminous Gielgud cloak in mind) to a beaver, a hawk, and finally to an old owl. The super-objective, which is the most important choice I make – because it goes over and beyond the play – was, at first, revenge. Rarely do I change my conclusions once I've made them, but in this instance my super-objective changed three or four times.

Revenge is there, of course, strongly, throughout the play, but it is re-solved within it. Alonso gives him back the Dukedom of Milan while his brother Antonio, who usurped it from him, famously says nothing. To play 'revenge' so strongly would, I assume, have led me to an angry and bitter performance, which I have, indeed, seen more than once. Then I had a brilliant idea: the revenge is achieved through the marriage of his daughter with Ferdinand – the son of the King of Naples. I would create an Italian dynasty; my offspring would rule not only Naples and Milan, but possibly Rome and beyond. About this time I began to read an assortment of prefaces and essays – by Frank Kermode and Harold Bloom, among others. They all referred to the dynastic theme being resolved within the play, so as a super-objective it became valueless, though essential as a course of action.

Rehearsals had begun by now and we sat around the all-too-familiar tables, pushed together to form a whole, to thrash out the meaning of the words. In this case it was little more than a bonding process for a fortnight. Nicholas Day, who is involved with a company that performs Shakespeare by working from a cue-script, gave a talk about punctuation and capitalization in the first Folio. We were, indeed, working from a typed-out script of the first Folio text of *The Tempest* and it has to be said that the 'corrections' in the editions we buy from our bookshops were a revelation. For example, the Folio's '. . . Urchins / Shall for that vast of night . . .' (I.ii.326–7) becomes (in some editions) '. . . Urchins / Shall forth at vast of night'. Why? Who decided to improve? Similarly, in the phrase I have chosen as a title for this essay, I see that the latest Arden edition has added a comma and an exclamation mark: 'O, you wonder!' Does it need them? In subsequent readings, and during performance, I have found that the punctuation of the first Folio, and particularly the capitalization of nouns, has been very influential on the way I stress some of the sentences:

> The Cloud-capped Towers, the gorgeous Palaces,
> The solemn Temples, the great Globe itself . . .
>
> (IV.i.153–4)

and before that

> Are melted into Air, into thin Air.
>
> (IV.i.150)

Look at the way Shakespeare writes and he'll tell you what he wants.

We, the cast, now superficially know one another. My daughter is black; my Ariel is black; my Caliban is fundamentally Indian. The Ferdinand, as far as I can ascertain, is from landed gentry in Cambridgeshire. The rehearsals become individualized and it is the most agonizing moment ever – as ever. I have a daughter that I hardly know at all who comes from Sierra Leone, and I am white. I have a stick – well, it's a staff and it's magic, but in fact it's a broomstick. It is a prop and it feels absurd in my hand. Now we have to begin to explore about the most difficult text I can remember. I don't let on that I already know the lines. The syntax is tortuous. Frank Kermode is so dismissive of the whole episode, saying that Shakespeare was attempting to stay within the unities of time and place (the whole action of the play takes place within four hours) and that his attempt to recount twelve years within a virtual monologue defeated him to such an extent that he had to resort to making Prospero question Miranda's attention span in order to maintain the flow. He has a point, and one that I went along with for a while.

The 'tempest' doesn't exist. It is a fabrication. The tempest is within Prospero: twelve years of repressing resentment, hatred and thoughts of revenge have distorted him. He has tried to speak about the pain, but prevented himself from doing so – many times. He can't let it go. Then . . . his enemies arrive on the island and he knows he has to *let go* – now. 'The very minute bids thee ope thine ear'(I.ii.37). She has to know now that she is a princess and at last he has to divulge the horror of their expulsion from Milan.

Now the difficult syntax becomes dramatic. He has to relive the betrayal; he has to tell his daughter what she is; he has to suppress his anger; and finally he has to admit that fate has handed him the gift of

an opportunity for reprisal. Every performance is hard: if I don't suc-
ceed in this I know I shall have nowhere to go. It sets up the evening
and the audience must be taken along – and they have to understand it:

> I, thus neglecting worldly ends, all dedicated
> To closeness and the bettering of my mind
> With that which, but by being so retired,
> O'er-prized all popular rate . . .   (I.ii.89–92)

It might just as well be Hungarian; but it has a meaning, although it
is tortured. I don't think anyone hearing that for the first time could
understand it, but the audience will understand the anguish and the
hurt from the actor.

Two things helped me. First, that I was taught to speak verse by John
Barton in 1960: spinning off a caesura on to the next thought, end-
stopping the line with a short beat; always flowing on. James MacDonald
made it his mission to slow me down. 'Give it time', he would say,
'breathe into it.' 'I can't', I would say, 'it slows me down too much.'
'Give it time', he would insist. Eventually I trusted him and took my time
and I truly think the audience went with me through every thought. The
Barton rules are still in place, but now I dare to examine each thought
before going on to the next – though the verse line has more pauses,
and I suppose is more broken, than has been my custom.

The second lynch-pin was my daughter. So often work is spoiled by
an actor, crucial to one's own performance, being inadequate – unable to speak the verse, or playing for laughs, or in some other way
inappropriate. But this is not the case with Nikki Amuka-Bird, who is
perfection. She's as scared, if not more so, than I am; and over the next
few weeks we work so wonderfully together, and in the process establish
a very recognizable father/daughter relationship (for all her black and
my white) that we go agonizing, step by step, from incomprehension to
a scene of pain, exposition, and revelation. I could never wish for more,
nor thank her enough.

There is a flyer that was printed for our production before rehearsals
began that seems to suggest that Prospero has no heart. I don't know
who dreams up such rubbish. Where do they get it from?

> I have done nothing but in care of thee,
> Of thee, my dear one, thee my daughter . . .
> (I.ii.16–17)

1 Philip Voss as Prospero with Nikki Amuka-Bird as Miranda, *The Tempest*, Act I, Scene ii: 'I have done nothing but in care of thee / Of thee, my dear one, thee my daughter.'

– the word *thee* occurring three times in the space of seven words;

> . . . he, whom next thyself
> Of all the world I loved . . .   (I.ii.68–9)

And to Ferdinand he says

> . . . for I
> Have given you here a third of mine own life,
> Or that for which I live.   (IV.i.2–4)

He adores her and, as he says, does everything for her.

Miranda and Ferdinand are at the centre of my performance of Prospero. Through them and their offspring I will accomplish my revenge over my brother. 'Heavens rain grace / On that which breeds between 'em' (III.i.75–6). They have to fall in love, but it must be real and untouched by magic. Each scene has its own objective for Prospero, and there are four sections to the very long establishing scene of Act One, Scene Two. The overall objective is to bring Miranda and Ferdinand together in such a receptive condition that they will fall in love. The second this is achieved successfully, my project is on course: 'It goes on, I see, / As my soul prompts it' ((I.ii.420–1), followed swiftly by 'O you wonder' (I.ii.427). At first sight he has fallen in love.

My objective for the first quarter of the scene is to tell Miranda that she is a princess, but it has to be harder than that. I change it slightly for each performance, so that it becomes a variation of 'I want to release the suppressed horror of our expulsion to my daughter.' It couldn't be more cumbersome, but it produces the right state of anguish and hatred in me.

In the following part of the scene, with Ariel, I want him to bring Ferdinand to me in a highly emotive and aroused state. When he grumbles about wanting his freedom, I remind him of the torment I released him from and when he capitulates – which he does very easily – I send him off on his mission, dressed (invisibly) as a nymph. All Prospero's fantasies are female, the harpy and Ceres being the other two. It must have relevance to his nature.

The episode which follows is with the monster, Caliban. It took me a long time to decide on the objective. Why would he want to take his daughter to see someone she dislikes so much? ''Tis a villain, sir, / I do not love to look on' (I.ii.309–10); and, later, she is provoked into 'Abhorred slave, / Which any print of goodness wilt not take . . .' (I.ii.351–2). Unwillingly I decided that Prospero wanted just that – to remind her of the foulness of the attempted rape and so make her emotionally alive to the first sight of Ferdinand. Ariel, as nymph, lures Ferdinand to the stage, singing, first the seductive song which involves a reference to the strutting cock, Chanticleer; he then follows this up with the sorrowful dirge that reminds him that his father is drowned. Then enter Prospero with his daughter and, in my view, the worst lines Shakespeare ever wrote: 'The fringèd curtains of thine eye advance / And say what thou seest yond' (I.ii.408–9). The conditions are well prepared for the two youngsters to fall in love, *for real*: 'O You Wonder'. My daughter's name derives from the Italian adjective *mirando*, meaning 'wondrous', and from the Latin *miror*, meaning 'to wonder' and 'to be astonished at': 'It works' (I.ii.495).

There are rages from Prospero in each section of this scene, but they are all different. The first, in the duologue with Miranda, is a release of twelve years' suppressed anger. The second, with Ariel, is much jokier and is designed to quell the rumblings of a mild rebellion and to get what he wants. The fury with Caliban is genuine. He is the one element in the play that Prospero cannot control, and in our production I treat him quite brutally here, grabbing the inside of his mouth while I threaten him with physical pain. I use my staff on him and kick him – and then react to my failure and my own anger with self-disgust. The rage with Ferdinand is, of course, faked and produced only to make winning the prize of Miranda more difficult. It is a scene of comedy, though frequently I feel the audience taking me seriously – but, then, they've seen me go through several mood swings in the short time since they've met me, so I suppose it's not surprising.

By the end of this long section of the play my plans are spot on course and I give Ariel a smile to thank him for his help. I have been introduced, before giving a talk about the play, as 'the Prospero that smiled'. And not only do I smile; I also have a sense of fun. The part is full of irony – what Shakespeare character isn't? – but the grandeur of most Prosperos tends to render them humourless. When I first read the play, knowing that I was going to play the part, the line that I loved most was 'Come with a thought. I thank thee, Ariel, come' (IV.i.164). That seemed to me to epitomize the best kind of relationship you can have with anybody: no need for speech; just think, and they know what you mean. In Ariel's case he is only air, and small enough to loll about in a leaf or suck honey from a flower, so I imagine him just around my shoulder, communicating simply by thought – wonderful!

Very few lines were cut in our production, which means that Prospero is off after the big exposition scene (I.ii) for fifty minutes, including the interval – hence the 'company show'. One huge benefit is that the lords' scene (II.i) is given full value. So often it's difficult to distinguish one person from another and I have seen a production with Alonso wearing a crown, just so that we shall know that he's a king. I suspect that Gonzalo is frequently cut to shreds, but with us his vision of Utopia remains intact. One other revelatory ingredient that bound us all as a company was the use of *a cappella* music from start to finish. 'The isle is full of noises' (III.ii.136) is interpreted literally. The spirits, in soft black garb, are played by actors with remarkable voices, each in their own right. The music was composed by Orlando Gough and the sounds are interwoven on stage and off throughout the action. They create the magic.

I read several books on magic early on. It is an art that enters 'through the ear', and it certainly does with us. My broom handle – which, after a week or so, begins to take on a life – should be a virgin staff of elder, one year old. But the real magic comes from the actors – and the designer.

The set is white, and designed on the theory of chaos. It rises to form a back wall upon which video images, many of them, may be played: sea for the storm, peacock feathers for Juno, a ring of fire for the breaking of the lords' trance, and so on. It falls in a slide to make a series of waves, or humps and troughs. Sometimes it looks like the sea, sometimes like a sheet of paper thrown across a desk. Ariel slides down it. Ferdinand, bemused, is lowered – as though through the sea – onto the shore below. We are dressed around the turn of the twentieth century, a period in which swords are still just about acceptable – for ceremonial occasions, anyway.

With about a fortnight to go my super-objective was still in flux. There was a short period of 'I want to be normal', but that is almost impossible to act. Eventually, and after a couple of walks around the field with the dog, I decided on 'I want to face up to the realities of life without the help of magic.' I don't know if I can make it clear how important these choices are to me: everything I do under the umbrella of the super-objective, or the objective of an individual scene, is affected by it. I want something, and I want it badly: so, for example, in Act Four I want to present my daughter and her future husband with the most wonderful betrothal gift ever, so I summon up Iris, Ceres and Juno, the best in the business for this sort of gift. Shakespeare, you see, never lets you down: he's in there before you, like Chekhov. Who does he give me? Ceres, who represents the fecundity of the cultivated earth (and remember I need grandchildren, sorely). Wheat and barley were sacred to her and she was known as the maternal fertility goddess. Juno is the goddess of light and of childbirth. They are summoned to the celebration by Iris, Juno's special messenger, a sister to the harpies, who could affect all the elements.

Our choreographer is Peter Darling, who worked on the film *Billy Elliot*, so, as an added bonus, James MacDonald had my daughter and her lover perform a joyous and exuberant dance with the help of magic shoes. My present, or my objective, couldn't have been more fulfilled. Then I remember that Caliban is coming to kill me. It is not the fact that I am in danger that makes me end the celebrations so abruptly, but the fact that for once, by enjoying the masque, I have lost control of events and *forgotten* the threat to my life. The course of action has gone against the objective and caused an explosion inside myself, making me wreck the very thing I set out to achieve. I dismiss the spirits in anger, denounce the futility of all such achievements, and then, realizing my error, I apologize to Ferdinand. Within the 'Our revels now are ended' speech, I stress the 'we' in

> We are such stuff
> As dreams are made on; and our little life
> Is rounded with a sleep   (IV.i.156–8)

and the 'our' in the last part of the sentence. It makes it more personal and, along with the anger, prevents the speech from becoming just a rather beautiful piece of poetry.

My objective for Act Five was, for many weeks into performance, 'I want to give up my magic'. But I didn't. How could anyone want to give up anything so useful and handy? When I changed it to the super-objective then I could give the 'Ye elves of hills . . .' (V.i.33) speech the dynamic it needs. I begin by calling to them, softly. It personalizes them and stops it becoming a 'set speech'.

I think what Prospero does is incredibly brave. He was never the best ruler in the world, retiring and library-bound. He achieves his magic powers through study, but unlike Faust he decides to let them go: letting go of his daughter, letting go of his need for revenge, letting go of Ariel (the best servant in the world), letting go of the island, and, biggest of all, letting go of his magical powers. When does he begin to let go? His answer to Ariel – who says that, if he were human, his feelings would become tender at the sight of the lords' distress – is only three words: 'And mine shall' (V.i.20). Yet, within seconds, he is swearing to break his staff. My feeling is that he starts to let go the moment his enemies set foot on shore, but the real release can begin the minute Ferdinand sees Miranda, falls in love on sight, and addresses her with the phrase: 'O you wonder.'

My all-important magic cloak is an extraordinary garment. Designed by Kandis Cook, it is based on an old Byzantine priest's vestment, but made of a very loose-weave linen. The fabric has been stressed throughout and the weave pulled into holes into which have been pushed, and then stitched, soft velours and velvets in muted shades. It has sleeves and is more of a coat than a cloak, but reaching to, and slightly trailing on, the floor. The costume has been embroidered by a craftsman whose normal job is to emboss the clerical robes of the church. He has decorated the entire garment in gold thread, with accepted magic symbols – trees, medallions, wands, and so on. It is extremely light, which means that I can wear it for longer and more frequently than many Prosperos. It looks as if it might be four hundred years' old and when dropped to the floor it seems to all but disappear.

My general look when being unmagical is of a man wearing his own clothes, clothes that have seen twelve years of wear and tear. So my trousers are frayed, the shirt torn, and I have a cardigan that is full of holes and loose threads. It absolutely fits with my idea of his appearance and seems logical. Only my beard is controlled and trim: it is the old owl.

For the moment when he says to Ariel 'I will discase me and myself present / As I was sometime Milan' (v.i.85–6), Kandis assembled an entire outfit – bow-tie, waistcoat, tail-coat, and overcoat in fake astrakhan. 'I'll never have time to get all that on', I said. 'We'll make time', she said, undaunted. And we do. While singing 'Where the bee sucks' Ariel helps me to dress and I am transformed into a Verdi-looking figure who could well have been the Duke of Milan twelve years since. 'Fetch me the Hat' (note the capital letter), I say to Ariel (v.i.84). And what a hat! – a specially made 1900s topper. The image is complete – well, after Ariel has adjusted the bow: it's not easy to tie a bow in public. I can't recall ever noting the transformation before, but it must always be done. Kandis has turned it into a real coup. I break my magic staff earlier than most Prosperos. I break it while Ariel is getting my ducal clothes, with the lords still coming out of their trance in front of me. When I am rigged out in my finery (I have changed the word 'rapier' (line 84) to 'finery' because in 1900 I would hardly have had a sword of any kind) I make particular use of the three 'So's' that the text provides (v.i.96): on the first I take the hat from Ariel and ask for his approval; on the second I give him my recently discarded magic coat; and on the third he receives the broken staff.

There is still some magic to perform and our thinking is that the relationship between Ariel and Prospero is so close that he performs these favours from love: 'Thy thoughts I cleave to' (IV.i.165) – the answer to my favourite line – and 'Do you love me, Master? No?' (IV.i.48). At the end of the play, when I do release him to the elements to be free, Ariel takes some little time to adjust to the idea that he can in fact go and does so with some reluctance, as if it takes him some time to get used to the idea.

2 Philip Voss as Prospero, *The Tempest*, Act v, Scene i:
'As I was sometime Milan.'

The Epilogue I have often seen effectively played as a charm offensive on the audience, but I stay within Prospero for most of it: 'My ending is despair' (line 15). That is the way I see it: 'Every third thought shall be my grave' (v.i.312). By renouncing magic some say he gains inner freedom and becomes a wise old man. I think he renounces magic to face up to the awfulness of life. I don't think he turns into a good ruler or becomes a much better human being. I don't fully believe he forgives Antonio:

> Since I have my Dukedom got
> And *pardoned* the deceiver . . .
> (Epilogue, lines 6–7; my italics)

He will still try to control. I think he takes Caliban back to Milan with him, poor beast. He can't be pinched any more, but Prospero will try to come to terms with him – not as his own dark side, though that is there, but as a deformed human being. Maybe Prospero will get to hear the benefits of teaching him his language, so that 'my profit on't / Is I know how to curse' (i.ii.363–4) will develop into sharing something as beautifully poetic as 'The isle is full of noises' (iii.ii.136).

To return to the labels so assuredly put on this play: yes, Shakespeare knew about the North Virginia Trading Company; the Earl of Southampton, his patron, was a director of the company. He was probably aware of the William Strachey letter, which would give him the background to the island. I do think the play is an answer to Marlowe's *Dr Faustus*. One of the most significant lines is the word 'No'. It is the answer to Sebastian, who says 'The devil speaks in him' (v.i.129). In the Folio it is the whole line in itself; it neither finishes the line before, nor begins the next. Shakespeare does not do things like that without a reason.

King James loved masques and always joined in the dancing at the end. Ben Jonson was a master of these extravagances; on occasions several were performed in a month, while the number of Shakespeare's plays presented at court diminished significantly; only three during one particular year. Was Shakespeare resentful? Did he want revenge? Does Shakespeare make Antonio usurp Prospero's dukedom as Ben Jonson usurped his position at court? What does Shakespeare do? He writes a brilliant masque but breaks it at the point where the audience would normally get up to join in the dance and thus creates a highly dramatic moment. 'Sod your masques!' – but it is certainly integral to the action and could never have been added later, as some claim. I wonder if by this time Shakespeare was in pain with some sort of rheumatism or repetitive stress syndrome: all the tortures in *The Tempest* relate to cramps and pinches and aches, and four years later he could hardly sign his name. As for laying down his pen – he didn't. The play is full of theatrical references: 'art', 'perform', 'the Globe', 'actors', everything is in there. As always, as with every writer (but he's the best), he mixes his ingredients so that it is theatrical, it is political, and, above all, it is human and thoroughly explored psychologically – as if he knew what that meant. Well of course he did. He wrote a play that explored the inner workings of a complex human being. It is a Wonder.

Dromio of Syracuse in
The Comedy of Errors

IAN HUGHES

IAN HUGHES played Dromio of Syracuse in Lynne Parker's production of *The Comedy of Errors* at the Royal Shakespeare Theatre in the summer season of 2000, and later at the Barbican Theatre. His other part that season was Faulkland in *The Rivals*. Earlier Shakespearian roles for the RSC include Sebastian (in *Twelfth Night*), John of Lancaster, Tybalt, Fortinbras, the Fool in King Lear, Puck and Autolycus. He has worked extensively in provincial (particularly Welsh) theatre, where roles include Khlestakov in *The Government Inspector*, Guildenstern in *Rosencrantz and Guildenstern are Dead* and Mercutio, and in London at the Gate, the Lyric Hammersmith and the Donmar. He has also done a great deal of radio work; television roles include Bernard in *Death of a Salesman*. He was the winner of the first National Theatre Ian Charleson Award for his performance of the title role in *Torquato Tasso*.

The fundamental things apply . . . as time goes by

I had never read, or seen a production of, *The Comedy of Errors* when I was offered Dromio of Syracuse for the RSC's summer season of 2000. My first thought was 'O, no, not another twin' – I had played Sebastian in an ill-fated production of *Twelfth Night* during my first season with the Company in 1991; and my second thought was 'O, no, not another obscure Shakespearian "comic role" ' – I had previously played the Fool in *King Lear* and Autolycus in *The Winter's Tale*, both parts seemingly funny, but difficult to flesh out and make real. *The Comedy of Errors* presented me not only with its fair share of obscure and obtuse language and set-piece 'funny scenes', but also with the added difficulty of playing my role in the same style and manner as the actor playing my twin. I was not enthusiastic.

Some of my fears were calmed on meeting the director Lynne Parker. Better, she thought, to concentrate on the differences between the Dromios, and let costumes, wigs, and make-up take care of the similarities. This sounded encouraging; and added to this Lynne had a slightly anarchic air about her. Making her début with the RSC, she would set her production in the 1940s world of film-noir, drawing heavily on film references as broad as *Casablanca*, *The Third Man*, *The Maltese Falcon*, *Key Largo*, and the films of Abbott and Costello and Laurel and Hardy. All this sounded interesting and exciting, but there was still Shakespeare's language to get to grips with – again.

There were a few weeks until rehearsals would start, but I chose not to seek out productions of the play, or videos, from which to get some overview of it. I would come to this as a novice, with no pre-conceived ideas or images – almost impossible if one is playing Hamlet or Richard III, but with this less frequently performed comedy the task would be easier.

The first week or two of rehearsals were spent very enjoyably crouched in the corner of the RSC's rehearsal rooms in Clapham, curtains drawn, watching some classic films. I had never seen *Casablanca* and was struck by the apparent similarities of its setting to that of Shakespeare's Ephesus. Both are melting pots of culture, both possess a strange, almost supernatural, hold over those who visit them:

> They say this town is full of cozenage,
> As nimble jugglers that deceive the eye,
> Dark-working sorcerers that change the mind,
> Soul-killing witches that deform the body . . .
> (I.ii.97–100)

And there is the all-pervading military presence that gives both locations an edge, with the threat of violence around every corner.

The Comedy of Errors has a history of directorial man-handling which an audience seeing the play almost seems to expect – Komisarjevsky's stylized 1938 production and Trevor Nunn's 1978 musical version, to name but two. But 'our' version did seem to sit well with the play. As we watched those flickering images in the corner of the rehearsal room it was Lynne's hope that by a process of osmosis we, as a company, would absorb the style of the period. The costuming would certainly help with that: 1940s suits and trilby hats. It was fascinating to watch some early 'screw-ball' comedies and observe the wonderful physical dexterity of the actors: there was a flair, a sophistication and an ease which were truly enviable. The Marx Brothers' own version of *Casablanca*, *A Night in Casablanca*, became a firm favourite of mine, and it was here that I had my first real thought about Dromio. It crossed my mind that the Dromios could be played in the manner of Groucho Marx – some of the one-line wise-cracks would certainly suit that delivery. But this, on reflexion, seemed too literal and would probably unbalance the production – a shame, for if we had followed this idea we could have included Groucho's famous remark in the programme: 'I didn't like the play, but then I saw it under adverse circumstances – the curtain was up.'

Coleridge wrote that farce is nearer to tragedy in its essence than comedy is and you only have to look at the opening scene of *The Comedy of Errors* for this to be proven true: the public beheading of Egeon, unless he comes up with the readies, is hardly side-splitting stuff. Yet the madcap antics that will shortly follow are given a deeper resonance by the audience's complicitness in the story as it unfolds. Central to this, of course, are Antipholus and Dromio of Syracuse, true innocents abroad – rather like the 'Road' films of Bob Hope and Bing Crosby. The world that Dromio of Syracuse and his master stroll innocently into is riddled with danger and the threat of death hangs over the proceedings – not the stuff of comedy, one would have thought.

Antipholus and Dromio of Syracuse are travellers – they've been on the road together for years. All that they own they carry (or rather Dromio carries). We thought a few suitcases and an umbrella ('Be prepared') would suffice. Early on in rehearsals a camera was added, if only to bring a little humour into the opening banter with the First Merchant: Antipholus and Dromio could pose for a snap which the Merchant could take. The camera and brolly found lots of other uses as rehearsals went on. So familiarity and good-humoured banter seemed to be the way that this Dromio and his boss worked and co-existed and this is what David Tennant (playing Antipholus) and I agreed should be the way we would proceed. Antipholus is willing to give Dromio all his money for safe-keeping, which also suggests a bond of trust between them. Dromio himself comments on this:

> Many a man would take you at your word
> And go indeed, having so good a mean.
>
> (I.ii.17–18)

Not a great opening line for a comic character, but one that shows us the true depth of feeling he has for Antipholus – born out of servitude, no doubt, but developed into something stronger. A great deal of the ensuing comedy revolves around the fact that both Dromios act instantly and enthusiastically in response to their masters' orders. How much of the court jester is in Dromio? Judging by Antipholus's comment that he regards him as a 'trusty villain', and one that 'lightens my humour with his merry jests' (I.ii.19,21), he does have a clowning side. As we tentatively began to put the play onto its feet, we felt that this 'clown' was more broad and basic than, say, a Touchstone or a Feste: it did feel like an early working-out by Shakespeare of just what a clown is. Maybe Shakespeare had seen some of the commedia dell'arte troups that visited London in the late sixteenth century: both Dromios seemed to have a touch of the broad Italian put-upon servant about them. I was also beginning to see the possibility of portraying my Dromio as a gentleman's gentleman: although he may make his master laugh, this could be tempered by his good manners and his breeding. To sum up: my initial thoughts about Dromio were of a slightly over-protective manservant who worries and fusses over his ward – not effeminate as such (though I did spend a week of rehearsals playing him camper than John Inman), but someone who does have a prissy, mothering feel. The fact that David Tennant was younger than most actors playing Antipholus of Syracuse certainly helped with this reading.

Dromio of Syracuse, in the first half of *The Comedy of Errors*, has three main scenes: (1) the discussion of Time with Antipholus; (2) the door scene; (3) the great comic 'Nell' scene, the description of the enormous kitchen wench. Having now added several Chaplin films to my viewing list and witnessed Charlie's physical deftness, as well as viewing the model box of our set, it seemed increasingly important to me that my Dromio should have a strong physical life, as well as great mental agility. The set was simple but effective: an Italianate market square with an iron staircase and two practical doors; it demanded a slightly heightened style of playing. There being no showy set changes, the emphasis would, quite rightly, be on the actors and the text.

In spite of the closeness of Antipholus of Syracuse and his Dromio, of which I have already spoken, when we see them at the beginning of Act Two, Scene Two they are arguing and fighting, Dromio presuming that this is his master's high spirits when in fact Antipholus is genuinely concerned about just where his money has gone. The stage direction indicated the level of tension in the scene: 'Antipholus beats Dromio'. Tom Smith and Anthony Howell, playing the Ephesus twins, were well on the way to realizing that violence and beatings were the foundation on which their relationship is built. There is hardly a scene between them when Antipholus of Ephesus does *not* beat his Dromio. But somehow, for David and myself, the very notion of beating went against our basic instincts about the relationship between the Syracusan boys. And yet the stage direction remained: 'Antipholus beats Dromio'. We couldn't just ignore it, or cut it: a lot of the ensuing humour of the scene comes from Dromio's indignation at having been hit and thought a liar. The only feasible way to make it work, we thought, was to make it quite playful: not that it wouldn't hurt Dromio, but that it came from playfulness and not from any deep-rooted violence. It is just one example of how the political climate has changed, I suppose. In Shakespeare's day maybe audiences found servants being whacked hilarious, but now a political correctness has crept into the theatre, as elsewhere. No, our 'violence' would be of the Laurel and Hardy school: Stan and Ollie often knock hell out of each other, but you, as the viewer, never think that either one is seriously hurt or that their relationship will permanently suffer because of it.

Out of the knockabout banter following the beating comes what for me was the trickiest scene that Dromio and Antipholus of Syracuse have – the discussion of the nature of time:

ANTIPHOLUS By what rule, sir?
DROMIO Marry, sir, by a rule as plain as the plain bald pate of Father Time himself.
ANTIPHOLUS Let's hear it.
DROMIO There's no time for a man to recover his hair that grows bald by nature.

(II.ii.73–8)

And so it continues. This is not, I would argue, the stuff of big laughs. And yet on the page the *look* of the scene, the *feel* of the scene, even some of the *language* of the scene, do have comic overtones. But the simple truth is, taken as a whole, the scene does not raise the smallest laugh – ask any member of the cast who sat through the read-through! The arguments are dense and difficult. If we were to play the scene 'straight' – just stand up and say it – it would surely fall flat; and not only that, but David and I would have missed a chance to play the comic double-act that we wanted our Antipholus and Dromio to be. Far better, maybe, to show how this relationship works while using the

33

language of the scene as our tool. Initial ideas included Dromio dressing Antipholus – too complicated; Dromio combing Antipholus's hair – too literal; Dromio shaving Antipholus – too fussy. What about them having a small bite to eat and drink before exploring the town? The suitcase could be the answer: I could produce, from inside the case, two small stools, a tablecloth (with the case acting as a table), a bottle of beer, glasses, bread, chicken and fruit. We could sit, have a spot of brunch, and idly discuss the notion of Time together. The language would not be forced, indeed would almost be secondary, but the audience would see the closeness of the two of us in action. The fact that we both use the same words, and pick up each other's images, reflects the fact that all animosity is over and we are friends again.

ANTIPHOLUS Why, thou didst conclude hairy men plain dealers, without wit.
DROMIO The plainer dealer, the sooner lost. Yet he loseth it in a kind of jollity.
ANTIPHOLUS For what reason?
DROMIO For two, and sound ones, too.
ANTIPHOLUS Nay, not sound, I pray you.
DROMIO Sure ones, then.
ANTIPHOLUS Nay, not sure in a thing falsing.

(II.ii.92–102)

It has always struck me that in a play so concerned with the passage of time, Dromio of Syracuse seems hell-bent on slowing up the action, either in the 'Nell' scene, which has no dramatic function other than making the audience laugh, or in this scene, where he actually instigates a debate on what Time itself is. It is almost as if Shakespeare wanted the audience to have a breathing space in which to 'catch up' on events so far, giving us a dramatic pause before cranking up the chaos. As soon as Dromio and Antipholus are re-united by their use of language (and, in our case, some stale bread, flat coca-cola, and over-ripe pear), the ante is raised by the arrival of the furious Adriana.

It is in this next section of the play – up until the exit of Antipholus with Adriana – that Dromio really begins to suspect that events are taking a very strange turn and introduces the notion of 'transformation', in this case into an ape (II.ii.208). Luciana quickly decides it would be better if he were an ass. It is the same image that my twin later takes up: 'I am an ass, indeed. You may prove it by my long ears' (IV.iv.27–8). This is where Shakespeare begins to weave his magic. Not only are both sets of twins beginning to be mistaken for each other, but increasingly the

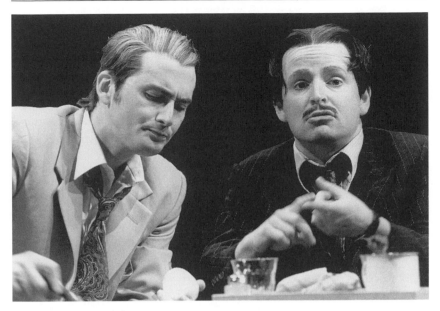

3 Ian Hughes (right) as Dromio of Syracuse with David Tennant as
Antipholus of Syracuse, *The Comedy of Errors*, Act II, Scene ii: 'For two,
and sound ones too . . .'

vocabulary they use echoes each other's, even if it be just in small phrases
like 'for God's sake', which both I and my twin use (I.ii.93, II.ii.24).
Ephesus would have been recognized by Shakespeare's audience as a
town full of mystery and magic, but also as a place with an underlying
darkness. In this apparently light comedy, there are continual flashes
of darkness (quite literally in our production in which large, looming
shadows would streak across the back wall of the market square – very
film-noir), but also flashes of uncertainty in the minds of those caught
up in the unfolding action. Dromio of Syracuse puts it thus:

> O for my beads! I cross me for a sinner.
> This is the fairy land. O spite of spites,
> We talk with goblins, elves, and sprites.
> If we obey them not, this will ensue:
> They'll suck our breath, or pinch us black and blue.
>
> (II.ii.197–201)

Dromio's anxiety is very real and yet audiences, given the set-up and
nature of the scene, would always find this speech very funny: it always

irked me that, even when playing the lines in my best 'concerned' way, I still managed to get a huge laugh off them. O well! It was interesting, too, I always thought, that Shakespeare should have Dromio introduce a very Christian image, his rosary beads, into this most heathen of places.

Having been ordered to 'keep the gate' by Adriana (II.ii.216), and watched Antipholus give in to her advances, Dromio follows his orders to the best of his abilities (of course), the result being what we came to call the 'door scene' (Act Three, Scene One). This is where Shakespeare really starts pulling out the stops – having one set of twins on stage at the same time, separated only by a door. I felt sure that the comedy of this would be heightened by having both Dromios visible to the audience, but our director had had other ideas. One of the problems of pre-designing a show before rehearsals start is that new ideas that spring up from the creative process cannot always be accommodated. So although Lynne agreed in principle to the idea of both Dromios on either side of a door, both visible to the audience, the practicalities meant that this couldn't happen. The off-stage Dromio would communicate to the on-stage Dromio by means of an intercom system. Although initially funny, Dromio of Syracuse does have a fair bit to say, and I suspected that an audience would feel slightly cheated of some of the dramatic possibilities. As a result of speaking my lines into a backstage microphone I never felt fully engaged in this scene. All I could do – and it was rather like being in a radio play – was to commit as fully as possible to the text of the scene. Dromio of Syracuse does seem unnecessarily earnest in carrying out his door-keeping duties, but it is this determination to keep people out that matches the eagerness of Dromio of Ephesus to get his master *in*.

What later happens behind that door is the spur to Dromio's deciding to leave Ephesus: his next appearance is swift and one gets the impression that he is set on leaving this strange town as quickly as possible: 'Why, how now, Dromio. Where runnest thou so fast?', his master demands of him (II.ii.71–2). We never see her, but Nell, his twin's girlfriend, leaves a strong impression. One can only wonder at just *what* occurred inside the house. This 'beastly creature' (III.ii.89) has laid claim to Dromio and is set on 'having' him (III.ii.83) – yes, in the sexual sense, no doubt. Touching on my earliest thoughts about Dromio, he does seem to be strangely sexless and, unless one believes his hugely exaggerated description of this kitchen wench, he does seem to over-react to her advances. A gay Dromio? Maybe – but impossible to play. All that I could do, as an actor, would be to play, fully, his horror, shock and revulsion at what has occurred behind closed doors. The fact that Shakespeare never shows us Nell on stage provides great fuel for our imaginations. Maybe she *is* the size of a bus – we shall never know! What we do know is that Dromio, entering the scene in a state of shock, begins, through the process of describing his plight to his master, to enjoy his predicament.

The scene that follows does nothing to further the plot, or advance the action: it is there to make the spectator laugh – and how! In contrast to the earlier Time sequence, this scene needs no special gimmick to sell it: stand and deliver is all that is required, for here the text takes care of everything, brilliantly. It did, though, take a few weeks of rehearsal to come to understand this. The more we tried to impose some set business on the scene – Dromio's global description of Nell – the more it seemed to interfere with the simple, but brilliant, text.

Marry, sir, she's the kitchen wench, and all grease; and I know not what use to put her to but to make a lamp of her and run from her by her own light. (II.ii.98–101)

My playful suggestion of producing a retracting tape measure to illustrate just how big Nell *might* be would stay with us from the rehearsal room into the final performance. Cheeky . . . audacious? Certainly.

The quality that one can't avoid while reading the scene is that of a comic double-act in full swing. And as David and I had always envisaged the boys from Syracuse being just that, here was our chance to play our version of Laurel and Hardy, or Abbott and Costello, using Shakespeare's text – and with the suitcase to stand on as a little stage and the brolly as a cane. It is a subtle thing, but instead of playing the scene to, and for, each other, you can, just by turning out front and playing the text straight to the audience, easily break down the so-called 'fourth wall' that separates actors and audience. Audiences tend to like this (in the right play) and find it exciting when applied to Shakespeare. You begin to get a feeling of what it might have been like playing to a packed Globe audience in the daylight, and talking directly to the audience as you would to a character in the play. The simple device of comparing parts of Nell's body to the countries of the world – 'she is spherical, like a globe' (III.ii.120) – is bold comedy writing and if *The Comedy of Errors* is often dismissed as an early apprentice piece, then give me early apprentice pieces any day. This one scene contains more laughs than Feste and Touchstone combined.

It was immediately before Act Four, Scene One that we took our interval. In the second half of the play, as the scenes of mistaken identity start to come thick and fast, so Dromio of Syracuse becomes the key figure of mayhem, delivering wrong messages and believing firmly that what he is doing is right, but only adding further to the anarchic confusion.

Having been sent to the bay by Antipholus of Syracuse at the end of his last scene to seek a passage out of Ephesus, Dromio now returns triumphantly with the news that there is indeed a ship waiting to depart, that their belongings are packed, and that the skipper of the vessel now waits only for Antipholus before the ship sets sail. All this, of course, he delivers to the newly arrested Antipholus of *Ephesus*. It is the first time that Dromio of Syracuse mistakes his master in the play, and from an acting point of view I could easily find motivation for this. The stakes are now higher than they've ever been and both Dromio and his master are desperate to get out of this mad-house. In this wound-up state I tried not to look Antipholus in the eye too often. I came into the scene wearing a fez – something I'd picked up at the harbour, I imagined. I wanted to show that I was ready to leave, relieved at having found the means to do so. I also brought a fez for Antipholus and promptly plonked it on his head – something that would have pleased *my* Antipholus no end but which only served to exacerbate the situation for his Ephesian brother. With my new instructions to take a key to Adriana to open a desk in which sits a purse of ducats, I am left alone on stage – though not before having the officer's gun held at point-blank range at my forehead. I felt it would be good thus to illustrate the danger and potential violence of the situation; it also became an excellent spur to motivate me into the next scene. After some cheap business with the two fezzes – 'She is too big, I hope, for me to compass' (IV.i.112): I'll leave you to judge for yourself what can be done with two fezzes – there followed what was, for me, the key to Dromio's actions throughout the play. Rarely do we find in Shakespeare a fellow of the lower ranks – in this case a servant speaking directly to the audience – describing just what it is like to be in a position of subservience:

> Thither I must, although against my will;
> For servants must their masters' minds fulfil.
>
> (IV.i.113–14)

I may not want to go, but I simply have no option: the masters give their orders and the servants act on them. I always liked Dromio of Syracuse as a character, but this line made me love him. Here he shows intelligence and feeling – no bad combination in a comic character.

With Adriana and Luciana reclining on a day-bed lamenting the fickleness of men, I rush in. I need to give the key to Adriana, explain that Antipholus is arrested, and ask her to bring the money to bail him out. Simple, one would think – but not so with Dromio. Why use a few words when several will paint a more elaborate image? I may be out of breath with 'running fast' (IV.ii.30), but I can still manage to give one of the most long-winded and over-elaborate descriptions that the play contains. Dromio seems to relish his new-found importance as the messenger who brings bad news. Once Luciana is despatched to find the money, the chiming of a bell spurs Dromio again to instigate a conversation on the nature of Time. Just when action is needed, debate is what we get – a breather for the audience, and for Dromio too, no doubt. I suggested that at this point I could produce a miniature brandy and a glass out of my little case and Adriana and I could have a swig together – a little moment of stillness amid the bustle. As he says:

> Have you not heard men say
> That Time comes stealing on by night and day?
>
> (IV.ii.58–9)

They are the thoughts of the home-grown philosopher, no doubt, but poignantly true for Egeon, his life in the balance, waiting for judgement at the end of the day.

Act Four, Scene Three presented us with several problems. Once Dromio finds Antipholus of Syracuse he gives him the money for his release. This Antipholus, of course, has never been arrested and my strange behaviour only adds to his growing concern that everyone in Ephesus is mad. The language that Dromio uses is obscure and obtuse – not funny. Yet the comedy dynamic of the play needs this scene to be humorous – at least it should be for the audience. Complicit throughout, the audience is beginning to sense that events are building now to a climax of confusion before the inevitable dénouement. Yet how to make this scene funny – and how to make this scene *understandable*? The extensive notes that accompany editions of Shakespeare were no help. A line like 'have you got the picture of old Adam new-apparelled?' (IV.iii.13–14) brought with it half a page of academic interpretation. It seemed to me that there was a code-like quality about some of the language, a deliberate strangeness. Images from the films we had watched came flooding in: how many spy films contain the meeting of two secret agents with an 'It is raining in Berlin' type of greeting? Could this be used here – spy-speak? We gave it our best shot: I would dress in overcoat, dark glasses and opened umbrella, and skulk about in the corners of the set half whispering the dialogue to Antipholus – very unnerving for him, yet strangely satisfying for me. We also seemed to achieve our aim of making the scene funny, and other cast members said they got the gist of what I was saying, if not every detail. From then on the scene became known as the 'spy scene'.

Antipholus of Syracuse has throughout the play been aware of Ephesus as a place of witchcraft and magic. The arrival of evil personified, in the shape of the Courtesan, confirms that we need to leave quickly. Antipholus identifies her as the 'devil' himself (IV.iii.50). Dromio takes him at his word, but instead of fleeing he stays to debate the nature of such a devil. Again, on paper, the scene reads badly, but in the playing of it, with the cumulative effect of the rest of the play behind it, Dromio's banal and tired use of biblical quotations identifying the Courtesan as an 'angel of light' (IV.ii.55) has an insane logic to it that works – especially when one considers where he is mentally. And yet his last statement to her – ' "Fly pride", says the peacock. Mistress, that you know' (IV.iii. 80) – suggests that he has, at some level, seen through her 'disguise' and recognizes her as a mere mortal: pride, the first of the deadly sins, was often presented as a prostitute.

A manic energy seems to pervade the last section of *The Comedy of Errors*. The re-entry of Antipholus and Dromio after the Pinch scene needed somehow to illustrate this. Could we appear from under the floor, as if from the sewers of the city – echoes of *The Third Man*? Having emerged from our man-hole, Dromio expresses the view that, were it not for the 'mountain of mad flesh' (meaning Nell, of course), he would consider staying in Ephesus as he finds the people there to be such a 'gentle nation' (IV.i.151–2). Quite where he gets this notion from it is impossible to tell, unless he is referring to the gifts that the

4 Ian Hughes (left) as Dromio of Syracuse with Tom Smith as Dromio of Ephesus, *The Comedy of Errors*, Act v, Scene i: 'I see by you I am a sweet-faced youth.'

townspeople have bestowed on Antipholus – or else one could conclude that Shakespearian characters, like real people, are a mass of layers and contradictions.

Dromio and Antipholus appear briefly at the start of Act Five. The spur for their departure through the newly noticed Priory door is the argument between Angelo and the Second Merchant. As this is the high point of the anarchy, before the relative calm of the imminent revelations, it seemed too straightforward simply to run off the stage. I rather boldly suggested a 'comedy-chase', which was greeted with enthusiasm by the other members of the cast, although Lynne needed some persuading. Great fun was had one afternoon coming up with various versions of Antipholus and Dromio being chased, first by Angelo and the Merchant, then gradually involving more and more members of the cast; umbrellas and suitcases were used, and anarchy reigned. Lynne not only loved it, but suggested that we add a camel to the chase, direct from the best traditions of pantomime – and with grateful thanks to the Marx Brothers. We had, it seemed, got the thumbs-up to perform an extended comedy-chase in the middle of a Royal Shakespeare

Company production. All I can say is that the two sat side by side very comfortably. In the fullness of time, actors from the *Henry IV* plays (being simultaneously performed next-door in the Swan Theatre) would join in the chase and thus the 'David Troughton Memorial Run-Across' was born.

The arrival of the Abbess in Act Five provided David Tennant and myself with a welcome break. Events then tended to take care of themselves as the mystery of the day's confusion was unravelled – although the staging here can be problematical in terms of the number of people on the set. But the sheer brilliance of Shakespeare was evident for all to see. For our arrival back on stage, with Antipholus and Dromio of Ephesus already present, very little was required in terms of acting: the scene pretty much takes care of itself. A line such as 'I, sir, am Dromio. Command him away' (v.i.337) never struck me as anything special, but on the rehearsal-room floor drew genuine gasps of laughter from other cast members.

It seemed right and proper that Shakespeare should leave both sets of twins together on stage at the end of the scene. No lines are given to the Antipholuses to express their joy at having found each other – one suspects a few awkward questions to come, behind closed doors – but Shakespeare puts the two put-upon and much maligned Dromios centre-stage to sum up their feelings for each other. The writing confirms what I had suspected all along: Shakespeare *likes* these servants. He, like all those watching from the sides of the rehearsal room, brushes away a tear of emotion, thankful that they have found in each other not only a brother, but someone to love.

The Comedy of Errors, more than any other play of Shakespeare I have been involved with, belongs to an audience. The twists and turns of the plot, on paper at least, can seem clumsy and awkward; but in the presence of the spectator they are transformed into pure theatrical joy. Likewise such a part as Dromio of Syracuse can appear to be a cog in the mechanism of the plot, not character-driven, but merely a function. Maybe this is why this 'fierce little play' (as Harold Bloom calls it in *Shakespeare and the Invention of the Human*) is sometimes dismissed by academics and given a wide berth by some actors. It now appears to me to be one of the most complete and satisfying of the plays, and Dromio of Syracuse one of the most enjoyable of the Shakespearian clowns.

Simple story-telling, well-drawn characters – the fundamental things apply . . . as time goes by. Play it again, Bill!

Puck (and Philostrate) in
A Midsummer Night's Dream

AIDAN McARDLE

AIDAN McARDLE doubled the roles of Puck and Philostrate in Michael Boyd's production of *A Midsummer Night's Dream* at the Royal Shakespeare Theatre in the summer of 1999. The production was later seen at the Barbican Theatre and at the Brooklyn Academy of Music in New York. His other roles that season, his first with the RSC, were Roderigo in *Othello* and Alexas and Thidias in *Antony and Cleopatra*. In 2000–1 he returned to the RSC to play the Dauphin in 1 *Henry VI* and Richard of Gloucester in 2 and 3 *Henry VI* and *Richard III*. Earlier roles at the Abbey Theatre, Dublin, include Dromio of Ephesus and Osric. In London he has worked at the Royal Court and at Hampstead Theatre and television roles include John the Baptist in *Judas and Jesus*.

A little while before I played Puck for the RSC I had auditioned for the part with the Oxford Stage Company. My audition speech was Puck's report to Oberon on his success with Bottom and the ass's head, and its effect on Titania (III.ii.6–34). The speech should be sprightly, speedy and funny, but I got the breath completely wrong and made a terrible mess of it – and, quite rightly, they didn't give me the job. I told myself that I would have been useless in the part, and that I couldn't see any attraction in it anyway. About a year later I was offered the role by the RSC (without an audition!) and accepted with delight. In spite of those earlier sour grapes, I'd really always known that it was a lovely part. The first twenty minutes after accepting it were pure joy; they were immediately followed, however, by a sense of terror that lasted until rehearsals began. The panic came, of course, from having no idea at all about what to do with this person – or, indeed, whether 'person' was the appropriate term for him.

That horrible wait lasted for about a month and a half. I spent much of it wondering what I would look like. *A Midsummer Night's Dream* in the modern theatre is such a design-based play that actors are more or less at the designer's mercy. Would I have horns, like a satyr; would

I be hanging upside down? Since I had no idea how Michael Boyd, the director, envisaged the play, it was hard to do any preparation or to eradicate those fears. A book by Katherine Briggs with the title *The Anatomy of Puck* sounded as if it would be enormously helpful and I tried desperately to get hold of a copy. But it was out of print and I didn't at that time have access to a decent library, so I just went on frustratedly thinking that it must hold the key to the role, not so much with regard to Puck's shape-changing (that's there in the play), but by providing information from the background in folklore on everything to do with Puck's characteristics and behaviour. After rehearsals had started I did finally get hold of a copy of the book, and though it was very interesting in its own right, it could obviously never have helped on the grand scale that I had once imagined, because it didn't set out to deal with that fundamental actor's problem of 'finding the character'. It is very difficult to deal in your imagination with ideas about what a fairy is like, especially when you don't know what sort of a world your play is going to be set in. You have to define boundaries within which you are going to try to paint the picture and at that point I didn't have any sense at all of what our boundaries would be. The character has to come, in the end, from what your relationships are, and that means, fundamentally, from some sort of humanity. Puck may come from the fairy world, but what makes audiences love him are the qualities of mischievous humanity that he constantly evinces.

When we started rehearsing it was immediately clear that the doubling of roles was absolutely vital to the director's vision of the play and thus to the way we would deal with the presentation of the fairy world. Duke Theseus's court in our production was to be a place of deep repression. Hippolyta, we felt, was clearly a victim of conquest and colonization, being forced into marriage with Theseus. We took at its face value the fact that the fairies' quarrel has put the weather out of kilter, so the court was immediately seen as bitterly cold and snowy, like a Russian winter. It is in this repressed and frosty world that we meet Philostrate, the Master of the Revels – revels unlikely to go beyond cold tea and cucumber sandwiches (on black bread). It was very good for me, in preparing Puck, to have his opposite, Philostrate, defining a boundary, presenting 'the other'.

Philostrate, we decided, was the most repressed member of a re-pressed court, the one who organizes everyone else's bows to the duke. All through rehearsals I had one of those little clickers – used, I think, in some churches to indicate when to stand and when to kneel and (before the days of automatic projectors) by slide lecturers to signal to the projectionist when to bring up the next slide. That clicker was of immense importance to me all through rehearsals, the symbol of Philostrate's petty, fussy authority, and it was going to continue through into the role of Puck. In the event the bowler hat that the designer Tom Piper decided Philostrate should wear proved more important in creating continuity.

To the bowler hat were added glasses and, at my request, white gloves. It then emerged that the First Fairy, in her court manifestation, was going to look like Philostrate, so she too was given glasses, white gloves, and a hat, and thus we started for the audience visual connexions that would be vital in what became known as the 'Transformation Scene' (the first part of Act Two, Scene One) as repression turned to release – but more of this later. My precious clicker was taken from me late in rehearsals and I was temporarily lost; but a battered and broken-down bowler hat was added to Puck's accoutrements during the previews and that became, throughout the performance, the visual key to relating the two roles – and a rather more identifiable one for the audience too, perhaps.

I was delighted when I saw the model of Tom Piper's set: absolutely simple, with its curved grey walls producing a sort of amphitheatre for us to play in. Michael Boyd and Tom Piper have a way of making audiences work with their imaginations: no 'pretending' to be in a wood for us, but a ladder could be imagined as a tree, while still having the functions of a ladder. The audience, through the language, will see what they want to see. It was clear from the start that the director knew exactly what he wanted Theseus's court to be, but that the fairy world was more of a process of exploration. The repressed, regimented, grey court, reminiscent of Cold-War Russia, would move to the forest by way of the transformation scene, which would begin with artificial flowers (the first colour in the play) sprouting up through the stage floor. We knew that the court characters would be transformed into the forest characters, but what that great central section of the play would be like was something we had to explore and discover – and Michael Boyd is very good at using actors' ideas and developing and improving them through the rehearsal process.

In a production that's about transformation, you have to tell that story of transformation very well. One particular scene embodies the transition. It was worked on over and over again by Sirine Saba (the First Fairy) and myself. Michael knew from the start that there would be an element of clothes being ripped off to it, but it turned into something more challenging and dangerous than that, a war of the genders, an encounter with the enemy – that's what we had to find a way to dramatize.

During rehearsals of the fairy scenes I went through a period of desperately wanting the RSC to provide me with special big contact lenses, so that my eyes would look like great cats' eyes, shining in the dark. I suppose I wanted to be marked out as being right-hand man, second only to Oberon. It seems irrelevant now, looking back on it, but at the time it was desperately important to me. I was full of ideas about Puck's speed, his ability to put a girdle round the earth in forty minutes, returning from his missions by exploding onto the stage looking as though he'd encountered everything en route – including pigeon feathers from the flocks he'd burst through in his haste.

One of these 'speed' ideas that we tried a lot but could never solve technically so had to abandon, was to have me depart down a trap-door while someone dressed as me would appear almost instantaneously at another trap, look round once, and go down again. We also had a bit of business in which I would disappear down a trap and come up again a few seconds later as if from a U-boat, checking with a periscope that all was well and that Oberon had calmed down sufficiently to make my return a safe proposition. Rehearsals, though, are always a process of discarding – even if sometimes with regret – and the simplest methods usually turn out to be the best.

The really valuable part of any rehearsal process, obviously, is working on relationships. Everything that Puck has to do is with Oberon, and everything that Philostrate has to do is with Theseus. I saw my character, in both worlds, as very much the lieutenant, the one who keeps everything together, whether that is in doing the best, or the worst, of things. I felt that Puck was definitely of a higher status than the other fairies, but that it was a status very much dependent on Oberon's humour: he might as easily give him a kick as a hug. But just as a loyal dog will not resent the occasional smack (provided, obviously, that it never becomes abuse) and will keep on coming back, so Puck doesn't begrudge the occasional slap from Oberon. Puck lives in a world where he hits others and Oberon hits him. Nick Jones (playing Oberon, and Theseus) and I, therefore, inevitably started to form a sort of double act. One bit of business we developed early on was for Oberon to chastise Puck, an action that would turn into a little dance, with Oberon asserting his authority by slapping me down again if I became too uppity.

We decided that Puck absolutely loves the disharmony in the fairy world, partly because he's fond of chaos *per se*, but mainly because a war between Oberon and Titania gives him the undivided attention of his master. This leaves the two of them free to range round the forest in partnership. One of the folklore stories about Puck is that he was a human child who was so naughty that Oberon marked him out as having a rare mortal talent for mischief and took him off to the fairy world to develop it further through training. We worked, therefore, on the idea of Oberon as surrogate father. Puck is no doubt a million years old, but he is for ever fixed in immaturity – not in any Peter Pan way, but in a more psychological sense. Because I was playing Philostrate, I could think of it as *ego* and *id*. These opposites were vital to the performance: 'how repressed, how obedient, can you get?' . . . 'how wanton, how disobedient, can you get?'.

I decided to use a standard ('RP') English pronunciation for most of the play, but to let my own Irish accent creep in at certain points in the later stages when Puck gets more earthy. Of course you can get away with almost anything with him because you're playing a fairy; I found it important not to ask too many literal-minded questions about how old he was or where he came from. But 'playing a fairy' still leaves you with the absolute need to find things that audiences will relate to and will empathize with. The idea of the duality of the personality was vital here, the *ego* of Philostrate and the *id* of Robin, and also the wants and needs that he has in both manifestations, the desire for self-expression, the fear of loneliness, the need for the surrogate father.

It thus became rapidly clear to me that there was no point in trying to play 'non-human'. I did make the actor's statutory visit to the zoo and looked at the meerkats, thinking that they might help with the physicality of the part. But this sort of thing never really helps me much, and it didn't on this occasion; for even if you get good animal physicality, you still have to find the motivation for the things you are given to say; and if you talk there is really no way that you can be non-human.

Among my reading was Peter Holland's Introduction to his Oxford edition of the play. I very much enjoyed his demonstration that there is nothing fluffy about the piece. In fact the play presents a volatile and dangerous sexual world. I wondered a little about his argument that 'puck' is not a personal but a generic name, the category of fairy to which 'Robin Goodfellow, *the* puck' belongs. In one sense it's pretty fundamental to have your character's very name questioned, and were it in a history play, where genealogy and inheritance are vital, it would obviously be crucial. When you're playing a fairy, however, it doesn't seem to matter so much. Perhaps to an Elizabethan audience he would indeed have been 'the puck', but Shakespeare's creation has overtaken folklore and actually changed word usage, turning 'the puck' into a universally known theatrical character who goes by the name of 'Puck' – yet another example of the effect that Shakespeare has had on the English language.

Merely to turn the pages of an edition of *A Midsummer Night's Dream* is to see Puck's verse forms constantly changing. All those little rhymes could, on occasions, begin to seem tedious:

> Through the forest have I gone,
> But Athenian found I none.
>
> (II.ii.72–3)

Luckily Michael Boyd had created such a good rehearsal atmosphere that we were able to work through the doldrums. Rhymes like this are obviously limiting in some ways, but they can also be liberating. For one thing they make the speeches very easy to remember – indeed, it's hard to get them wrong! Sometimes, although you have always to serve the rhymes, it's good to play against them a little. It is altogether too easy to play a skittish Puck, but you must never let the audience forget that you are dangerous; you may be making them laugh at the tricks you are playing on the lovers, but you are also leading those lovers further and further into a dark wood where they could easily die. You are making the audience laugh at the lovers' grief and pain; for the misfortunes of others frequently make the funniest comedy – provided that the sense is clear that they are within a structure that guarantees to deliver them to the happy ending.

I decided that Puck's attitude to the human characters wasn't directly malevolent: he would never deliberately kill them. He does, however, behave with indirect malevolence by putting people into situations where something seriously bad could happen to them. Some of his behaviour is pure curiosity, like the child pouring salt on the slug to find out what happens, or losing the arm off its doll by throwing it across the room to see if it can fly. Human beings are play-things to Puck; his aim isn't the destruction of mankind, but if the head should fall off one of his toys – well, he found out what happened to it if he banged it on the table. His attitude is really one of experimental curiosity based on emotional indifference to humans. 'As flies to wanton boys . . .': Puck is the boy having 'sport' and the humans are the flies. He is thrilled by the improvised destruction that derives from the situations he creates:

> Those things do best please me
> That befall preposterously.
>
> (III.ii.120–1)

He sets things up as if he were creating his own soap-opera and invites Oberon to watch it with him: 'Shall we their fond pageant see?' (III.ii.114).

These, then, were some of the general questions I faced, and some of the main ideas I worked with, as we prepared the play in rehearsal. I want now to examine some of the important moments for Puck (and Philostrate) through the play and to describe the decisions we made about them and the reasons we did so. I have already mentioned the crucial importance to our production of what the editors call Act Two, Scene One, but which was known to us as the 'Transformation Scene'. After the cold, repressed world of the court, and the equally grey world of the mechanicals' first rehearsal, brightly coloured flowers pushed their way through the stage floor as Sirine Saba, Philostrate's side-kick in the court scenes, came on in her white gloves, fur hat, and spectacles. Philostrate appeared in the doorway behind her as she bent down – ostensibly to pick a flower, but somehow in a rather suggestive manner. Philostrate would then stalk her down the stage, moving every time she moved, stopping every time she stopped, in comic syncopation. Then he would catch her up and thus be right behind her the next time she bent down.

Philostrate had had an idiosyncratic little gesture, in the court scene, of stepping forward and rocking on his heels. This movement behind a girl bending down was, obviously, very sexual – although ostensibly nothing at all out of the ordinary, as though he were just out for a walk looking at the scenery, entirely unaware that there was a young woman bending down in front of him. She would then turn, and slap me across the face. I would take that in, then remove her hat, pull off its ear-flaps,

49

5 Aidan McArdle as Philostrate (just prior to transformation into Puck) and
Sirine Saba as an Athenian courtier (just prior to transformation into First
Fairy/Peaseblossom), *A Midsummer Night's Dream*, Act II, Scene i (prelude).

and throw it away. She would acknowledge that, then remove my glasses
and break the arms off them (one at a time), take off my bowler hat,
spit in it, and throw them all into the wings. Things would then begin
to escalate. I would tear an arm off her coat, she would tear an arm off
mine . . . et cetera et cetera until we would be ripping the clothes off
each other with frenzied energy. This was followed by energetic kissing,
the fierceness of the love/hate relationship descending rapidly into pure
sexuality. She would then run away in a very coy, teasing manner, which
was the cue for the first line of the scene: 'How now, spirit; whither
wander you?' (II.i.1). When she came back in, always playing lightness,
the scene became directly about desire and passion – everything that
they had both been repressing at court. We were always playing off the
idea that, because of the quarrel, there had been no communication
between the genders of fairies for a very long time, so through these
few, wordless moments we had moved from cold, grey repression to
colour, and light, and passion.

But the scene was aggressive and dangerous as well. The First Fairy
would imagine that she could tease me:

> Farewell, thou lob of spirits, I'll be gone.
> Our Queen and all her elves come here anon.
>
> (II.i.16–17)

– said as if from a position of power. At one point, too, she used to wrench my arm, demonstrating her superior strength. My response was to make a signal that caused the door to slam; she would then realize that she was trapped as I said 'The *King* doth keep *his* revels here tonight' (II.i.18), as if to say 'My boss is bigger than your boss – and, by the way, don't you imagine that you can tease me sexually and then run away.' On 'Either I mistake your shape and making quite . . .' (II.i.32), the mood turned flirty again and she would treat me like a pop-star, but with the entrance of Oberon the threat was back, and much greater. The rest of the male fairies would suddenly appear through trap-doors behind Oberon, and the First Fairy was clearly in great sexual danger until Titania burst in with her female fairies and rescued her.

As I have already described, we had a number of ideas in rehearsal about how to suggest Puck's speed and diligence in putting a 'girdle round the earth' (II.i.175) in obedience to his master. What we finally decided on (and the image became central to the presentation of Puck) was that he would set off appearing very lackadaisical about the whole thing – 'I'll sort this out, there's just no problem' – and that he would come back, absolutely exhausted, as if he'd been through deserts and floods, and seven kinds of beatings, tumbling back onto the stage absolutely knackered. I used to cover – really *cover* – myself with fuller's earth (not good for the vocal chords) so that the dust would be flying off me, like one of those old pictures of the miner returning from the pit to his tin bath in front of the fire. And the flower I had brought, of course, was the entire plant, foliage, roots, and all – and a barrow-load of compost to plant it in. There was obviously a certain insubordination to Oberon in this (after all, he had asked only for 'a *little* western flower' (II.i.166)), as well as a good laugh for the audience, but the real reason for the choice was that it aligned precisely with my conception of Puck. He is the sort of person who would rip plants up by clumps, who wouldn't take care or pay attention. Puck is rough and ready; there is an essential *rudeness* about him.

Robin's next important scene is the one in which he administers 'Love-in-Idleness' to Lysander. Following on from the notion of Puck's 'rudeness', there was none of that delicate squeezing of the flower-juice

6 Aidan McArdle (left) as Puck with Nicholas Jones as Oberon, *A Midsummer Night's Dream*, Act III, Scene ii: 'Still thou mistakest.'

into his eyes: with a wheelbarrow load of potting compost, Puck dumped a good stout clump of the plant in Lysander's groin, and used his watering-can to water it well in. He is accused by Oberon of getting the wrong man deliberately, but this always seemed to me grossly unfair. Oberon tells him that he will recognize the youth 'by the Athenian garments he hath on' (II.i.264), so why should he be expected to know that there are two young men wandering about the woods in Athenian clothes? It's in Puck's interests to do what he's been told if he's going to prolong his special new relationship with Oberon. Oberon, though, thinks he has done it deliberately:

> This is thy negligence. Still thou mistakest,
> Or else committest thy knaveries wilfully.
>
> (III.ii.345–6)

Puck's explanation, however, seems to me quite genuine:

> And so far blameless is my enterprise
> That I *have* 'nointed an Athenian's eyes.
>
> (III.ii.351–2)

But all the time, of course, he is delighted with the results of his mistake and with the wonderful scene of chaos that it produces: 'this their jangling I esteem a sport' (III.ii.353) – 'sport', the very term used of the wanton boys, and the flies, of the gods and the deaths of men.

In the matter of the love-juice he acts under Oberon's instructions; presenting Bottom with his ass's head is entirely his own idea. And he's very lucky, for it's entirely fortuitous that the first thing the awakening Titania sees is Bottom. Puck goes off to seek his master, absolutely desperate to tell him the story: 'My mistress with a monster is in love' (III.ii.6). He is here at the top of his game – for this was what he ordained. The speech is Puck's longest in the play and one of his few in blank verse. It's wonderful, but I made rather a mess of it at first – shades of my Oxford Stage Company audition! In our production it followed immediately after the interval. Nick Jones as Oberon would be downstage, pondering how Puck had fared – 'I wonder if Titania be awaked' (III.ii.1) – and, of course, the audience knew exactly what had happened, having been roaring with laughter at Titania and Bottom in compromising positions immediately before the break.

I always feel it's important, if a character in a play uses a conspicuous prop, that it shouldn't be a 'one-off' but should reappear and become, if possible, part of him. Hence my appearance at this point with the watering-can which I'd recently used in the planting of the love-herb on Lysander, blowing a bit of an entrance fanfare for myself down its spout – usually the theme from *The A Team*. This is Puck's chance to share his genius properly with Oberon. But it's a huge speech, and he's very excited, and (as I'd discovered at that audition) if you don't have its shape and thoughts clearly down, it's easy for it to turn into nonsense. Puck starts at an enormous speed: one must honour that, because he's hugely excited, and he won't grab Oberon if he doesn't convey that excitement. He offers streams of comparisons for the terror of the mechanicals – 'wild geese', 'russet-pated choughs', and so on – and the whole thing needs to be done with an energy matching his excitement at telling the news. It required a lot of work before I found a technical way of starting it with the right amount of excitement, but not so much that I blew a gasket before I'd finished. To be so excited that you can barely speak, and yet to make sure that the audience understands the whole thing, is an interesting challenge. It was so easy to start at too high a pitch and go right off register; and it's a speech that you have to push, because you know that Puck would push it; anything that sounded moderated and controlled wouldn't work at all. Puck here is like a child, bursting – absolutely *bursting* at the seams – to relate what a great job he has done, how perfectly brilliant he has been, what an absolute genius he is.

'Lord what fools these mortals be', says Puck (III.ii.115) as the 'fond pageant' of the lovers' big quarrel gets under way. In one sense it's just a callous, almost pitiless, remark about the plight of the four young people he's going to watch on stage, but Nick Jones and I developed a way of turning it out into the audience too, so that the 'fools' Puck refers to were also sitting there watching. I would whisper to Oberon as if to say 'Look at them. My God, look at the idiots! Have you seen them?' The resultant laugh was always rather uncomfortable. I felt it necessary to keep playing against the idea of a 'cute' Puck: audiences are always apt to love him and it's essential to remind them to watch out, to remember that he's dangerous. As an actor, too, one needed to be careful of this: it's too easy to succumb to wanting to be liked, vital not to let an audience get too comfortable with you or with Puck.

The 'quarrel scene' entails a lot of watching for Oberon and Puck, and although we performed the production well over a hundred times I never stopped finding it funny. Indeed, except for the last few performances in the huge theatre at the Brooklyn Academy of Music in New York, playing the part was never anything but immensely enjoyable. And the only problem even in Brooklyn was that the theatre was simply too big for our production; and it was miked, so that we didn't feel we had proper control over it. Sometimes there is an optimum space for a production and it won't work properly if you go bigger than that. Our production was absolutely right for the main house at Stratford and worked well enough at the Barbican; in New York I thought we had to push it too hard.

Watching the lovers' quarrel, then, was always a pleasure. I was quickly aware, though, that the actor of Puck has to be careful here not to do anything to distract attention from the main story. There's a temptation to make it Puck's star turn, to have him leaping out into the audience and jumping on people's laps, or chasing the lovers around the stage. But do this and the audience will lose track of the play. You might suppose that as Puck you could do anything you wanted to: you're play-ing the King of Chaos, so anything goes. This is simply not true: the curious thing about playing Puck is that you have to keep it within the bounds of what you might call taste when the character you're playing has absolutely no taste at all. If you do things that will distract from what Oberon is saying, the audience will lose the play, so you have to convince them that you're the King of Chaos without the scene becoming in the least chaotic; you have to keep a grip on your own taste without for a moment allowing Puck to seem one bit tasteful. The scene doesn't need a lot of extraneous business from Puck anyway: he just winds up the clockwork toy and watches it run. That's how it works best.

At the end of the quarrel Puck is left by Oberon to put the lovers to sleep and to sort out their confusions. Before Oberon's departure, however, Puck has an intense little exchange with him about his fear of the coming dawn:

> For night's swift dragons cut the clouds full fast
> And yonder shines Aurora's harbinger.
>
> (III.ii.379–80)

We had it in our heads as we played this (though there's no way that it could come across to the audience) that they were afraid of turning back into their daylight selves. As it gets light Puck must be transformed into that monster Philostrate – and Philostrate is as much a monster for Puck as Puck is for Philostrate. Even without this element, particular to our production, however, it is clear that Puck is only truly at home in the darkness and much in need here of Oberon's reassurance. He is wonderfully back in his element again at the next transformation, at the end of the play – 'Now the hungry lion roars' (v.i.361) – claiming the darkness as his territory, warning those who trespass in it of the dangers that threaten them.

Puck closes the long central scene of the lovers' quarrel by getting the pairings right at last:

> Jack shall have Jill;
> Naught shall go ill.
> The man shall have his mare again and all shall be well.
>
> (III.ii.461–3)

I had my fun leading the men 'Up and down, up and down' (III.ii.396) to exhaustion, and then, from the top of my ladder, used the tin tray on which I had first presented 'Love-in-Idleness' to Oberon (another characterizing prop re-used) to reflect the light and dazzle them into confusion and collapse. Michael Boyd was brilliant in allowing me to mix with these sophisticated (well, relatively) tricks from up the ladder some good old-fashioned slap-stick when I got down to stage level and whacked them one by one over the head – Lysander, Demetrius, Helena – with the tray. But they didn't play being hit on the head: they played being suddenly overcome with drowsiness and collapsing to sleep, one beside another (after a little arranging by me). Hermia came last, crawling onto the stage 'Never so weary, never so in woe' (III.ii.442), and I would ride her like a horse, giving her a crack on the backside with the tray to hurry her up until she collapsed to sleep just before I was able to give her a bang on the head like all the others. I then had simply to dump the rectifying plant in Lysander's crutch and set it to grow, and pull Hermia across to put her hand on the sprouting flowers. And there they all were like a tidy little row of parcels and I could check them off; 'Jack shall have *Jill*' (which I said rather interrogatively, while making sure that it really was the right coupling this time), 'Naught shall go ill' (checking again), 'The man shall have his mare again and all shall be well' (III.ii.461–3). 'Di dum, di dum, di dum', Puck thinks; it's just a mechanical little solution as far as he's concerned. I tried to draw attention to the mechanical nature of the language, hoping that its rhythms would point up the mechanical nature of the actions he is performing to get them all paired up. Yet a few moments earlier, Oberon has spoken of a 'league whose date till death shall never end' (III.ii.373), as though Puck's activities here are to be dedicated to the restoration of true love. Mechanical coupling (with Hermia's hand on the excrescence in Lysander's groin), or true love – as usual Shakespeare leaves the audience to make up its own mind.

In his next scene, the reconciliation of Oberon and Titania, Puck has only three lines, one as he removes the ass's head from Bottom – 'Now when thou wakest with thine own fool's eyes peep' (IV.i.83) – and a couplet again expressing anxiety about the coming of daylight:

> Fairy King attend and mark:
> I do hear the morning lark.
> (IV.i.92–3)

It is the scene that marks the end of all the fun for Puck. Titania used to give me a very dirty look when she woke up. Oberon always seemed to me surprisingly relaxed in telling her that she's not been dreaming and that she really was in love with an ass; and she, it seemed to me, takes all this remarkably well when you consider what a horrible thing it is that he has done to her. The fairies and I used to laugh a horrible raucous laugh and Oberon would take control of the moment and shut us up: 'Silence awhile!' (IV.i.79). I played that I was bored, annoyed, and almost throwing a tantrum at the fact that Oberon is removing the spell and that everything is going to be normal again. Puck is silent here (having had lots to say for himself through most of the play) simply because he is sulking. I used to try to get in between Oberon and Titania when they kissed, but was just unceremoniously dumped out of the way. Yes, the scene is the end of all the fun for Puck. The daylight is coming, with the morning lark; he's got to become Philostrate again.

In the second court scene Philostrate has a great deal more to say than he had in the first. I played him here as utterly snobbish – the main similarity between him and Puck being the fact that they're both like contemptuous kids. I tried playing him straightforwardly at first, but then we realized that what's needed here is a reprise, in a different key, of the double act between Oberon and Puck. Philostrate is the front man: 'What have you to offer me?', asks Theseus – 'Say, what abridgement have you for this evening?' (v.i.39); and it quickly emerges that Philostrate's choices aren't up to scratch, with Theseus dismissing each of his offerings in turn and Philostrate going slower and slower, and his collar getting tighter, as Theseus becomes more disapproving.

Philostrate's proposals are a remarkable selection for a 'manager of *mirth*' (v.i.35) and come straight from the style of the old court. I think his favourite (he certainly puts it first) would be

> *The Battle of the Centaurs*, 'to be sung
> By an Athenian eunuch to the harp'
> (v.i.44–5)

but *The Riot of the Tipsy Bacchanals*, or the lament 'for the death of learning' (v.i.48, 51) would have suited him too. Unlike the rest of the court, he is unreformed. I was still in the black and white costume I had worn in the first scene, while all the rest of them were in pastel colours. For the first time in his career Philostrate finds himself outside the court loop, wondering why they are all dressed like this, what can have happened. The dry and arid entertainments he is proposing would have been perfectly in accord with the ethos of the old court, but while Philostrate has remained fixed in the earlier intellectual snobbery and pretentiousness, Theseus has been transformed, like everyone else, and refuses to be bored by any of these proffered performances. He has found a new humanity in himself and knows that the mechanicals will have made a huge effort and must not be laughed at:

> For never anything can be amiss
> When simpleness and duty tender it.
> (v.i.82–3)

He has found a new self and it was here, in our production, that he got his first kiss from Hippolyta.

Watching the mechanicals' play was always as enjoyable for me (as an actor) as watching the 'play' of the lovers' quarrel had been earlier. For Philostrate, of course, the experience is rather different. The court dance that follows heals everything and brings the court into a different realm, more liberal, perhaps, and more fun; less about mass discipline, more about the individual. The dance in our production broke down all the class barriers as Bottom the Weaver asked Hippolyta the Duchess to dance with him – a moment that made everyone draw breath and that seemed to Philostrate an offence that ought to be punishable by death. Philostrate was shocked and horrified by Hippolyta's acceptance, and by Theseus's joining in; I used to stand side-stage, ram-rod straight, watching these idiots dancing. Then, when they had all gone out, Philostrate was left on the stage alone and a spotlight came up on him; after a moment's stillness I did that old trick of seeming to say 'I wonder what it's like if I just do *this*' – and Philostrate did a step or two from the dance. And that was the start of his going back into Puck. He turned round, and he was becoming Puck:

> Now the hungry lion roars
> And the wolf behowls the moon,
> Whilst the heavy ploughman snores
> All with weary task foredone.
> (v.i.370–3)

And he took off his bowler hat, threw his glasses away, pulled off the tearaway shirt, and he was Puck again: 'You thought I was Philostrate. I'm not Philostrate now, I'm somebody else. And you're back on my turf now, so watch out!' It's no accident, of course, that the first two things he mentions are a lion and a moon, while the mechanicals have spent their rehearsals, and their entire performance, failing to create both a lion and a moon. Puck just says it in two little lines, and you can see them as if they were there. I loved to take control of the audience at that moment, and try to send a shiver down everyone's spine. Sometimes, when there were young schoolchildren in the audience, they would join in by doing a lion's roar – it completely destroyed the speech, but it was gratifying to find them listening so closely and so involved with the performance. By the end of this speech even Puck seems to be endorsing the idea of peace:

> Not a mouse
> Shall disturb this hallowed house
> (v.i.377–8)

– though I used to take the 'house' to mean the *theatre* and push the line out to the audience: 'Don't you dare make a noise! Shut up and listen to the last bit of the play while we do our dance and sing our song.' And during that dance, flowers fell onto the stage.

Unlike the plastic flowers of the transformation scene, these were real flowers, with real 'field dew consecrate' (v.i.405) – well, they were wet – and at the end of the Epilogue I used to throw them out into the auditorium. I loved doing the Epilogue. Early in the run we'd had a party from a convent school walk out in protest at what they thought was the too-overt sexuality of the first scene between Bottom and Titania, so the line 'If we shadows have offended' (v.i.413) took on a rather particular meaning; 'just imagine you were asleep and forget about it; it wasn't our fault – you were dreaming'. On the press night I tried to suggest that I was talking to the critics, indicating to the rest of the audience that we all knew that they were scribbling away furiously. I did the Epilogue 'in character' as Puck, but of course as an actor you are well aware that you are rounding things off and have to put a full stop at the end of the evening. It's very similar with the epilogues to *As You Like It* and *The Tempest*. For the final couplet I used rather to enjoy going a bit 'lovey-dovey' as I asked them to

> Give me your hands if we be friends,
> And Robin shall restore amends.
> (v.i.427–8)

And then I would throw the flowers out to them, as far as I could. 'If we shadows have offended . . .'; 'If you didn't like the production . . .'; 'If you pardon, we will mend . . .'; 'I do hope you enjoyed the evening . . .'; 'Gentles, do not reprehend . . .'; 'Maybe it wasn't *too* bad . . .?'.

Viola and Olivia in
Twelfth Night

ZOË WAITES AND MATILDA ZIEGLER

ZOË WAITES AND MATILDA ZIEGLER played Viola and Olivia in Lindsay Posner's production of *Twelfth Night* at the Royal Shakespeare Theatre in the summer of 2001, and later at the Barbican Theatre. Zoë Waites's other role that season was Kelima in *The Prisoner's Dilemma*; earlier parts for the RSC had been Juliet, Desdemona and Mary in *The Family Reunion*. Among her roles elsewhere are Ophelia (Greenwich and West Yorkshire Playhouse) and Victoria in *The White Devil* (Lyric, Hammersmith), as well as modern plays at the Almeida and the National Theatre Studio. Her television work includes *The New Adventures of Robin Hood* and *Love in a Cold Climate*. Olivia was Matilda Ziegler's only role in the 2001 RSC season, her first with the RSC. A wide range of roles elsewhere includes work at the Royal Court, Hampstead Theatre, and the Lyric, Hammersmith, and several plays (*Volpone* and *Look Back in Anger* among them) at the National Theatre. Her television work includes *Mr Bean*, *Armadillo*, and *Harbour Lights*, and her films *Jilting Joe* and *Mr Bean*.

At the beginning of rehearsals Lindsay Posner took us through his aims and ideas for revealing the heart of *Twelfth Night*. He was most concerned that it was essentially a love story, that the love triangle of Viola, Olivia and Orsino should be central to the play, and that any comedy should emerge from that truth. He wanted to strike a tone that would enable all the characters to come vibrantly to life. We all felt that one potential danger for this play is for it to become episodes of serious boring bits followed by comic turns to cheer up a flagging audience. We believed that the lovers' adventures are dark and deep enough to present real issues that in themselves can be paradoxical and painfully funny. With this idea of forefronting the lovers' contribution to the play, Lindsay called rehearsal with both of us and our Orsino a week before the rest of the cast. This gave us the opportunity to read our scenes quietly together, to hear how these people think, and how they express their feelings, desires and fears. It was during this time that we began to discuss the obsessive love that entangles our characters together:

> How will this fadge? My master loves her dearly;
> And I, poor monster, fond as much on him;
> And she, mistaken, seems to dote on me.
> What will become of this? (II.ii.33–6)

We all felt strongly that the pain experienced by all the characters was crucial to a reading of the play; that their agonies are what make the play so vivid, so desperately funny and so moving. Viola witnesses in Orsino an insatiable passion for a woman he barely knows, whilst Olivia, who totally rejects his advances, falls desperately in love with Cesario, whom she has only just met. Viola finds herself completely in love with Orsino, but, unlike the other two, she does not actively pursue the object of her affections. Not only is she prevented from doing so by her disguise, but her love for Orsino has a maturity and selflessness that makes her prepared to 'let concealment, like a worm i' the bud, / Feed on her damask cheek' (II.iv.110–11).

We felt that our version of the play needed to live in a place and time that was very much an age of innocence. Lindsay and our designer Ashley Martin-Davies chose 1910. Our Illyria was an island somewhere off the coast of Edwardian England. Lindsay felt that this Englishness was crucial to a reading of the play and we were enthusiastic about the period setting. We felt that it could release and illuminate aspects of the play without overwhelming or obscuring it. We were excited by the sense of adventure that seems to have flourished in England at the time. Despite the rigid formality of society, people were beginning to experiment more openly, both artistically and sexually, yet it was still unusual for a woman to wear trousers. The impact of Viola's disguise would therefore be tangible and the cross-dressing have a genuine frisson, placing Viola as a true adventurer. We also chose to make Orsino a military man, and to people his court with a host of young men relaxing between commissions; and Sebastian a young uniformed officer. So for Viola to become Cesario meant not only slipping into a uniform, but also stepping into a recognizably gender-specific world. For Olivia too the period seemed a helpful one, particularly in view of the atmosphere of deep mourning which pervades her house – something the Edwardians seem to have elevated to an art-form. It being an accessible period to research, we found ourselves with lots of material to work our imaginations and to provide us with an Illyria that, despite the fantastic things that happen there, we could all believe in.

We then began to unravel the relationship between Viola and Olivia; how they come together and what experiences bring them to that meeting. At least in Viola's mind, the connexion between the two women is established even before they meet, within Viola's first conversation in Illyria. It is key to their ensuing relationship that Viola discovers so early that Olivia is another young woman suffering the bereavement of both a father and, more recently, of a dearly loved brother (I.ii.39). In the throes of profound grief and disorientation, thrown ashore on a strange land from a violent and terrifying storm, Viola shows immense spirit and optimistic determination. Her energetic imagination is stirred by the strange synchronicity of Olivia's plight, and her first impulse is to serve this woman who 'hath abjured the sight / And company of men' (I.ii.40–1). She then leaps even more enthusiastically onto the idea of serving Orsino and as her relationship with him develops, so her strange connexion with Olivia becomes increasingly fraught, complicated and ambiguous. They are, of course, destined to meet, and the scene in which they do so is of enormous importance to them both, and for us as actors constituted a large part of rehearsals.

We found it important to consider how vulnerable both the women are in this initial meeting and how they are both hiding their true identities. The unconventional freedom this allows them makes playing the scene a really exciting prospect. Viola's disguise has a glorious liberating power, allowing her to tackle Olivia with unusual frankness and enabling her to make an unprecedented exploration of her own thoughts and desires. Olivia seems at a very low point. She is hiding in mourning and is probably very depressed and disillusioned by her problematic household. Malvolio seems to be the only source of strength and piety and he suits her current mood. Yet it is he who awakens her curiosity in the young man at the gates: someone new, half man half boy, beautiful and with a shrewish voice. It is all too tantalizing, but she takes the protective precaution of veiling her face.

For us as actors this was a curious experience. We rely so much on our senses. We need to see each other's faces and sometimes it was frustrating not to see clearly or be seen. Later, when we attempted a rehearsal without the veil, we realized how much the scene depended upon it. Our frustration as actors was synonymous with that of the characters, particularly Viola. For her, having already struggled to get past Belch and Malvolio, this is a bad start. She immediately blunders, launching into an unrestrained eulogy of Olivia's 'unmatchable beauty' (I.v.164). Too late she realizes the irony of praising the beauty of someone whose face she cannot see: the veil has successfully disempowered her and given Olivia the upper hand, a situation that Olivia builds upon by remaining silent and unforthcoming whilst an increasingly desperate Viola tries to coax forth some hint as to which is 'the lady of the house' (I.v.164). Their evasiveness only strengthens her resolve and indeed we always felt a kind of enjoyment in the slightly edgy exchange that ensues. There was a particular pleasure for us in the way that they spark off one another so quickly, deftly appropriating one another's words and ideas and developing shared metaphors very ably. For Olivia particularly, starved of conversation in her self-imposed isolation (especially with anyone so youthful and fresh-faced!), this is pretty exciting.

Even this early on, they express some quite significant and contradictory attitudes and philosophies. They are at this time naturally inhabiting quite different worlds as far as their thoughts on love and wooing are concerned. 'I will on with my speech in your praise', says Viola, 'and then show you the heart of my message'. 'Come to what is important in't. I forgive you the praise', retorts Olivia, and to Viola's plea that ''tis poetical' she silences her with 'it is the more likely to be feigned' (I.v.182–8). Where Olivia distrusts the language of wooing and suspects its sincerity, Viola is captivated by the idea of being able to articulate love through poetry and believes in its ability to transfigure and stir. Viola also makes another intriguing point which we found striking in our conversation: 'Most certain, if you are she, you do usurp yourself; for what is yours to bestow is not yours to reserve' (I.v.180–1). Here again their ideas are in direct conflict. Olivia has done exactly that, 'reserved' herself from the world, and to Viola this seems not only unnatural but wrong. To her it is clear that one has no right to withhold oneself; one only has the right to give, not to keep hidden away. This seems a basic tenet of Viola's approach to life, a clue to her openness, her generosity, and her readiness and desire for a loving relationship.

Although Olivia now tries to end their 'so skipping a dialogue' (I.v.193), we believed her to be already aroused by Cesario's presence – by his wit, his boldness, his strong-headed perseverance, and his youthful energy – since she allows herself to be persuaded to continue their conversation and to despatch Maria. Viola's 'what I am and what I would are as secret as maidenhead; to your ears divinity, to any others profanation' (I.v.207–9) is finally irresistible. The two are left alone together – a small victory for Viola which is immediately undercut by Olivia's refusal to let her get more than three words into her speech. Referring to Orsino's text, Olivia's wit becomes even sharper: 'O, I have read it; it is heresy' (I.v.218). Viola, increasingly offended by this apparently glib dismissal of Orsino's passion, wearies of the veil which prevents any genuine eye-contact and demands its removal: 'Good madam, let me see your face' (I.v.220). Olivia finally removes her veil. At last, actors make proper contact! Interesting that Olivia uses the analogy of drawing back the curtain to show 'the picture' (I.v.223), as if she is used to thinking of her face in this way – as a thing to be stared at, desired, coveted. Her relationship with her beauty is fascinating. Hitherto she has perhaps felt badly served or almost betrayed by it, for it has drawn Orsino to her and made him think he knows her or has some right to own her. Yet now, we thought, she is a little excited by the idea that this young man might be moved by that beauty. We felt that she wanted to use it positively to her advantage.

In the playing of the scene this moment seemed like a definite turning-point – at once a test, an invitation, a challenge, a provocation: 'Is't not well done?' Viola delightfully confounds Olivia, undercutting the intrinsic melodrama of the gesture: 'Excellently done – if God did all' (I.v.224–6). Despite the mischievousness of her retort, she then falls into some heartfelt verse (the conversation has been in prose to this point), her own voice bubbling up out of Cesario as she considers Olivia's beauty and its implications:

> 'Tis beauty truly blent, whose red and white
> Nature's own sweet and cunning hand laid on.
>
> (I.v.228–9)

Finally seeing the face of Orsino's beloved and being able to look into her eyes is strange and intimate for Viola too. She seems even more determined to make Olivia take responsibility for that evident beauty, to make herself available and not to 'lead these graces to the grave, / And leave the world no copy' (I.v.231–2).

Olivia, having made herself suddenly vulnerable, protects herself once again with her wit, trying to undermine Viola's urgent sincerity with her flamboyantly ironic inventory speech, which returns (for the last time in the scene) to prose. She finishes, however, with a genuine question: 'Were you sent hither to 'praise me?' (I.v.238). (Incidentally, since ''praise' here means 'appraise' we decided that Olivia should actually say the latter, since otherwise a modern audience could easily miss the real meaning.) Finally Viola has had enough of what she perceives to be Olivia's glib, haughty refusal to engage in a proper conversation, let alone to take Orsino's love seriously, and she asserts herself: 'I see you what you are, you are too proud' (I.v.239).

We felt that it is here that Olivia is shocked into engaging more seriously. The frankness of Cesario's analysis leaves her a little stunned. Her growing fascination for the boy makes her keen to hear him answer the question 'How does he love me?' (I.v.243), to hear him say the words. Viola is desperate to impress upon Olivia that Orsino's love is not fickle or superficial, but a deeply felt, life-defining passion:

> With adorations, fertile tears,
> With groans that thunder love, with sighs of fire.
>
> (I.v.244–5)

Unbeknownst to Viola, she has shot an arrow into Olivia's heart and spilt real feeling. It is even clearer to Olivia now that she 'cannot love' Orsino (I.v.246), and leaving aside her earlier tone she seriously voices her feelings about him. In the face of this well-articulated and thought-through explanation, Viola's only hope is to make it clear that such an all-consuming passion cannot take no for an answer. Crucially she empathizes with Orsino to such a degree that she quite naturally imagines herself as the desperate lover:

> If I did love you in my master's flame,
> With such a suffering, such a deadly life,
> In your denial I would find no sense;
> I would not understand it.   (I.v.253–6)

So we come to the clinching part of the scene: 'Why, what would you?' (I.v.256).

We tried different ways of playing this over time. For a period Lindsay was keen for Olivia's question to be a demand by which she hoped to deflate Cesario's fervour, or scorn his argument. This meant that Viola's willow cabin speech was almost in defiance of this ridicule. Later we felt that Olivia's question could be a more genuinely curious one: that she had moved on from her tactics of scorning and rebutting and was already more open and available. Either way it was always fun to play this section of the scene because there is something so satisfying about

7 Matilda Ziegler (left) as Olivia and Zoë Waites as Viola/Cesario, *Twelfth Night*, Act I, Scene v: 'Make me a willow cabin at your gate.'

the anger and discord and frustration melting into the gorgeously intimate and utterly sincere expression of love that Viola makes to Olivia. In the moment between question and answer there was a particular quality of anticipation and erotic charge generated by Olivia's sudden desire for him and Viola's unmistakably genuine identification with Orsino. Her consequent determination to win Olivia means she cannot hold back and her confession of the lengths she would go to as a lover tumbles out of her. We understood it as a kind of longed-for relief, to be able legitimately to express the feelings she has for Orsino. There is no element of play-acting: she is painfully honest and it is this evidently deeply felt truth which so captivates Olivia. There is, we found, a tremendous connexion between them, not just because Olivia is knocked sideways by the strength of feeling she is experiencing, but because Viola has conjured a situation that is real and unprecedentedly intimate for her too.

Of course Viola has played the role so convincingly that Olivia's suspicions are aroused, although in the wrong direction. She wonders if a servant could speak such words: 'What is your parentage?' Viola's reply, 'I am a gentleman' (I.v.266, 268) brings on a sudden rush of excitement and fear. This young man is a potential suitor after all. He was, as a servant, perhaps someone with whom flirting could be safe. Now she realizes she has played with fire. It was at this moment that we felt she began to 'speak . . . distractedly' (II.ii.21). She abandons herself to 'the plague' and cannot resist its power: 'Well, let it be' (I.v.284, 287).

As yet oblivious of this and only aware that she has failed in her mission, Viola lays a kind of parting curse on Olivia's obstinacy and lack of compassion:

> Love make his heart of flint, that you shall love,
> And let your fervour like my master's be
> Placed in contempt. (I.v.276–8)

Little does she realize how soon that suffering will begin, and that she will be its cause.

By the time we next meet Viola is of course in full knowledge of Olivia's feelings for her and we naturally found a new element partly defining their relationship – embarrassment. Viola was obviously even less keen to return to Olivia's house than she was to go there the first time and her careful formality at the beginning of the scene suggests her anxiety neither to mislead nor upset Olivia. It is a complicated and agonizing scenario for her. Now that she knows how Olivia feels she has great empathy for her, understanding as she does 'what thriftless sighs shall poor Olivia breathe' (II.ii.39). Despite her conviction that time will 'untangle this' (II.ii.40), it is excruciating for her to have to continue, particularly when she has to tread such a careful path between annoying and encouraging. This explains her reticence in this scene, which is driven by Olivia's new-found ardour. We found that the first section of the scene was characterized by a rather formal awkwardness and that it is Viola's struggle to make Orsino rather than herself the subject of the conversation – 'Madam, I come to whet your gentle thoughts / On his behalf' (III.i.102–3) – which provokes Olivia to throw caution to the wind:

> But would you undertake another suit,
> I had rather hear you to solicit that
> Than music from the spheres.
> (III.i.105–7)

Viola can do nothing but listen to the confessions and questions that flood forth. It finally becomes inevitable that she must give some kind of response to Olivia's plea 'so let me hear you speak' and she expresses herself as honestly as possible: 'I pity you' (III.i.119–20). It struck us as interesting that she is here echoing her earlier instruction to Olivia:

> O, you should not rest
> Between the elements of air and earth,
> But you should pity me. (I.v.263–5)

When she said that, it was as if she believed that compassion for some-one's plight should be enough to make you love them, or at least let them love you. Experience has made her realize that pity is not always 'a degree to love' as Olivia hopes, but that 'very oft we pity enemies' (III.i.120, 122). In the playing of it, it seemed that we both heard the harshness of those words as they were spoken. Olivia seemed quite shocked by what in retrospect sounded a little cruel, although Viola had meant only to be clear, and indeed honest. Olivia recovers herself valiantly – 'Why, then, methinks 'tis time to smile again' (III.i.123) – and shortly afterwards a clock strikes. We decided early on to make a feature of this reminder of the day passing and of the world beyond Olivia's garden. In terms of the play as a whole, time (or, perhaps, Time) obviously plays a significant role. Olivia has attempted to bend time to her will and refused to acknowledge it as a force of change, whilst Viola depends faithfully on time as her trustworthy ally who, in due course, will 'untangle' all their knotty problems. We originally had a big grandfather clock in Olivia's house. Despite having the happy side-effect of providing a hiding-place for Belch's wine stash, we lost the clock, along with all our other furniture, when the production moved to London. Our clock chimes, though, came from somewhere outside Olivia's garden and we allowed them to interrupt our conversation completely. Given that the clock struck twelve times, this was actually quite a substantial length of time without speaking and the embarrassment intensified with every stroke. We were free to experiment with how we responded, and there was always an interesting combination of guilt, desire, connexion and isolation hovering in the air between us. We did, however, sometimes question whether such subtle flickers were rendered imperceptible by the large spaces of the theatres we played in.

After the agony of 'your wife is like to reap a proper man', Olivia allows a mortified Cesario to leave: 'There lies your way, due west' (III.i.130, 131). It seemed to us that Viola's 'Then westward ho!' is a rather desperate attempt to leave on a jokier, lighter note, which she immediately regrets and tries to make up for with her heartfelt 'Grace and good disposition attend your ladyship' (III.i.132). Olivia clearly isn't ready to let her go, however: 'Stay. / I prithee tell me what thou think'st of me' (III.i.134–5). She is desperate to hear him speak to her, to hear his opinions, perhaps to rekindle the intimacy of the earlier wooing scene. The ensuing exchange sees Viola becoming quite angry as she finds herself increasingly trapped by the necessity of playing games with words which make Olivia think she understands something that she cannot. The dynamism of the argument, however, and the passion it engenders, only further fuel Olivia's desire:

> O, what a deal of scorn looks beautiful
> In the contempt and anger of his lip!
> (III.i.142–3)

Horrifyingly for Viola, she launches into her own wooing speech:

> I love thee so that, maugre all thy pride,
> Nor wit nor reason can my passion hide.
> (III.i.148 9)

Viola is now, of course, forced to experience unrequited love from the other perspective. Where she and Orsino earlier wooed Olivia, now Olivia tries to woo her and she experiences, perhaps for the first time, how alarming this can be. Olivia's final suggestion to Cesario seemed to us, however, extremely interesting as a point on which they might concur: 'Love sought, is good; but given unsought, is better' (III.i.153).

Out of this flicker of recognition, Viola's empathy with Olivia's plight, and (mainly) the sheer heights of Olivia's passion, we decided early on in rehearsals that Olivia should kiss Viola. This later proved controversial, and often came up in discussions with audience members. Lindsay's suggestion was that after Olivia initiated the kiss, Viola, rather than pulling away instantly, should respond for a brief moment. Lindsay's intention was to highlight the sexual magnetism of their relationship and the thematic notion of cross-gender sexual ambiguity that reverberates through the play. What it represented for these characters was a welcome moment of pure sexual curiosity. Although Viola's instinct might initially be to pull away, the experience of such a loving kiss became fleetingly seductive for her too. Brimful as she is with love for Orsino, she is living with her own unexpressed erotic charge and readiness, and the joy, or comfort, of sensual human contact is not to be

8 Matilda Ziegler (left) as Olivia and Zoë Waites as Viola/Cesario, *Twelfth Night*, Act III, Scene i: 'Love sought is good, but given unsought is better.'

underestimated! It also seemed to us that the threads of their uncanny connexions could come together in this moment: their empathy, grief, loneliness and readiness for love. Whether an audience feels these things is, of course, entirely their own business, but this was a story that we felt was valid and that we wanted to tell. It also proved a really interesting take-off point for Viola's speech that follows, giving her more of a journey and a heightened sense of responsibility towards both Olivia and herself.

Despite Viola's parting assurance – 'never more / Will I my master's tears to you deplore' (III.i.158–9) – Olivia sends after Cesario and begs him to return. Although the servant 'could hardly entreat him back' (III.iv.58), the audience does get to see the two women alone together one more time. For some reason we always found this tiny scene really tricky, and particularly early on it didn't seem to sit very easily. We felt that it suffered a bit from perhaps seeming a little repetitious, and obviously it lacks the reach and complexity of the other two scenes. It is just a short, awkward parting in which Olivia tries to secure some future between them. Not only does she demand that Cesario 'come again tomorrow' (III.iv.212), but she gives him a brooch of her own portrait. Viola meanwhile offers no words of sympathy, but tries doggedly to wrest Olivia's thoughts back to Orsino. It did become more fun to play after the production moved to London, when, with a bit of re-rehearsal, we chose a more violent, almost hysterical, journey for Olivia which gave us a bit more to play with. It does also finish wonderfully with Olivia's parting shot which so encapsulates the horror of unrequited love:

> Fare thee well.
> A fiend like thee might bear my soul to hell.
> (III.iv.212–13)

The play culminates in a series of revelations and resolutions in Act Five which, in our experience of playing them, can be either completely joyful or tortuously extended, depending on the evening! Olivia enters for what feels like a long-awaited confrontation with Orsino, in which Viola is cast as the largely silent conspirator. Early on she is certainly very eager to maintain a low profile – 'my duty hushes me' (v.i.105) – and later, as the revelations abound, she often appears to be rendered speechless, presumably with astonishment. The initial spat between Olivia and Orsino brilliantly captures the different perceptions of those involved in unrequited love: 'Still so cruel?', asks Orsino. 'Still so constant, lord', is the unarguable reply (v.i.109). Viola, uniquely, understands both positions.

Orsino, almost unhinged in his passion, decides to punish Olivia the best way he can imagine: by threatening to kill her beloved Cesario. Viola's evident willingness to let him go to such extreme lengths, and her unequivocal decision to go 'after him I love . . . More by all mores than ere I shall love wife' (v.i.132–4) devastates Olivia, who feels that she can no longer keep secret what she believes to be their betrothal. The shared sense of despair and betrayal is finally pricked by Sebastian's entrance, and so begin the reconciliations. It seemed to us that one of the most striking observations comes from Sebastian himself when he says to Olivia 'You are betrothed both to a maid and man' (v.i.260). Viola will always be the person that Olivia fell in love with, even when she gives up her 'masculine usurped attire' (v.i.247). It was, after all, to the woman as much as to the man that Olivia was drawn. It is also true that when Orsino pledges his love for Viola, he never uses what he now knows to be her real name, but deliberately refers to her as Cesario or 'boy'. He finds it difficult to shift his perception of her; hence his eagerness to see her in her 'woman's weeds', when she can legitimately become his 'fancy's queen' (v.i.270, 385).

The public reconciliation between Viola and Olivia has to wait a little longer and it is Olivia who initiates it. Given all that she has been through and how vulnerable she has made herself, it is with grace and strength of character (and a little desperation) that she proposes that 'One day shall crown th'alliance on't' (v.i.315). Interesting, too, that she makes the offer of 'at my house, and at my proper cost' (v.i.316). Everyone seems very conscious of paying for things in Illyria – for servants, messengers, fools and even pleasure: 'Truly, sir, and pleasure will be paid, one time or another' (II.iv.69–70).

Olivia further cements her bond with Viola after Orsino has made his pledge: 'A sister, you are she' (v.i.323). We always found this such a welcome moment and embraced with joy – another reference to the sexual ambivalence of the relationship and a tribute to Olivia's determination to get over how deeply she has exposed herself to pain and ridicule. This sense of the recognition of the journey they have made together, and the intimacy of their relationship, was very instrumental in our decision about how to conclude the lovers' story – and a source of even greater controversy than the kiss between us in Act Three, Scene One. There are a multitude of choices we could have made, since Shakespeare leaves the ending of the play very open and shrouded in ambiguity. Will the two pairs of lovers have happy marriages? Will Orsino forget his passion for Olivia and be able to honour Viola with the profound commitment she promises him? Do Olivia and Sebastian know each other? Does that matter? Who is really attracted to whom? Have Orsino and Olivia returned to the conventional boxes of their upbringing, or are they irrevocably transfigured by the eruption into their lives of Viola and Sebastian? Where will Olivia and Viola's relationship go from here? And where does Antonio fit in, if anywhere?

These and other questions seemed to us to lie half-submerged at the end of the play and even the simplest choices, such as who leaves the stage with whom, can seem to imply quite different potential answers. The alternative choices were a source of much debate over the rehearsal period and even into the performing there was some anxiety about the possible inferences of the decisions that we did finally hit upon. The process began with determining who should exit with whom and we were both keen to leave with each other rather than with our respective future partners, thereby enabling us to share a final public affirmation of our connexion. To this end it was decided that after Orsino's final declaration of love to Viola, Olivia should approach her, extending a hand of friendship. We had already decided that it would be lovely to see Orsino and Viola kiss whilst Viola was still dressed as Cesario. We felt that, despite his repeated assertions that only when she is dressed as a girl can he take her as his mistress, we wanted to show his desire for her when she still looks like (and so to all intents and purposes is) the boy he has known all along. At the same time Olivia and Sebastian also kissed with a similar intensity of passion, the sexual charge of both relationships being left in no doubt. Then, after taking Viola's hand, Olivia leant in and kissed her full on the lips. This obviously echoed our previous less comfortable kiss and for us felt entirely appropriate and quite enjoyably provocative. Audience members seemed either horrified or delighted and we did initially suffer some anxiety that it was being misconstrued as nothing more than a cheap gag, but as time went on it felt more and more right. Not only was it a celebration of their affection for one another, it was also a recognition of the sexual confusion of their relationship. For us this wink towards self-knowledge seemed to ring very true.

There are obviously individual decisions, and indeed whole aspects of the play, that we have not been able to go into here. Viola and Olivia act independently of one another a great deal, but we have tried to explain our mutual experience of this play. Over the year and a half that we worked together on *Twelfth Night* we had enormous fun, loving the play and our characters as we did, and we have tried to illuminate the specifics of that pleasure. There were undoubtedly difficult times too. Our confidence in our decisions often wavered, despite our conviction. The production received some criticism on all fronts and we did suffer feelings of acute disappointment and sorrow that we seemed to be failing to serve up the brilliance that is undoubtedly in the play. Our experience of playing the play did in fact often bear out our early fears that the audience might find our scenes less immediately engaging than those of all the clowns, and this at times could feel very disheartening. It was therefore with a degree of trepidation that we committed our thoughts to paper. People have very different responses to *Twelfth Night*. This was ours. Developed as it was through our eighteen-month association with the play, it is inextricably bound up with our own joy, fear, recognition, confusion and, especially, our friendship.

Hermione in
The Winter's Tale

ALEXANDRA GILBREATH

ALEXANDRA GILBREATH played Hermione in Gregory Doran's production of *The Winter's Tale* at the Royal Shakespeare Theatre in late
1998 and early 1999; the production was later seen at the Barbican
Theatre. Earlier roles for the RSC include Maria in *Love's Labour's Lost*,
Regina in *Ghosts*, and Roxanne in *Cyrano de Bergerac*. In the RSC's 2000
season she played Rosalind and Juliet, and in 2003 Katharina in *The
Taming of the Shrew* and Maria in Fletcher's *The Tamer Tamed*. A wide
range of work in provincial and London theatre includes performances
of Regan and of Ophelia; she played Celia in the film *Dead Babies*;
and among her television appearances have been roles in *A Wing and
a Prayer*, *Out of Hours*, and *Monarch of the Glen*. In 1996 she won the
Ian Charleson Award for her performance in the title role in English
Touring Theatre's production of *Hedda Garbler*.

> 'After sharp showers', says Peace, 'the sun shines brightest;
> No weather is warmer than after watery clouds,
> Nor any love deeper, or more loving friends,
> Than after war and woe, when Love and Peace are masters.
> There was never war in the world, or wickedness so keen,
> That Love, if he liked, could not turn to laughter
> And Peace, through Patience, put an end to all perils.'
>
> (William Langland, 1332–1400)

I was sitting on the tube, stopped, as usual, between stations, and my
eye wandered from the newspaper to the sections of advertising on the
upper walls of the train carriage. This poem caught my eye, and there
was Hermione's character staring down at me. Or it describes a part of
her character, at least, that of forgiveness, something she seems to have
in abundance – a living saint and yet a real woman, living and breathing.

The Winter's Tale is quite the most beautiful, most violent, and most
satisfying of plays. It is a late play, probably written in 1611. It also
seems to have a bit of everything: tragedy, comedy, fairy-tale romance,

the most famous of all stage directions ('*exit, pursued by a bear*'), the obsessive jealousy of a man who accuses his pregnant wife of infidelity, which apparently brings about her death and does cause the death of their only son; he tries unsuccessfully to murder his closest and oldest friend and throws out his baby daughter onto the mountain side to suffer whatever fate has in store. And yet, the final scene, with Hermione as the statue coming back to life, was the most moving and most satisfying to play. To quote Greg Doran, the director: 'It is the desire that it should be possible to find forgiveness for the unforgivable that makes the play have the impact that it has.'

So, to start at the beginning: Greg Doran had called me up one day and asked me if I'd like to play Hermione in his forthcoming production of *The Winter's Tale*, with Antony Sher playing Leontes. We had all worked together the previous year on *Cyrano de Bergerac*, and I had had the most inspiring time working with them both, so I was keen to repeat the experience. The 'Sir, spare your threats . . .' (III.ii.90) speech from the trial scene had been one of my audition pieces for drama school, and here I was being offered the role for the RSC! We talked initially about the domestic violence in the play, that essentially it is about a family disintegrating; it just so happens that it's all very public and that the family is of the royal variety.

I talked at about this time to a very well-known actress who exclaimed, when she discovered that I was playing Hermione, 'well, you're too young to play her. . .'. I was twenty-eight. But you know, there's no right age to play this woman: I'm old enough to be a wife and a mother and therefore old enough to play Hermione. For that is all she is, a devoted wife and mother; it's as simple as that. You begin with a very uncluttered, uncomplicated character. She's not difficult to understand: first and foremost that 'wife and mother'; secondly, a queen. The most extraordinary quality she has is the way she reacts to the situations she finds herself in: her honour, her patience, her state of grace, and her overwhelming ability to endure. I was reminded of Nina in *The Seagull* when she explains to Konstantin what it has been like working as an actress: 'The main thing is the ability to endure. Learn to bear your cross; have faith. I have faith, and for me the pain is less.'

So, after this initial conversation with Greg I dug out an old copy of the play and tried to find any notes I might have made when I was a wee small eighteen-year-old in the process of preparing for the audition at LAMDA. Unfortunately everything had been thrown away in various moves since then, so back to the beginning. Hermione is rather a small part. She has only four scenes, and yet her impact in the play is immeasurable and it was this extraordinary quality that I was anxious to start to discover. Having read and reread the play, I came to the conclusion that, first and foremost, she is an innocent falsely accused. Now you can play this as ambiguously as you want, but it is essential that her world falls down on top of her and she is powerless to change it. Let's consider exactly what she loses: first of all her husband and the throne, but most importantly her children, her young, sickly son Mamillius and her baby daughter. And who is responsible for this? The man she trusts and loves most in the world, the father of her children, her husband. And how does she respond? 'I must be patient till the heavens look / With an aspect more favourable' (II.i.106–7). This response was such a clear indication of who this woman is: not a victim incapable of shaping her own destiny, not passive and submissive, but someone who places her trust in fate and the undeniable belief that her husband will repent his sins and her baby daughter be returned to her.

Now this leads me to the rehearsal process . . .

Greg Doran has a very clear and precise way of starting work, which always involves the entire company. For two weeks or thereabouts we all sit around a big table and read through the play from beginning to end and unravel every sentence, so that all concerned have a fair understanding of what is happening. Each actor will respond to a line of Shakespeare in a completely different way and this method means that the company shares thoughts, stories, opinions and so on, and (without being pretentious) a kind of collective 'bonding' takes place. When the language has been dissected and digested, we then take it in turns to read each character as it unfolds during the play, not reading your own character: for instance, I could be reading Leontes, Tony Sher could be reading Paulina, etc. This certainly takes the strain off the first read-through – which usually has the most seasoned performers sweating in nervous anticipation.

Greg and the designer, Rob Jones, had already spent some considerable time planning the design and concept, which always has to be in place as rehearsals start, for the sets and costumes are built and made in six weeks, simultaneously with the average rehearsal time at the RSC. Shakespeare seems to have given the director and designer various problems to overcome in terms of time and place in this play:

(a) two crowned heads of state, Sicilia and Bohemia, with the power of life and death over their subjects;
(b) a coastline;
(c) the fact that the final jurisdiction in the trial scene is given to Apollo and the oracle at Delphi;
(d) Julio Romano, apparently the sculptor of Hermione's statue, who lived in the sixteenth century;
(e) a sheep-shearing feast that seems to take place in Shakespeare's rural Warwickshire.

The list goes on: Shakespeare seems to be defying place and time, mixing gritty realism with mythic resonance. Greg and Rob have to find a world that could conceivably link all these pieces together. Eventually they set the play in a Romanov world at the end of the nineteenth century – and it's always helpful for actors if the setting is specific. (I also refer, in the trial scene, to my father as being the Emperor of Russia (III.ii.118).)

The costumes were therefore rather restricting and formal. The set was a long galleried room, reaching back to an acute perspective, with no ceiling, just a huge piece of silk, threatening to engulf us all. There were no windows, and when Leontes's jealousy gathered momentum the walls could move in and out, making the life of the court smaller and more claustrophobic, the world that we were living in seeming capable of breath. At the end of the trial scene, when everyone's world has crashed in on itself, the huge piece of silk fell and enveloped the set and suddenly we were in a beautiful winter landscape, fit for marauding polar bears!

So, anyway, back to the beginning: Hermione is eight-and-a-half months' pregnant; her husband is Leontes, the King of Sicilia. They have been entertaining Leontes's closest and oldest friend Polixenes, the King of Bohemia, for some nine months and the play opens with Polixenes planning to return home. It seems on the surface that everything is completely ordinary. We opened the play with a triumphant tableau, both Kings and the Queen greeting the crowds below them, the two heads of state presenting a happy and congenial relationship.

Relationships as complex as Shakespeare's need preparation and discussion, resulting in each actor sharing the same history. Tony and I invented a past life, a world to which we could both relate. On the whole our marriage was a very happy one, fruitful and contented. And yet

Shakespeare plants a little seed of doubt: the fact that it took Hermione three months to agree to his marriage proposal, for one thing. Now there could be a variety of reasons for this – all innocent – and yet there it is, an undeniable hint that all was not well at the beginning:

> HERMIONE But once before I spoke to th'purpose? When?
>   Nay let me have't; I long.
> LEONTES   Why, that was when
>   Three crabbèd months had soured themselves to death
>   Ere I could make thee open thy white hand
>   And clap thyself my love: then didst thou utter
>   'I am yours for ever.'
> HERMIONE   'Tis Grace indeed.
>   Why, lo you now, I have spoke to th'purpose twice:
>   The one for ever earned a royal husband;
>   Th'other for some while a friend.
>
>   (1.ii.100–8)

This innocent teasing could be interpreted in so many different ways: from my point of view, sweet, gentle humour; from Leontes's point of view, the beginning of a dangerous game.

Tony Sher, renowned for his intensive research, had (as he describes in the next essay in this volume) been talking to a number of psychologists and psychotherapists and had discovered a medical condition known as 'morbid jealousy', a condition particularly affecting men in their forties, that leads to unreasonable, paranoid, and violent behaviour. This led him to develop a number of telling minor details for Leontes, the smelling of Hermione's belongings, the frantic searching through her sewing bag, always looking for that vital piece of evidence.

As I have said, Hermione is eight-and-a-half months' pregnant. I wanted her to be as 'ripe', as 'female', as possible. I wanted her to glow with the expectancy of her unborn child. Motherhood to Hermione is a beautiful thing. Pregnancy suits her; it therefore makes her supremely vulnerable. It was also important to make it conceivable that she delivers the child as a result of shock, and therefore the baby should be near to full term, making its survival in the wilderness as viable as possible. Having never been pregnant before, I took myself off to some pre-natal classes, which caused no end of mirth with the expectant mums. There was I, happily stroking my rehearsal 'bump', listening to the conversation, considering what was possible in terms of movement, watching them as they prepared for the imminent arrival, a keen sense of terror and excitement!

When one is developing a character, the first clues are in the language and, with a character as sparsely drawn as Hermione, one combs through to glean as much as possible; and then it's down to one's imagination. I was first struck with her informality: whether she is addressing her husband or Polixenes, there is a rather gentle, teasing quality that runs through her dialogue, as if she always seems to be conversing with a twinkle in her eye. I was very keen to promote this quality – that she has a sense of fun, a sense of mischief, never to be taken too seriously but gently persuasive and very, very charming. After all, it doesn't take Polixenes long to decide to stay for that extra week. Hermione has already given her permission that when Leontes goes to stay with Polixenes in the future, she will consent to his remaining for a month after the set departure date.

I suppose that what I really wanted to achieve is the sense that she has absolutely no idea what is happening in Leontes's mind, that her flirtatiousness with Polixenes and her teasing of her husband are oblivious of the volatile emotional situation that, very soon, she will discover. It always seems to me that discoveries for each character in the moment and as the play unfolds are far more interesting for the audience to experience; that an actor should 'bump into' situations, not prepare for them.

Having tried so hard to promote Hermione's innocence, I found it very hard to deny the certain 'something' in the language that Polixenes and Hermione have together, especially during the exchange in which Polixenes explains the relationship between himself and Leontes as young boys, with the suggestion that it was their meetings with their respective future wives that ended their innocence. I suppose I wanted to communicate that Hermione was consciously aware of the subtle sexual overtones behind this dialogue, yet graceful and dignified enough not to yield to them:

> HERMIONE   By this we gather
> You have tripped since.
> POLIXENES   O my most sacred lady,
> Temptations have since then been born to's; for
> In those unfledged days was my wife a girl;
> Your precious self had then not crossed the eyes
> Of my young playfellow.

HERMIONE   Grace to boot!
   Of this make no conclusion, lest you say
   Your queen and I are devils. Yet go on:
   The offences we have made you do we'll answer,
   If you first sinned with us, and that with us
   You did continue fault, and that you slipped not
   With any but with us.

                         (I.ii.75–86)

During Leontes's 'Too hot, too hot' speech (I.ii.108), we decided that
Polixenes and Hermione would begin a courtly dance together, reminiscent of old times when they were all younger (Leontes having given his
permission, with pressing matters of state drawing his attention away).
At the moment when Leontes says

   But to be paddling palms and pinching fingers,
   As now they are, and making practised smiles
   As in a looking-glass . . .   (I.ii.115–17)

the baby moved in my womb, at which I would let out an involuntary
gasp, thus prompting his next line 'and then to sigh, as 'twere / The mort
o'th'deer', and so gradually setting the inevitable momentum of what
is to come, with the next scene being a very public, violent, humiliating
and shocking one for Hermione, and for all the others who witness it.

It starts with Hermione, her young son Mamillius, and her ladies in
waiting. It is a scene of harmony and peace, a domestic one, and because
it ends in the extraordinary way that it does I was keen that it should
begin with merriment and fun. I wanted the scene to be as relaxed as
possible, a brief glimpse, behind the formality of the world outside, of
a private world and of the speed with which it is turned around – which
leaves one breathless, literally.

The scene begins with Hermione asking for the boy to be taken away
from her:

   Take the boy to you: he so troubles me,
   'Tis past enduring.   (II.i.1–2)

Now I didn't want this to be a serious request, just a momentary desire
to be left in peace, and when settled I soon called for him to tell his
'spooky' tales. Leontes then enters and accuses his wife of adultery
with Polixenes; he doesn't mince his words, he doesn't make it easy.
Hermione's supposed treachery is out in the open, for all to witness,

and it happens with such speed and physical ferocity, and in such a public manner, that everyone is rendered speechless:

> LEONTES Bear the boy hence; he shall not come about her.
>   Away with him, and let her sport herself
>   With that she's big with: for 'tis Polixenes
>   Has made thee swell thus.
> HERMIONE   But I'd say he had not,
>   And I'll be sworn you would believe my saying,
>   Howe'er you lean to th'nayward.
>
> (II.i.59–64)

If one strictly follows the clues that Shakespeare gives us, the shared verse line means that there is no pause between these two speeches, thus resulting in Hermione's response being acutely direct and honest, with absolutely no room for shocked incomprehension. Does this mean she is aware of what is coming – or, in my case, that I have understood the accusation at once and deny it immediately? I did find this rather complicated to play, for as modern actors we desire time to reflect or consider. Shakespearian characters are too quick for us and their speed of thought is illuminating: they say what they think on the line and in the moment, without subtext. The language *is* the subtext.

Not only did Leontes (in our production) wrench Mamillius away, much to Hermione's distress, but he turned on her with physical violence, throwing her to the floor and pulling at her clothes. Hermione tries to appease her husband, maintaining her innocence and claiming, in her usual selfless way,

> How this will grieve you,
> When you shall come to clearer knowledge, that
> You thus have published me! Gentle my lord,
> You scarce can right me throughly then to say
> You did mistake.   (II.i.96–100)

Hermione bears this accusation with extraordinary dignity and simply states

> There's some ill planet reigns.
> I must be patient till the heavens look
> With an aspect more favourable.   (II.i.105–7)

Her language in this scene is so clear and so precise that all an actor need do is follow the course of her arguments. It was very hard not to feel anger or outrage during this scene, but to try to play her with resolute patience. Her gentle, reassuring language to her ladies-in-waiting suggests huge personal courage and self-belief:

> Do not weep, good fools:
> There is no cause. When you shall know your mistress
> Has deserved prison, then abound in tears
> As I come out. This action I now go on
> Is for my better grace. Adieu, my lord.
> I never wished to see you sorry: now
> I trust I shall. (II.i.118–24)

At this point I happened to find myself on the floor, having been roughly pushed by Leontes; he was then standing in front of me, and as I tried to stand I reached out my hand to ask for his assistance, which he resolutely denied. It was at this moment that I found Hermione's extraordinary strength: very carefully and quietly I tried to stand up, no one moving a muscle to help and my last words being 'My women, come, you have leave' (II.i.124). Still no one moved. I don't think that I was consciously challenging Leontes to deny me my women, considering my state. Eventually Leontes gave his consent and, as I was led away to prison, the physical pains of imminent childbirth as a result of his brutal treatment were for all to see.

There is a certain gender division in the scene. Leontes and his lords enter a 'female' world, and literally pull it apart. For me, however, it wasn't so much gender division as the destruction of a family, a child being taken away from its mother by the father, a wife being accused of a horrible deed by the husband. I think it is the fact that the accusation is so cruel and unexpected that gives Hermione her extraordinary strength. She cannot believe that this is happening, she hopes that Leontes will eventually see the folly of his ways and restore her to her rightful place; but it is all so incomprehensible that it almost beggars belief.

There is almost an entire act between this scene and the trial scene, though probably no longer than a few days in terms of 'play' time. Hermione has given birth to a baby daughter:

> EMILIA She is something before her time delivered.
> PAULINA A boy?
> EMILIA   A daughter, and a goodly babe,
>   Lusty, and like to live. (II.ii.25–7)

I find it interesting that Paulina's first instinct is the hope that the child will be a male heir, a more convincing option to try to steer Leontes from his madness. Paulina has become Hermione's champion and believes that her best chance of resolving this horrific situation is to take this tiny new-born child to Leontes in the hope that it will miraculously bring him to his senses. It fails, of course, and I know that Estelle Kohler, playing Paulina, found it hard to understand how she could possibly leave this little child with Leontes. Paulina is taking the most remarkable risk: how can she return to Hermione and explain that she has left the child with Leontes? It seems the most extraordinary gesture, openly sacrificing the baby.

I wanted Hermione's fall from grace to be not only textually shocking but visually shocking too. My Hermione was a young woman at her peak, a glamorous queen with beautiful clothes and exquisitely luxurious hair. After her imprisonment I imagined that Leontes would strip her of all comforts, her beautiful clothes replaced by a long and filthy sack dress and her beautiful hair hacked off; so my entrance into the trial scene was as visually alarming as possible. I also wanted the effects of childbirth still there for all to see, with a huge blood-stain on the back of my dress. It is alarming to imagine what childbirth was like before modern medical techniques. How horrific and painful had this birth been, in a dirty, rat-infested cell? Was she still experiencing pain? Did she require medical attention – without going into too much graphic detail. I wanted her physical traits to make her as vulnerable as possible, thus highlighting her remarkable strength of character and her ability to endure enormous suffering.

The beginning of the trial scene was very formal. We tried to include the audience as much as possible, pushing the fourth wall behind them and addressing them as if they were themselves witnessing the trial. The previous 'accusation' scene had been a public one, and so is the trial scene – even more so. Leontes entered amid much pomp and ceremony, lavishly attired, the crown firmly in place. A huge six-foot-high throne had been carried on and seemed to dominate the stage. (I remember at times glancing at Tony, who seemed to make himself terribly small, as if his clothes were too big for him – a little boy on the top of a huge chair.) I would then be summoned and make my way very slowly to a small dock. Even though I imagined that Hermione was still suffering immense pain I wanted her to bear herself with as much dignity as possible, even as she found the step up to this small dock almost too much to cope with. And now to the most difficult part to play: how on earth would anyone find the strength to speak, let alone form concise and persuasive arguments. But she does.

Hermione has three speeches during this scene. I just had no idea of where to start – until I got careful advice from the RSC Voice Department, in the person of Andrew Wade. (When one has an idea of where to start, the rest of the scene has a chance of taking care of itself – in response to what Leontes throws at her.) Andrew and I spent a long time looking at her first speech, understanding the rhythms of it, the rather complicated sentence structure. It appears to be rather formal, suggesting that I have spent time preparing something to say. Occasionally, when one is working on a character, it can take one little detail and suddenly all is unlocked. In this case Andrew brought to my attention the fact that Hermione uses single beats in her first sentence until she reaches the centre of her argument at 'contradicts my accusation'. This made the beginning of the speech very clear and very simple. It is not easy to rush the speaking of monosyllables; one has to take one's time:

> Since what I am to say must be but that
> Which contradicts my accusation . . .
>
> (III.ii.21–2)

As I progressed through the scene I found it so hard not to lace every choice with anger, resentment or bitterness – the ways I would react to this situation. Hermione is absolutely and categorically not bitter or resentful. I tried to read as much as I could about this very famous scene. I found three phrases (they can remain anonymous) that at first seemed very helpful, but which proved impossible to play without her appearing submissive and passive:

a majestic sweetness, a grand and gracious simplicity, an easy, unforced, yet dignified self-possession;

still waters run deep;

. . . passions are not vehement, but in her settled mind, the sources of pain or pleasure, love or resentment, are like springs that feed mountain lakes, impenetrable, unfathomable and inexhaustible.

Now this is all very lovely and poetic, but how on earth can you play it all and make her real and human at the same time? The answer to that question, obviously, is that you can't – but that doesn't stop

9 Alexandra Gilbreath (right) as Hermione with Antory Sher as Leontes, *The Winter's Tale*, Act III, Scene ii: 'Read the indictment.'

one trying, and the scene for me was therefore a continual balance between my own instinctive hot-headedness and her 'still waters run deep'.

There is a very clear indication in the middle of the scene that Shakespeare was suggesting something:

> LEONTES You knew of his departure, as you know
> What you have underta'en to do in's absence.
> HERMIONE Sir,
> You speak a language that I understand not.
> My life stands in the level of your dreams,
> Which I'll lay down.
>
> (III.ii.76–81)

That huge pause in Hermione's reply between 'Sir' and 'You speak a language' seemed to speak volumes to me. It suggested a vital change in the scene and at this point I stepped down from my dock and walked over to Leontes, perched on his massive throne, and appealed to him directly, not as my accuser and my king, but as my husband and my friend. He then spat back at me, as my husband:

> Your actions are my dreams.
> You had a bastard by Polixenes,
> And I but dreamed it . . .
> . . . so thou
> Shalt feel our justice, in whose easiest passage
> Look for no less than death.   (III.ii.81–90)

I reply with a speech which, in my humble opinion, is the most exquisitely phrased in all of Hermione's language. When I spoke it ten years earlier for my audition it seemed so clear to me; I had understood it immediately and loved this effortless feeling of Shakespeare flowing out of me, without my usual 'but what does it all mean?' It is essential to quote the speech in full:

> Sir, spare your threats!
> The bug which you would fright me with I seek.
> To me life can be no commodity:
> The crown and comfort of my life, your favour,
> I do give lost, for I do feel it gone,

> But know not how it went. My second joy,
> And first fruits of my body, from his presence
> I am barred, like one infectious. My third comfort,
> Starred most unluckily, is from my breast –
> The innocent milk in its most innocent mouth –
> Haled out to murder. Myself on every post
> Proclaimed a strumpet; with immodest hatred
> The childbed privilege denied, which 'longs
> To women of all fashion; lastly, hurried
> Here to this place, i'th'open air, before
> I have got strength of limit. Now, my liege,
> Tell me what blessings I have here alive
> That I should fear to die. Therefore proceed.
> But yet hear this – mistake me not: no life,
> I prize it not a straw; but for mine honour,
> Which I would free – if I shall be condemned
> Upon surmises, all proofs sleeping else
> But what your jealousies awake, I tell you
> 'Tis rigour and not law. Your honours all,
> I do refer me to the oracle:
> Apollo be my judge!   (III.ii.90–115)

In my mind Hermione finishes her argument, and her appeal, after 'Tell me what blessings I have here alive / That I should fear to die'. I then walked to the foot of the stage, with my toes almost curling over the edge, and spoke directly to the audience. Hermione at this point scales her most powerful moment, for the actor and for the character; she is absolutely 'centre-stage'. At no other point in the play does she communicate her supreme strength of character so powerfully; her language is simple, direct and utterly convincing.

And in her next speech she also reminds the audience of who she is and where she has come from:

> The Emperor of Russia was my father.
> O that he were alive, and here beholding
> His daughter's trial!   (III.ii.118 20)

The scene then moves with extraordinary speed. The oracle is read and Hermione is vindicated. Its final sentence is, I believe, a great clue as to how Hermione exists for the next sixteen years: '. . . and the King shall live without an heir, if that which is lost be not found' (III.ii. 133–4).

Could this be a suggestion that Hermione spends all that time patiently waiting for her daughter to be returned? What absolutely pushes her over the edge is the news that her son Mamillius is dead. Without her children she has no reason to live, for what is there left to defend? Her life? – 'I prize it not a straw.' Paulina then takes a grasp of the scene and controls it with remarkable dexterity. If Hermione is already dead there is no reason for Leontes to kill her; so in one fell swoop Hermione's life has been saved, and the long wait begins.

So what did I do for the next two hours? Keeping in touch with the play was essential, just listening over the tannoy, trying to keep the momentum in place . . .

And so to the next huge challenge of the play: what does Hermione do for the next sixteen years, hidden away by Paulina, patiently waiting for the oracle to be true to its word and for her daughter to be returned? I believe that Hermione's supreme faith in some way pulls her through: she has no doubts that she will see her child again, or in some way prove that her little baby didn't perish on the mountain side. I remember watching a documentary at the time concerning the American hostages in Iran, the families and the hostages themselves reliving those painful memories. And in some way their experiences helped me understand Hermione: she was both the hostage held captive and also a member of the family waiting patiently for her loved one to be returned. I shall never forget the images of the families meeting again after all that time. How does one cope with the waiting? – and suddenly it all made sense. So for me the statue scene was not about the reconciliation of Hermione and Leontes, but the meeting of a mother and daughter.

So why the statue? I needed some reason. I haven't seen Leontes for sixteen years. Of course Paulina has, during the years, told me how he has changed, but the last time I saw him he was destroying everything around me. Would you trust him? So I just gave myself a little reason: if I stand perfectly still, I can see for myself and it's my choice. I might not want to move; I might remain just where I am. So for me the scene wasn't just an exercise of me standing as still as I possibly could until the allotted time in the script for me to move. I was living and breathing through every painful moment: I could see my daughter standing in front of me, a beautiful young woman; I could see my husband standing in front of me, a changed man. And so the moment when Hermione 'comes to life' was, for me, a moment of choice:

10 Alexandra Gilbreath (right) as Hermione with Antony Sher as Leontes and Estelle Kohler as Paulina, *The Winter's Tale*, Act v, Scene iii: "Tis time: descend.'

'Tis time: descend; be stone no more; approach;
Strike all that look upon with marvel. Come,
I'll fill your grave up. Stir; nay, come away.
Bequeath to death your numbness, for from him
Dear life redeems you. You perceive she stirs.

(v.iii.99–103)

How can I describe this moment for you? Every attempt I make seems inadequate. It seemed to encompass every aspect that an actor strives for, to be effortlessly in the moment without having to 'work' it, the desire in all of us for there to be a second chance, for there to be forgiveness, for there to be redemption. Shakespeare gives Hermione and Leontes no dialogue – how could you possibly put into words what they must be feeling? And leaving all that unsaid, of course speaks volumes. Without wanting to labour the point, I loved playing the scene. Shakespeare so beautifully recognizes the desire in all of us, the need, for forgiveness – and, to quote Greg Doran again, 'that is why the play is so life-affirming, and that, I think, is its special Grace'.

I found that playing Hermione was one of the most rewarding experiences of my life; playing someone with so many life-affirming qualities is in itself life-affirming. She's not as complicated as Leontes, and yet she creates the same amount of 'power'. The challenge of her is her simplicity, her immovable dignity, her state of grace:

Love is patient and kind; it is not jealous or conceited or proud;
Love is not ill-mannered or selfish or irritable;
Love does not keep a record of wrongs;
Love is not happy with evil, but is happy with the truth; Love never gives up;
    and its faith, hope and patience never fail.

(1 Corinthians 13: 4–7)

Leontes in
The Winter's Tale,
and Macbeth

ANTONY SHER

SIR ANTONY SHER is an Associate Actor of the Royal Shakespeare Company. He played Leontes in Gregory Doran's production of *The Winter's Tale* at the Royal Shakespeare Theatre in late 1998 and early 1999 and later at the Barbican Theatre. He played the title role in Gregory Doran's production of *Macbeth* at the Swan Theatre in Stratford in the autumn and winter of 1999–2000, and, in the following months, on a national and international tour, at the Young Vic in London, and for a video recording. Antony Sher's earlier work for the RSC includes the title roles in *Richard III, Tamburlaine, Tartuffe, Singer,* and *Molière,* as well as Shylock, Malvolio, the Fool in *King Lear* and Vindice in *The Revenger's Tragedy.* For the National Theatre he has played, among much else, Arturo Ui, Astrov in *Uncle Vanya* and the title role in *Titus Andronicus.* A wide range of film work includes *Mrs Brown* and *Shakespeare in Love,* and he has appeared extensively on television. His numerous awards include two Olivier Awards for best actor. He has also published several novels and exhibitions of his paintings have been held in London and in Stratford. His essay on his performance as the Fool in the RSC's 1982 production of *King Lear* was published in *Players of Shakespeare 2.*

Two kings: one Sicilian; one Scottish. Two kings who become tyrants. Two men who make a terrible mistake, and venture into the darkest places within the human experience: madness and murder. Two men who destroy themselves and everyone else within reach. One of these characters was written at the height of Shakespeare's creative powers, a time when the artist must have been alight with achievement, and yet he describes a journey which is utterly bleak and nihilistic: life is futile, Macbeth concludes towards the end of the play, it's just a pointless queue of tomorrows shuffling towards eternity. The other character, Leontes, was written at the end of the playwright's career, and is given a miraculous second chance, redemption, resurrection, reunion with his beloved, everything he could ask for.

By chance I played both roles in the same year, 1999, and both were directed by RSC Associate Director (and my partner), Greg Doran. I began by believing that Leontes and Macbeth were like brothers, or first cousins at least. I ended convinced that they were barely related at all. And yet their differences, particularly the differences in their language, illuminated each role vividly. Half way through the year I thought I'd cracked something which is at the heart of this book – the playing of Shakespeare – but by the end I came to a different realization again. There's no definitive solution to be found: you open one window only to find yourself gazing on another that still seems locked . . .

Let me make a confession. Although I've spent much of my career with the Royal Shakespeare Company, until recently – in fact, until that year 1999 – I harboured a secret fear that Shakespeare was forbidden territory for me. I felt that he was the preserve of a certain type of English actor – honey-voiced, middle-classed, tall and noble; Gielgud's children – and that my Jewish South African background put him out of bounds. Whatever Shakespeare's gifts as a portrait painter of humanity or as a stage magician, it is his language that matters most. The words, rhythms, images which lift into the air when the plays are performed, these become like the oxygen itself in the theatre auditorium, an invisible power in the ether. And the source of that power rests in the actor's voice. I spent years studying under the two great voice gurus in the country – Cis Berry at the RSC, Patsy Rodenburg at the National – but something wasn't clicking inside me. When I ventured into Shakespeare I could get away with some roles, those that corresponded to my own circumstances, the foreigner (Shylock), the outsider (Richard III), but anything else, any 'straight' playing of Shakespeare, and I simply sounded wrong in it, my voice sounded wrong to my ears – it sounded like the noise of someone trespassing.

Two things happened to change that. The first was the experience of playing other verse dramatists: Tourneur's (or whoever's) *The Revenger's Tragedy* and Marlowe's *Tamburlaine*. Whatever their individual strengths, they make the writing of verse seem a rather difficult task, either because the language is so jagged, as in Tourneur, or so thumpingly regular, as in Marlowe. They send you hurrying back to Shakespeare, marvelling at his ease with the form. There's a pure connexion between thought, emotion and speech. We all do it effortlessly in every-day situations – we can whisper or roar without a moment's hesitation – and this is what Shakespeare captures: a spontaneous expression of feeling. It's nothing as self-conscious as trying to sound poetic or mel-lifluous: the character simply *has* to express himself through these long, rich sentences. They are second nature to him. The actor need only go with it – by absorbing everything he's learned, all the techniques, all the theories, and then forgetting about them. In the end the language must just pulse through him like blood and come out fresh as air. A good recipe for performing Shakespeare is one part technical skill and one part personal passion.

To achieve this mixture myself – the second stage in my liberation as a Shakespeare actor – it took a crisis in my life. Here is not the place to go into details (and anyway I'd much rather the reader hot-footed it to the nearest bookshop and bought my autobiography *Beside Myself*), but suffice to say that acting had started to give me some bad frights. After being forced to withdraw from two roles in quick succession, something snapped; snapped in anger and snapped into place at the same time. With rehearsals for *The Winter's Tale* already under way, I suddenly didn't care how I sounded in Shakespeare. The point is not how you speak him, but whether or not he speaks to you – as an actor, as a person.

It was in this frame of mind – angry and reckless – that I set out to tackle Leontes, and it proved quite a good starting point.

The Winter's Tale is a 'problem play', and the first problem is solving what happens to Leontes at the beginning. This motors the first three acts. And it's a powerful motor, a runaway motor, heading for a cliff-top. It's make-or-break for the play, and the production.

Leontes is King of Sicilia, which appears to be a prosperous and sta-ble society. He's married to Hermione, happily married – apparently – and they have one child, with another on the way. When we first meet him he's been reunited with his best, childhood friend, Polixenes, and is thoroughly enjoying it – apparently. The atmosphere seems light, joyful, celebratory.

But then – bang! – suddenly the audience are hearing Leontes's thoughts, and these are troubled, strangely troubled. He's convinced that Hermione and Polixenes are having an affair. They're not – we instinctively know that they're not – but there's no stopping Leontes;

his jealousy is gathering force, rising in temperature ('Too hot, too hot!' (II.i.108)), spiralling out of control. Within ten minutes of the play starting, we're in the presence of a very disturbed, very dangerous man. And now we find ourselves asking 'What on earth has just happened?'

Shakespeare provides little help. There is one passing reference to Leontes's feeling of insecurity when he first proposed to Hermione –

> Three crabbèd months had soured themselves to death
> Ere I could make thee open thy white hand
> And clap thyself my love   (II.i.102–4)

– but otherwise nothing. No rumours, no proof, no circumstantial evidence even. Just a man convinced that he's been betrayed, growing more impassioned with every passing moment:

> Inch-thick, knee-deep, o'er head and ears a forked one.
> (II.i.186)

A wonderful image – of flesh, of sewage, of devils and cuckolds – it provided the first clue for me. His subconscious is bubbling up into his wide-awake brain. And there's peculiar arousal to it: lovers kiss with 'inside lip', wives are 'sluiced', they're 'slippery' (II.i.194, 273, 287). He's expressing disgust, yet – like a tabloid journalist – with juices flowing. The normal functions of self-censorship, of self-control, are leaving him. The world is becoming dream-like, or nightmarish, exactly as it does when you have a fever. During the stage history of the play Leontes has sometimes been branded with crude labels – a fairy-tale villain, a wicked king, an evil monster. But no, the writing is too particular, too personal. The rage and destructiveness in Leontes feel familiar to me from my own recent past. Even if I can't explain him, I know this isn't about 'evil' behaviour; this is about someone in trouble, in pain. Look how Shakespeare sprinkles the text with references to illness, as when Leontes says

> Many thousand on's
> Have the disease and feel it not.
> (I.ii.206–7)

But *what* disease, though? This isn't jealousy, just ordinary common-or-garden jealousy, that prickle of competitiveness we've all felt in our love lives or professional careers. This is deeper, darker, much more violent: twenty minutes into the play and Leontes is plotting the death of Polixenes. Thirty minutes in, he's imprisoning his pregnant wife. When the baby is born, he sentences it to be carried into the wilderness and abandoned. By now – and we're still only in Act Two – he has torn apart his whole world. Nobody can reason with him, not even that heroic tigress Paulina (powerfully played by Estelle Kohler in our production). At this point in the play, Leontes is on a collision course with disaster.

'What *is* this disease?'

In search of an answer, I spoke to many experts in mental disorder – a neurologist, a psychiatrist, a psychotherapist – and asked each to put Leontes on the couch. The first thought the patient might be schizophrenic, the second that he was manic-depressive, the third that Shakespeare was possibly creating a portrait of himself in old age, raging against the dying of the light, consumed with frustration and impotence. Then I met Maria Ronn, Professor of Psychiatry at the famous Maudsley Hospital, and she diagnosed Leontes with complete certainty. She explained that he was suffering from a condition known as 'morbid jealousy' or 'psychotic jealousy'. Descending out of the blue, mostly affecting men, mostly in their forties, the dominant characteristic is a delusion that the patient's partner is betraying him. This leads to wildly obsessive behaviour (a frantic search for clues, for smells or stains on clothes or bed-linen, misinterpreting every blush, every slip of the tongue, hiring detectives and lawyers) as well as gruesome visions and fantasies, often on the themes of poisoning and the paternity of children – as in the play – and these frequently lead to paroxysms of rage and violence, even murder, followed by intense periods of remorse. It's amazing: every symptom mirrors those that Shakespeare puts in *The Winter's Tale*. He must have experienced, or witnessed, some similar brainstorm – he must have known about this!

I returned to rehearsals with renewed confidence. Gone were those nagging doubts that the play's hostile critics might be right about Leontes – simply a one-dimensional villain. No, no, my character was ill, and I could prove it. Learning about the condition of morbid jealousy affected Greg too, and everyone in the production; they all began to view Leontes more compassionately. If he's ill, he's as much a victim of what's happening as those whose lives he wrecks. But how to make the audience understand this? Leontes can try your patience terribly: he tears through scene after scene, ignoring all reason or offers of help. The clue, again, was in Act One, Scene Two. There's a remarkable point in the 'inch-thick, knee-deep' soliloquy when Shakespeare suddenly breaks all the rules and allows Leontes to lean through the fourth wall, that invisible barrier protecting audience from actors, and vice versa, and lets him say:

> And many a man there is, even at this present,
> Now, while I speak this, holds his wife by th'arm,
> That little thinks she has been sluiced in's absence . . .
>
> (I.ii.192–4)

He's saying 'stop thinking of this as a play. I'm talking to *you* – sitting right there, right now. Have a think about who *your* wife might be screwing!'

In any soliloquy you are, of course, talking to the audience, but they can still remain in a safe, hazy middle-distance. Not with these lines though. Now you're *really* talking to them. And they rather enjoy the moment – well, everyone except the couple I've singled out in the front row; they enjoy both the *chutzpa* of Shakespeare's device and the salaciousness of Leontes's suggestion. I became increasingly fascinated by this exchange. It set my mind racing. Having established a special relationship with the audience, a kind of hotline, why don't I keep it up, return to it again and again – this hole I've torn in the fourth wall – confide in the audience, ask their advice? As in the soliloquy which begins Act Two, Scene Three:

> say that she were gone,
> Given to the fire, a moiety of my rest
> Might come to me again. (II.iii.7–9)

I tried posing this as a question, even adding 'Hmn?' at the end, imploring the audience to guide me: 'I don't want to kill her, but do you think it might be best – to cure this torment? – please help me.' They're seeing a side to Leontes that no one else does, a vulnerable side, a confused side. They're becoming his confessor – priest or shrink – and now they can't just dismiss him as a fairy-tale monster. They're seeing the world through his fevered vision, and seeing the pain he's in.

Pain: this is essential to the playing of the part, I'd say. Leontes and Hermione have a happy marriage. There's evidence of this before his brainstorm and even during the worst of it – Hermione tries repeatedly to reach for the man she knows and loves – and right at the end of the

11 Antony Sher as Leontes, *The Winter's Tale*, Act II, Scene iii:
'Nor night nor day no rest!'

play, too, at their reunion: she doesn't flinch from it, she embraces him. So if this is true, if they have a good relationship, imagine how he would feel if she betrayed him – which is what, in his illness, he believes. I think the actor playing Leontes has to grieve as well as snarl. I think he has to try to reach for Hermione too, even during his rages – 'if only this was the woman I trusted yesterday, just last week'; and there are tiny opportunities, such as

> Praise her but for this, her without-door form –
> Which, on my faith, deserves high speech
>
> (II.i.69–70)

– opportunities in which the actor can allow glimpses of the real Hermione, the pure Hermione, to confound his suspicions, to trip him up, as in, two lines later, '. . . O, I am out!'

If the performance is not to become one long rant, the actor must sometimes resist the remorseless trajectory on which Shakespeare sets the character. He needs to create little islands of stillness, of sanity, of sorrow, of humour, however brief, before being sucked away by the force of the illness again. Alexandra Gilbreath (Hermione) and I agreed to play our scenes very spontaneously, changing them from night to night, surprising one another, and surprising the other actors, in a way that was appropriate – the court scenes require an atmosphere of genuine danger. Alex and I resolved also to search for the moments of *love*, not just the obvious ones of hate and fear. Greg was passionate about this too. Whenever he directs Shakespeare he encourages his casts to seek what he calls 'the crossroads'. What if we didn't know these great plays inside out? What if events took a different turn? What if Hermione could absolutely prove her innocence, or if Paulina could shake Leontes out of his delusion – where might these moments happen? And what if we let them happen – almost? It's a method of rehearsal that can lead to the most invigorating discoveries: you learn to embrace the ambiguity and contradictions which govern much of human nature and which are sometimes ironed out in stage behaviour. In my case it produced a startling revelation: Leontes requires a strange lightness of playing. As written, it's the heaviest of roles, stuck in a mire of irrationality and stubbornness, and yet it only works when the character becomes buoyant and sprightly – when the actor dances with him.

Leontes uses this word himself, early on: 'my heart dances' (I.ii.110). His thoughts are dancing too – fractured and jumbled, maybe, but deft, very speedy. By this stage in his career Shakespeare has learned to use the iambic pentameter like a master jazz musician: he can keep to the beat, he can play against it, he can improvise round it, he can do all these things at once. The results are almost like modern speech: the broken sentences, the hesitations, the sudden streams of consciousness. I've heard some scholars describe Leontes's early speeches as incomprehensible. Well, I'm afraid they're simply demonstrating one of Cis Berry's favourite adages: Shakespeare was written to be spoken, not read. The same thing that thrills the actor inside the role – inch-thick, knee-deep inside it – is perhaps baffling to the learned brow staring at words on a page. Yes, Leontes does become incoherent, yet he is struggling to make sense of a world which has become unrecognizable. And this is absolutely exhilarating to play.

In fact when I came to do Macbeth, whose language is much steadier, more regular, more rhythmic, I would sometimes long for the tumbling unpredictability of Leontes's speeches, whether the abrasive, stop-start jerkiness of

> Ha'not you seen, Camillo –
> But that's past doubt, you have, or your eye-glass
> Is thicker than a cuckold's horn – or heard –
> For to a vision so apparent rumour
> Cannot be mute – or thought – for cogitation
> Resides not in that man that does not think –
> My wife is slippery? (II.i.267–73)

or, a few moments later in the same scene, the soaring, almost ecstatic explosion of jealousy, repeatedly echoing the word *nothing*:

> . . . is this nothing?
> Why, then the world and all that's in't is nothing;
> The covering sky is nothing; Bohemia nothing;
> My wife is nothing; nor nothing have these nothings,
> If this be nothing. (II.i.292–6)

But, as I would learn, it isn't just that *Macbeth* is an earlier play, and its author perhaps more conservative with the metre; no, there's a far better reason why its protagonist speaks in a more measured way. Both Macbeth and Leontes make a terrible mistake, commit terrible misdeeds, and go on nightmarish journeys; in these things they are similar. But the profound difference between them is that Macbeth remains horribly sane throughout; he watches himself throughout, increasingly appalled by what he sees. He never enjoys the wild, almost liberating oblivion that Leontes knows.

When Leontes does 'wake up' – at the end of the trial scene (III.ii) – it shakes him to his core. I found this the hardest moment to crack, and quite frankly never really did. The onset of jealousy is supposed to be the big challenge in playing the role, but I think the departure of jealousy, the coming-to-his-senses, is much more difficult – particularly if you root his behaviour in mental illness. Professor Maria Ronn had confirmed that sufferers from morbid jealousy can indeed 'wake up' and come to their senses, but it's a gradual process. Shakespeare makes it happen suddenly and dramatically. Even so, I suspect his instincts were better than ours – Greg's and mine. We decided to reduce one of Leontes's speeches at this point, the one that begins 'Apollo, pardon / My great profaneness 'gainst thine oracle' (III.ii.160–1). Here Leontes does a résumé of the events at the beginning of the play. We felt that this was slightly banal, rather like what happens at the end of Agatha Christie stories when someone unravels the mystery, and so we cut most of it. But in retrospect I think a slow piecing-together of what happened might have helped the transition. If elsewhere we were successful in fleshing out the character of Leontes, adding a few more colours and tones than the author necessarily indicates, here we were less so; here I think the master knew best.

Leontes disappears from the action after the trial, as does the court and the whole Sicilian setting. The Bohemian scene takes over: that peculiarly aimless if enjoyable play-within-a-play. By the time we return to Sicilia in Act Five, sixteen years have passed and much has changed. In our production, the set (imaginatively devised by designer Rob Jones) was itself different. For the first three acts the palace was represented by a long gallery, a weird, deep-perspective corridor, the nightmare tunnel down which Leontes tumbles, a tunnel with mobile walls, creeping together, squeezing tighter as the illness worsens. In Act Five the corridor had become wide and disjointed, its lines no longer straight, with gaps evident between sections of wall. The soldiers, whom we had seen immaculately uniformed and upright before, are now sitting around playing cards and smoking, their tunics unbuttoned. The kingdom has ceased to function efficiently; it's on hold. The King himself is a recluse, an untidy figure with long hair and long coat. At the end of the trial, when told that Hermione was dead, he vowed to make mourning his 'recreation' (III.ii.238) – a word which can be emphasized as 're-creation' – but I never imagined him as succeeding, and becoming a resurrected, healed man. (He is sometimes played quite saintly in Act Five.) I imagined him as someone still in torment, though in a different, quieter way to earlier. The realization of what he did, the damage he caused, this is a source of constant, small, active pain. He is like a man with no outer layer of skin; every breeze hurts. Tears flow freely, almost peacefully. If before he was an unstoppable force, now he is inactive, passive, and totally reliant on Paulina: I literally clung to Estelle Kohler during these last few scenes. He is tender – in both senses of the word: raw and gentle. His language is less convoluted than before and has a strange beauty, as when he remembers Hermione's eyes:

> Stars, stars,
> And all eyes else dead coals.
> (v.i.67–8)

Much of his imagery is about the sky, about air, his thoughts are constantly going upwards, upwards. When first seeing Perdita and Florizel he says:

> Alas,
> I lost a couple that 'twixt heaven and earth
> Might thus have stood, begetting wonder, as
> You, gracious couple, do.   (v.i.130–3)

Although I resist the saintly option, which implies an inner tranquillity, there's no doubt he's become more religious, more spiritually aware. But it's also excellent character-writing on Shakespeare's part: in the same way that his rage had that unexpected elation, now his guilt too has a distinctive buoyancy. Much has changed, perhaps, but this is definitely the same man.

And so finally to the famous last scene, the 'statue scene'. I approached it quite sceptically. The situation seems improbable. It turns out that Hermione never died at the trial, but was secretly spirited away and, for these past sixteen years, hidden by Paulina. Now she is revealed, disguised as a statue. It 'comes to life' during the scene, allowing Hermione and Leontes to be reunited. On paper this looks unlikely, as I say, but in practice its power is irresistible; it works utterly. It works like a dream – literally; a dream come true. Who has never fantasized about a lost one returning? Or about being granted a second chance? Everyone is stirred by these thoughts. I've never known a scene that works its magic so consistently. In rehearsals we could never just mark it through or do it technically. It always affected us deeply. In performance its impact on the audience was enormous, and palpable.

In his Shakespeare workshops John Barton points out that whenever a moment in the action is meant to be particularly intense or emotional, the language becomes very simple. Gone is all the spectacular imagery, the flowing poetic rhythms, the rhetoric, the word-play. Suddenly the character speaks plainly, in a way that every human being recognizes, whether they be seventeenth-century Jacobeans or twenty-first-century modern men. Lear says 'O let me not be mad'; Hamlet says 'To be or not to be'; Macbeth says 'Tomorrow and tomorrow and tomorrow'. And Leontes, in the moment of reaching out to touch his wife again, the wife he thought was dead, says something so ordinary yet so poignant that it seems to me as fine as anything this playwright ever wrote:

> O, she's warm!
> (v.iii.109)

I emerged from *The Winter's Tale* with a fresh understanding and love of Shakespeare's language, and with a growing confidence in my ability, or right, to play him. Somewhat arrogantly I also believed I'd found a definitive way of doing his soliloquies – the button-hole method: you crash through the fourth wall, you talk straight to the audience, eyeball to eyeball. Now at last I was perhaps ready to tackle something I'd never done before, one of the great tragic roles.

*

'We're calling it *Macbeth*', Greg told the company on the first day of rehearsals; 'not *Mackers*, not *The Scottish Play*, none of the euphemisms. There's supposed to be a curse on this play. Bollocks! The only curse is that it's so hard to do.'

This is true, but why? Why is this play so difficult to stage? I said earlier that it's better to perform Shakespeare than to read it. Well, here's a curious reversal. Read *Macbeth* and it's a superb, totally successful piece of writing: it's lean, fast, urgent, dangerous; it contacts like a blade, a sharp and vicious blade; it gets under the skin, it's truly disturbing. See it in performance and it's most often risible or tedious, or both. Why? Perhaps because of its themes: horror, witchcraft, the supernatural. The Elizabethans took these things seriously, as do certain unwesternized societies still – one of the best stagings of the play in recent times was the Zulu version *Umabatha* – but the rest of us try not to. We've learned to satirize the things that frighten us, to laugh rather than whimper. This is so deeply embedded in our psyche that we don't even know we're doing it. Greg reports that when he was auditioning for the witches, he'd begin by emphasizing that he wanted to avoid cliché, yet actress after actress would proceed to read the lines in eerie, cracked, hag-like voices. Who says witches sound like this? Walt Disney does. Meanwhile in *Umabatha* the witches are young, clear-voiced, ordinary-looking, their feet firmly planted on the earth – for that's where the dark forces are rooted: the darkness in the real world, in us all. But to acknowledge this is to acknowledge primitive fears. They sneak up on us at night, in real darkness, and in our dreams (or, in Leontes's case, his waking life), but for the rest of the time we try and laugh them away. The 1980 Old Vic *Macbeth*, with Peter O'Toole, caused much laughter, not always intentionally. Backstage, buckets of orangey blood were poured over the actors' heads to denote they'd just experienced an act of violence. But who says violence looks like this? Hammer Horror does – with tongue firmly in cheek. Yet I'm sure that O'Toole and company didn't set out to be funny. Somehow they just muddled the difference between real horror and its fictional counterpart.

Shakespeare doesn't, though. He's not describing the easy ride, the spooky, gasp-and-giggle, ghost-tunnel ride; he wants to consider the real thing. This is what you encounter when you read the play privately. And this is what eludes most productions. A famous exception is Trevor Nunn's in 1975. Greg and I felt daunted by this, yet also inspired, and resolved to learn what we could from it: the use of an intimate theatre, forcing the audience to become involved, not just to observe – they had The Other Place, we had the Swan; the casting of a heavyweight leading actress as Lady Macbeth, ensuring that the story works as a two-hander – they had Judi Dench opposite Ian McKellen, we were lucky enough to get Harriet Walter; simplicity of concept – inner not outer horror. The last is most crucial – easy to identify and target, incredibly difficult to achieve. They had nothing but a circle, darkness, and impeccable acting. Now . . . what would we have?

Time would tell. Meanwhile we began to explore the themes of the play – most especially fear. Every single character in the play experiences fear: even the most powerful, even Duncan (he's very vulnerable when we first see him, his kingdom in chaos), even the witches (Greg wanted them played as people who wish they didn't know the end of the story), and certainly the Macbeths themselves (they create a reign of terror, yet suffer as much as anyone else). Members of the *Macbeth* company were asked to describe their own experiences of ultimate fear. An astonishing range of stories emerged: natural disasters, near-fatal accidents, deep-seated phobias, recurring dreams. These sessions were often gruelling and upsetting to sit through. But if we were to do justice to the dark heart of this play, if we were to contact the *reality* of terror, we would have to open ourselves to some unpalatable stuff.

My private research became fairly testing too. With Leontes it had been a calm, dispassionate process: methodically tracking down the nature of the illness. Piecing together clues from the text, visiting the different experts in mental disorder, I felt like a kind of detective. But now I had to cross sides and immerse myself in something altogether more criminal. Murder: what is it like to commit murder? What is it *actually* like?

The RSC contacted various parole boards round the country and arranged for me to meet two murderers – on separate occasions – two men who'd served their time and were back in society. By chance both were Scottish, and both had committed knife murders.

The first man was younger, more innocent, if I can use that word. He suffered from a gambling addiction and ended up killing his best friend rather than confess what happened to the fifty pounds meant for an electricity bill. The second man was older, tougher, a hardened criminal. He had visited the home of a suspected grass, intending just to give him a lesson, but lost control and by the time he walked home his boots were squelching with blood. The first man was haunted by the crime (he reminded me of that image I had for Leontes in Act Five, a man with no outer layer of skin, nerve-ends hurting in every breeze), while the second man was haunted by the punishment – the long prison sentence, made even longer by fighting the system. You felt that if he hadn't been caught he'd never have given it a second thought.

I immediately identified Macbeth as the first man, and I would say – though Harriet Walter might not agree – that Lady Macbeth is the second: she simply wants to get away with it. But Macbeth is haunted by the crime even before he commits it. Just contemplating it in the 'If it were done' speech, he sees an astonishing image of the consequences:

And Pity, like a naked new-born babe
Striding the blast, or heaven's cherubim, horsed
Upon the sightless curriers of the air,
Shall blow the horrid deed in every eye,
That tears shall drown the wind.   (I.vii.21–5)

I described my first murderer as an innocent man. I'd go further, and call him a good man. He knows right from wrong. That doesn't mean he can't make a mistake and commit wrong. We've all done that. We may not have committed murder, but we've all done something wrong and suffered the consequences, if only in our own minds. Guilt: it's where the writing of the play is so brilliant. Shakespeare created two potential monsters in the Macbeths, but then made them so human, and eventually so vulnerable, that everyone can identify with them.

My meetings with the two murderers are among the most unique encounters of my life. The first man provided an invaluable early insight into the character of Macbeth, and even into the kind of images he uses. For the first murderer had a strange eloquence, born of seeing things that most of us are spared. He described the moment of doing the deed (and he did call it 'the deed') as 'crossing a barrier, going somewhere we're not supposed to go'. Macbeth also talks of primal boundaries:

And his gashed stabs looked like a breach in nature
For ruin's wasteful entrance.   (II.iii.110–11)

And when the deed was done, my first murderer saw a terrible vision: 'And there's me now. Alone. Naked in the world. For always.' It's strangely like Macbeth's image of a naked new-born babe.

A kind of birth, then; but a negative birth, a destructive birth, a birth not into light and life, but darkness and hell. Shakespeare sets both Leontes and Macbeth on these terrible rebirth journeys (though only Leontes is allowed to escape the tunnel, emerge into fresh air again, truly reborn), and both have real births, real new-born babes triggering their action. Leontes fears that the baby inside Hermione's womb is not his own and when it's born he banishes it, intending it to perish. Macbeth is also haunted by a baby, I believe, and by the death of a baby. It first surfaces in that image of the new-born babe, yet is most shockingly described in Lady Macbeth's speech in the same scene:

> I have given suck, and know
> How tender 'tis to love the babe that milks me;
> I would, while it was smiling in my face,
> Have plucked my nipple from his boneless gums
> And dashed the brains out, had I so sworn
> As you have done to this.   (I.vii.53–8)

Some Shakespeare editors invent all sorts of fiction to explain these lines, fiction about the baby being the product of a previous marriage, and so on. Cis Berry's point is proved again: you shouldn't just read Shakespeare, you should perform him. You can't play a previous marriage – never referred to in the text – but you can play a married couple who have had to deal with the death of a baby. For Harriet and me it became a pivotal factor in our relationship, and a pivotal point in that short scene, which begins with Macbeth resolving not to kill Duncan and ends with his dramatic u-turn. Why? Because she brings up the taboo subject, we decided, the tragedy at the centre of their partnership, the dead baby. This has an enormous impact on him. From an emotional point of view he suddenly needs to stand by her at all costs. There's a practical side too: the baby was their hope for the future. Nothing else is left; so they need to grab power now – now, in their own lifetimes.

Macbeth's dependency on Lady Macbeth is fascinating. As with Leontes's marriage to Hermione, it's a curious mixture of love and fear. Lady Macbeth and Hermione couldn't be more different as wives, yet both husbands are twisted on the rack in these relationships. Maybe this tells us something about Shakespeare's attitude to marriage, and to women (look at Othello and Desdemona too, or even Iago and Emilia), but whatever the autobiographical value, it's terrifically rich, complicated stuff to play, and feels very authentic: the shifting nuances of power which occur in any partnership. Harriet Walter and I developed one of the best on-stage chemistries I've ever experienced. To play a marriage you have to become one in a way, sensing what the other actor is thinking, feeling, needing. We were a couple who could switch from affection to anger very quickly, who at times still enjoyed a strong physical attraction, while at other moments were just very ordinary and comfortable with one another – breaking into mutual laughter at the end of that dinner-party from hell, the Banquet, when she suggests he's just over-tired and needs 'the season of all natures, sleep' (III.iv.140). ('Sleep? Yeah, sure, sleep would be nice . . .')

Macbeth's motivation seems to slip in and out of focus in relation to his other half. Look at what happens. The moment he meets the witches (three more powerful women mesmerizing a rather passive man), and hears their prophecies of kingship, a certain word immediately floats to mind:

> My thought, whose murder yet is but fantastical . . .
>
> (I.iii.138)

And in the next scene, at Forres, after Duncan announces the succession to Malcolm, Macbeth is still entertaining illicit thoughts:

> That is a step
> On which I must fall down, or else o'erleap,
> For in my way it lies.　　(I.iv.49–51)

But the moment Lady Macbeth joins in and articulates the plan, in Act One, Scene Five, he suddenly takes fright. Two scenes later he's decided not to do the murder. Then she brings up the baby. Now he resolves to do it. Yet *still* he hesitates. In the next scene he needs the whole dagger speech, with its curiously sensual, dangerous electricity –

> Now o'er the one half-world
> Nature seems dead, and wicked dreams abuse
> The curtained sleep.　　(II.i.49–51)

– finally to spur him into Duncan's chamber. But then, having done the deed – perhaps because he's done it *alone*, without Lady Macbeth – his fear escalates into something very strange. He panics at the sight of blood, forgets to leave the daggers at the murder scene, almost botches the whole thing. What's going on inside his head?

I found the early part of the role very difficult to crack until I finally realized that there weren't a series of neat solutions: Macbeth behaves inconsistently, and I needed to embrace that. We don't always proceed in straight lines. In fact, in *The Winter's Tale*, Shakespeare shows how certainty can be a kind of madness. In *Macbeth* he shows how uncertainty is very human. 'A soldier and afeard', Lady Macbeth says of her husband in the sleep-walking scene (V.i.36). On the battlefield his capacity for violence seems to go beyond the call of duty – he's unseaming people

12 Antony Sher as Macbeth with Harriet Walter as Lady Macbeth, *Macbeth*, Act II, Scene ii: 'I am afraid to think what I have done.'

from the nave to the chops, he's trying to memorize another Golgotha (I.ii.22, 41) – yet this same butcher can't kill one old man in his own house. Brilliant writing once again! When committing murder he behaves like you or I would – or that man I met, the gentle first murderer – and so we identify.

Greg's need to make the audience identify with the play was the driving force of our production. A third of the way through rehearsals we changed from a Jacobean to a modern setting. During early design discussions Greg identified one particular element as vital to the story – darkness. The literal darkness of night – when several major scenes occur – and the darkness nesting in the human spirit. At that stage he dismissed the idea of doing a modern-dress production, saying 'This can't be a world where you just flick a switch to banish the darkness – it can't go away that easily.' But by the time we reached rehearsals, two images had become very familiar on the television screen: the war in Kosovo and the earthquakes in Turkey – modern societies made primitive again; modern societies with all amenities gone; modern societies in deepest darkness. As rehearsals progressed, and as Greg became increasingly concerned that we, the cast, weren't contacting the *reality* of the play (and if *we* couldn't, how could the audience?), he and designer Stephen Brimson Lewis decided to change course, and make ours a modern-dress production. I say 'modern', yet they achieved a clever sleight of hand: it was clearly the contemporary world, but so scorched, blackened and blasted you couldn't say exactly where or when this was. I don't enjoy Shakespeare productions where everyone's using mobile phones and pocket calculators – these give the plays' universality little room to breathe. An early twentieth-century setting is always a good choice for modern-dress Shakespeare – it carries a feel of both past and present – and indeed we had just used this option for *The Winter's Tale*. But I think the burnt look for *Macbeth* was an even better solution: clothes and props recognizable, yet smudged with dirt, oil, soot; virtually no set, just a black space; nothing to interfere with the pure thrust of the narrative.

Our change to modern dress also benefited one of the trickiest sections of the play: Act Five. *Macbeth* propels itself like a jet through the first three acts, then pauses for a long (some might say too long) stop-over during the England scene, and then takes flight again with Lady Macbeth's sleep-walking scene, and in fact reaches its height: a scene of such disturbing emotion, so graphically resolving the theme of crime and conscience, that it's hard to follow onto the stage. (Particularly if you've got, as we had, a great actress at the top of her form.) Both the play and the title-role become less interesting after it. War scenes take over: two sides squaring up, booming and boasting – a bit Marlovian, a bit predictable. 'Tomorrow and tomorrow' in the middle of it, yes, but otherwise little to compare with the sharp, unsettling force of the earlier acts. Searching for a meatier way of doing Act Five, we renamed Macbeth's scenes the 'bunker scenes' and had him retreat to some well-fortified hideaway in the palace, together with his last remaining supporters, the Porter (taking Seyton's lines) and the Doctor: the first a drunken character in a grubby vest, the second a crumpled establishment figure; Macbeth himself, dishevelled and odd, wearing flak-jacket and crown, enthroned on a battered suitcase. A strain of black comedy was suddenly available to us: it was almost as if we were in a play be Beckett or Jarry. So by the time we got to 'Tomorrow and tomorrow' I didn't feel any of the usual pressure that descends when you're called upon to speak resoundingly famous lines. Half Fuhrer, half Godot-tramp, Macbeth could simply gaze into the future with terrible, nihilistic clarity:

> Life's but a walking shadow, a poor player
> That struts and frets his hour upon the stage
> And then is heard no more. It is a tale
> Told by an idiot, full of sound and fury,
> Signifying nothing.　　　　　　　(v.v.24–8)

Good God, I thought, when I saw this speech, he's doing it again – like in *The Winter's Tale* – Shakespeare's pushing the actor through the fourth wall, breaking all the rules, all the barriers. He's saying 'Life is like a performance by a not-very-good-actor; it's like a story by a not-very-good-author, who makes a lot of noise but has nothing to say.' It's as if, in seeking to portray Macbeth's ultimate despair, Shakespeare wants to shock the audience and can find no better way than by stripping away the layer of make-believe in the theatre itself, and asking; 'What are we all doing here – isn't this pointless?'

When the fourth-wall-breakage happened in *The Winter's Tale* I simply went to the very edge of the stage and selected a couple in the front row to address. In *Macbeth* I climbed off the stage completely, spoke to the people on the nearest aisle, then walked to the exit, threatening to abort the play. It seemed in keeping with the jolt which Shakespeare seeks to achieve here.

If the experience of doing *The Winter's Tale* proved to be a bonus for 'Tomorrow and tomorrow', the same wasn't true for the soliloquies earlier in the play, like 'Two truths are told' (I.iii.126) and 'If it were done' (I.vii.1). Throughout rehearsals and even into previews I was using the button-hole method here too: crashing through the fourth wall, confronting the audience eyeball to eyeball. And it simply wasn't working. 'It's making you *explain* the lines too much', Greg said; 'and you mustn't – *can't* – explain them. They are genuinely, thrillingly mysterious. They make us ask "What is he going to do next?" '

It's ironic: Leontes's soliloquies are frequently described as incomprehensible, and I had to do a lot of work to make sense of them. Yet now, with Macbeth, I was being asked to do the opposite – to keep an element of enigma in what he says. As, for example:

> The eye wink at the hand; yet let that be
> Which the eye fears, when it is done, to see.
> 　　　　　　　(I.iv.53–4)

I was at a loss how to achieve this. Greg came to the rescue: 'Try doing nothing on those speeches tonight', he urged; 'try just *thinking*'.

At that evening's preview I went very still on the Act One soliloquies. The audience had to come to me now, not the other way round. And immediately things started to fall into place. Freed from the need to explain Macbeth's rationale, I could let each new idea surprise me, faze me, horrify me, or excite me – or all at once, as in

> Stars, hide your fires,
> Let not light see my black and deep desires.
>
> (I.iv.51–2)

This was much more realistic. We don't always know why certain thoughts come to mind, or what we're going to do about them. We have to just stop and think.

Think: it's the clue to playing the part, I believe, and why I found it so difficult at first. I've never played a character who thinks so much. That sounds ridiculous – we all think all the time – but Macbeth is operating on quite another level. He's a man with an existential headache. By the end he's imploring the doctor 'Canst thou not minister to a mind diseased?'(v.iii.40). He's ostensibly talking about Lady Macbeth, but both men know who he really means, shown by the gender-use in the doctor's reply: 'Therein the patient / Must minister to himself' (v.iii.46–7).

Macbeth's 'diseased' mind is nothing like that of Leontes. Leontes is afflicted with temporary madness. Macbeth is tortured by sanity, by clarity, by both consciousness and conscience. Even when he sees visions like Banquo's ghost, or the apparitions, or the air-drawn dagger (and we brought back a real one to haunt him just before his death), even on those occasions he remains a sane man peering at assorted nightmares. Macbeth and Leontes possess extraordinary, yet very different, imaginations. If I were to choose an artist to portray each, I would say that Leontes's imagination is like something painted by Bosch – it teems with horrid little sticky pink nudes – while Macbeth's imagination is by Dali – elegant, epic pictures of lonely figures in empty landscapes: a newborn baby carried on the wind, one bloody hand turning the oceans red. Macbeth sees these astonishing images in his brain, and is stopped in his tracks. He may be a soldier, yet he's not really a man of action. These tend to be more impulsive, more reckless people. Macbeth is ambitious, but not at all costs: I'm certain he would never have got round to doing the deed without the impetus from Lady Macbeth. He just can't stop watching himself, watching the world, thinking, *thinking*. This is why Macbeth's language is so much steadier than Leontes's – less fractured, less spontaneous. I was finally sure that the two characters share no family genes: if anything, Macbeth is far more closely related to Hamlet.

I'd say that Macbeth is the hardest part I've ever played. And one of the most rewarding. Previously I've always tended to play doers rather than thinkers. I now realize what I've been missing.

So in many different ways 1999 was for me a year of learning and growth. Above all it was the year in which I was lucky enough to appear in two remarkable RSC productions (you're not supposed to say that of your partner's work, but what the hell – both shows taught me to break the rules), and although I never found the definitive way of playing Shakespeare – if such a thing exists – at least I felt I'd made a start: I was on familiar ground at last; I wasn't trespassing any more.

Romeo in
Romeo and Juliet

DAVID TENNANT

DAVID TENNANT played Romeo in Michael Boyd's production of *Romeo and Juliet* at the Royal Shakespeare Theatre in the summer season of 2000, and later at the Barbican Theatre. His other roles in that season were Antipholus of Syracuse, and Jack Absolute in *The Rivals*. Earlier roles for the RSC were Touchstone, Jack Lane in *The Herbal Bed*, and Hamilton in *The General from America*. His other stage work includes a wide range of classical and modern roles at the Manchester Royal Exchange (where he played Edgar in *King Lear*), the Royal Lyceum, Edinburgh, and in London, at the Donmar, the Almeida and the National Theatre. He has worked extensively on radio and televison and among his films are *LA Without a Map* and *The Last September*. His essay on his performance of Touchstone in the RSC's 1996 production of *As You Like It* was published in *Players of Shakespeare 4*.

The thing about *Romeo and Juliet* is that everyone seems to think they know what it's about. You don't have to talk about it for long before people start saying things like 'the greatest love story ever told' and spouting famous lines. ('Wherefore art thou Romeo' has to be one of the most overused and most misunderstood quotations in the English-speaking world.) When I found out that I was going to be playing Romeo for the Royal Shakespeare Company I was at first thrilled, then nervous, and then rather snowed under with unsolicited opinion: 'O, it's a wonderful part'; 'terribly difficult'; 'such beautiful poetry'; 'O, he's so wet'; 'he's so wonderfully romantic'; 'Why on earth do you want to play Romeo? Mercutio is the only part to play'; 'of course Romeo is always upstaged by Juliet'; 'it's the best of Shakespeare'; 'it's absolutely Shakespeare's worst play' – and so on, and on, until it soon became evident that to attempt such a part in such a play might be at best ill-advised and at worst total and utter madness. It was certainly clear that I couldn't hope to please all of the people all of the time and that even pleasing *some* of the people *some* of the time was going to be pretty tricky.

However, I had always wanted to play Romeo. I thought it was a great part full of very recognizable emotions and motivations, with a vibrant youthful energy and a sense of poetry with which anyone who has ever been a self-dramatizing adolescent can identify. It is suffused with the robust certainty and cynicism of youth, but crowned with a winning and rather beautiful open-heartedness.

And it's a great story brilliantly told, full of passion, wit, politics, intrigue, life and death, and topped off with lashings of sex and violence.

And we had a great director at the helm in the shape of Michael Boyd, whose work I had been thrilled by for years at the Tron Theatre in Glasgow and more recently at the RSC itself. His productions had always seemed to me to have the power to make the theatre a truly magical place where things happen that could only happen in a theatre, so that theatre isn't the poor relation of the feature-film but a genuine living art form specific to itself and nothing else. I'd always been desperately keen to work with Michael and to do it with this play was a dream come true.

And Juliet was to be played by Alexandra Gilbreath whom I had met several times and knew would be great to work with, as well as having seen her be very brilliant as Roxanne in *Cyrano de Bergerac* and as Hermione in *The Winter's Tale*. So the whole package was shaping up rather irresistibly.

And I was running out of time. There is no explicit reference in the text to how old Romeo is, but he is, undeniably, a *young* man. I didn't have very many years left. I'd always said to myself that it was a part I would have to do before my thirtieth birthday or not at all. Actors older than that have played the part, of course, and I don't doubt that they've done it very well, but I wanted to set myself a deadline. (There are, after all, few more tragic sights than a balding, middle-aged actor, corsetting in his paunch and inelegantly bounding across the stage as an ageing juvenile!) So, at twenty-eight (I would be twenty-nine before the show opened) it was now or never.

And I suppose that playing Romeo had always represented to me the first rung on a ladder that every great classical actor had climbed before ascending to Hamlet, Iago, Macbeth, and so on, finally culminating in a great, definitive King Lear before toppling over and retiring to an old actors' home and telling ribald anecdotes into a great, plummy old age. Not that I am, for a second, categorizing myself as a 'great classical actor', or even aspiring to such a term, but the opportunity to follow a path through these famous parts in the wake of actors like Irving, Olivier, Gielgud and others seemed thrilling, and something that, ever since drama school, I'd dreamed of doing. This is the sort of egocentric thought-process that is not entirely helpful to an actor when it comes to actually approaching a role, and I'm not particularly proud to admit to it now, but I can't deny that it was a part (only a relatively small part, but an important one nevertheless) of what made me say yes to the RSC and to begin to find my own way through the sea of received notions of what the part meant to everyone who was so keen to give me their opinion.

As the play was to be part of the RSC's 2000 season, I would be involved in more than one production, so I was duly signed up to play Jack Absolute in Sheridan's *The Rivals* and Antipholus of Syracuse in *The Comedy of Errors*, as well as Romeo. *Romeo and Juliet* wouldn't even start rehearsals until the other two plays were up and running, which meant that I was thrown into the first rehearsal day on Romeo only a day or two after my second opening night of the season. This meant that I had had little time to brood over the script before we started. I had been reading the play, of course, and I had made a few observations and suggestions for myself, but I came to the initial read-through relatively open-minded as to how I was going to approach the play and the part.

On the first day Michael Boyd spoke about his own initial impressions and ideas. He talked about the enormous amount of baggage this play seems to bring with it, and his desire that we should shed it all as soon as possible. He said that he'd been surprised, when rereading the play, how unsentimental and muscular it was, and he noted how full of sexual innuendo and darkness it was too. He was interested to find that it was a play about generation, and that the story of the parents was not to be forgotten in the story about their children. He talked about how he wanted to approach the play simply and truthfully, and he introduced us to the set design that he had been working on with designer Tom Piper.

It was a non-specific design, basically two curving walls, facing each other, that could represent different things throughout the evening – whether they were the orchard walls that Romeo climbs, the wall under Juliet's balcony, or, more symbolically, simply a representation of the two families, ever present and immovably solid. Costumes were to be vaguely Elizabethan, without any attempt to be pedantically specific. Statements about generations could be made through the costumes, so that the old world-order of the ageing Prince Escalus would be represented in full doublet and hose, while I, along with Benvolio, Mercutio and the other young men, would look more modern, using shapes and fabrics from contemporary designers. Anachronisms were not to be shied away from if they helped to tell the story.

So, with the world of the production taking shape, I had to start figuring out who Romeo is and how he fits into this society. He's the heir to the Montague fortune – a not-inconsiderable position either socially or politically – but he seems altogether without interest in the family's conflict and much more concerned with his own inner turmoil:

> O me, what fray was here?
> Yet tell me not, for I have heard it all.
> Here [*i.e., in my heart*]'s much to do with hate, but more with love.
>
> (1.i.173–5)

Before his first entrance we learn that Romeo has been seen wandering gloomily through the woods at dawn and holing himself up in his room. He's become distant from his parents – unlike the Capulets, the parent/child dynamic in the Montague household is barely touched on in the play. There doesn't appear to be any antagonism between Romeo and his parents, just a lack of any communication at all, despite Mr and Mrs Montague's obvious concern for their son. It suggests to me that Romeo finds his 'family' elsewhere. Certainly the parental *confidant* in his life seems to have become the friar (but we learn more of that later on) and it is Benvolio who is employed to find out what's wrong.

Central to this first Romeo scene is his relationship with Benvolio. Anthony Howell (playing Benvolio) and I were keen that the two should enjoy a familiar, relaxed relationship. We have just been shown that Benvolio has a trusting relationship with Romeo's parents and, since Benvolio's parents are never referred to, we began to assume that they had been brought up together, so that, although only cousins, they would interact like brothers. (And as Anthony and I were playing identical twins in *The Comedy of Errors*, it seemed churlish not to make the most of any 'familial' similarities.) Having someone who knows Romeo so well helps, I think, to mitigate the worst of his excesses. It struck me that Romeo's first entrance doesn't necessarily help to endear him to an audience, but Benvolio's presence provides an affectionate cynicism which allows the audience, and perhaps even Romeo himself, to see the extremity of his self-indulgence.

When we first see him, Romeo is in the throes of a huge and unrequited crush on a character we never even get to meet; not the 'Juliet' that the play's title has led us to expect him to be pining for, but some girl called Rosaline, who appears to have taken a vow of celibacy rather than reciprocate his advances. Michael encouraged me to think of Rosaline as a novice nun – the ultimate sexual lost cause for Romeo to be mooning after. And this, it seems to me, is part of it: Rosaline's very remoteness and inaccessibility are part of her appeal to the self-aware, emotionally immature and indulgent Romeo. A reciprocated love (such as he later enjoys with Juliet) would not grant him the opportunity to bemoan his own lot, in that peculiarly adolescent way:

> She hath forsworn to love; and in that vow
> Do I live dead that live to tell it now.
>
> (I.i.223–4)

It certainly allows him to cock a superior snook at Benvolio – a kind of 'you who have never loved couldn't hope to empathize with the transcendental pain that I am feeling to a degree that no other human being alive or dead could ever equal'. I'm not suggesting that Romeo is lying to himself, or anyone else, about how he's feeling, but I wanted to suggest that some part of him is enjoying his own drama. (That also allows you somewhere to go later when he experiences a very visceral passion and a very real drama which he can have neither time nor inclination to enjoy or indulge in.) It was a difficult balance to strike: on the one hand I didn't want to patronize the character by portraying someone who doesn't know himself – though in a way he doesn't (yet) – but at the same time I wanted to tell the story of a disaffected youth at odds with his predicament, his environment, and himself and full of the 'nobody-understands-me' ire of adolescence. In discussion with Tom Piper, the designer, it was decided that he would dress himself in black – a self-conscious Hamlet, in mourning for his life. He is therefore in a state of flux, full of unfulfilled passion and directionless purpose – ripe for a journey and looking for exactly the sort of experience that he is about to stumble upon. 'The readiness is all' – and without it there could be no inevitability about what happens and no journey for the character.

So if Benvolio is the familiar harbour where Romeo begins his journey, and Juliet is the northern star which guides him forward, Mercutio is the storm that tries to blow him off course and, in our production at least, goes all out to sink him.

Mercutio is a close friend of Romeo and Benvolio, but whilst he is undeniably fun to be around and the life and soul of the party, he is a 'high maintenance' personality, and when we first meet him the strain in his relationship with Romeo is beginning to tell. It certainly seems from the text of the play that Mercutio doesn't entirely applaud Romeo's interest in girls. He bombards Romeo with criticism and lewd innuendo about his mooning after Rosaline. Adrian Schiller (playing Mercutio) felt sure that this endless vitriol must be based on something more than locker-room horseplay and that the character's fury must stem from a feeling, however subconscious, of sexual jealousy and betrayal. We had no trouble finding this in the playing of the scenes. The further Romeo moves away from his 'childhood' friends into the grown-up world of heterosexual desire, the more Mercutio rages and the less Romeo is affected by him. Whether Mercutio himself is aware of his crush on Romeo, we chose to play that Benvolio and Romeo *are*, so that when Mercutio pushed me over and mounted me during the climax of his Queen Mab speech –

> This is the hag, when maids lie on their backs,
> That presses them and learns them first to bear,
> Making them women of good carriage.
> This is she –   (I.iv.92–5)

Romeo's interruption ('Peace, peace, Mercutio! / Thou talkest of nothing') is a rejection of his cynicism and innuendo as well as a rejection of his advances. Romeo has already set off in a direction that can't include his friend if he is going to demand his complete attention.

The playing of this unspoken sexual tension helped us to unlock some of the more opaque dialogue elsewhere in the play. The scene (II.iv) between the three lads in the midday heat – the morning after the party following which Romeo has (Mercutio presumes) spent the night with Rosaline – contains one of those Shakespearian interchanges that can make actors despair: an exchange of pun-laden witticism crammed full of Elizabethan references that make the pages of the play-text groan with footnotes. The challenge is always to make a modern audience who, on the whole, enjoy a relatively slim appreciation of the finer points of sixteenth-century *double entendre*, feel that they can follow your argument. When Romeo and Mercutio set off on their battle of wits (a battle, incidentally, that they both seem to enjoy and revel in – an interesting clue to why they have found each other as friends and something that Adrian and I were keen to show, for there is little to mourn in the break-down of a friendship if you have no idea why they were friends in the first place, and Shakespeare's economy of storytelling offers these clues sparingly enough), it's difficult to follow the thread of what they are saying even on the printed page, let alone in the heat of performance. We found, however, that if we played the subtext of their relationship it not only let the characters say what they were thinking about each other without *actually* saying it, it also lent the exchange a dynamism and clarity that transcended the problems of Elizabethan pun-age. So when Romeo says 'Pink for flower' (II.iv.57) he is calling Mercutio – and probably for the first time, since he has the security of his new life with Juliet now and doesn't need to humour Mercutio any more – a homosexual. Mercutio chooses not to take the bait ('Right', II.iv.58), but before long they are into a debate about 'geese', and again Romeo is quite bold with Mercutio:

ROMEO Thou wast never with me for anything when they wast not there for the goose [*i.e. my 'goose'*].
MERCUTIO I will bite thee by the ear for that jest.
ROMEO Nay, good goose, bite not [*i.e. get off me, I've had enough*].

Nothing is explicitly stated, but Romeo is cutting Mercutio off, and while it is Mercutio who ultimately wins the race of wits it is Romeo who is leaving him behind. I didn't want this to seem vindictive as Romeo is undoubtedly deeply fond of Mercutio – he has to be for the later scenes to work – but it is simply inevitable and necessary that he pushes Mercutio away. The choice our production took was that Mercutio's rage at his rejection and eventual death at the hands of his beloved transformed itself into a vengeance that would extend beyond the grave. When Mercutio is taken off stage to die shouting 'a plague a' both your houses' (III.i.106), he is fully intending to be the author of that plague and will (in our production) reappear later in the play, first handing over the poison that will kill Romeo and then, as Friar John, regretfully informing Friar Lawrence that he couldn't deliver his letter. This notion that the fates were a real and motivated influence on events in the world of the play had resonances throughout the production. In the purely pragmatic sense this device of Mercutio as an evil avenging angel neatly justified one of Shakespeare's less integrated plot twists

13 David Tennant (left) as Romeo with Adrian Schiller (centre) as Mercutio
and Anthony Howell as Benvolio, *Romeo and Juliet*, Act II, Scene iv:
'Nay, good goose, bite not.'

(the play is no longer a tragedy about a dodgy postal service), but the
broader implication of a divinity that shapes our ends was something
that I found particularly interesting in terms of Romeo himself and his
entire world view.

It struck me very early on that Romeo had a fairly well-developed
sense of the world of fate and destiny. He talks of his dreams and makes
numerous references to the stars and what lies in them. It seemed to
make sense that someone trapped in a world of very real physical conflict
that he wants no part of, should yearn to exist in a world outside himself,
and should be searching for something new to believe in. This became
a very important touchstone for me as I tried to draw this character
and it provided the backbone of my understanding of his emotional
responses. The first explicit reference I found was his justification for
not going to the Capulet ball by saying 'I dreamt a dream tonight'
(1.iv.50) – a protest soon demolished and sneered at by the decidedly
earthbound Mercutio, but something which nonetheless is a very real
fear for Romeo. After the others exit at the end of the scene he is left to
mull over his trepidation:

> I fear, too early. For my mind misgives
> Some consequence, yet hanging in the stars,
> Shall bitterly begin his fearful date
> With this night's revels and expire the term
> Of a despisèd life, closed in my breast,
> By some vile forfeit of untimely death.
>
> (I.iv.106–11)

It's an unspecific, yet creeping, panic that threatens to overwhelm him. I played this speech with my eyes glued to a particular space in the auditorium, as if these malignant stars that shaped his end had a physical location. It was a spot my eyes would return to later. This wasn't superstition on Romeo's part but a very palpable dread and one that would continue to haunt him. I began to wonder what this dream he had had could be, and the answer came from an idea of Michael Boyd's to have Romeo speak the Prologue.

> Two households, both alike in dignity
> In fair Verona, where we lay our scene . . .
>
> (*Prologue*, 1–2)

is one of those bits of Shakespeare that the audience can practically chant along with you. It is usually spoken at the very top of the play (as written), often by the actor playing Escalus. Michael's idea was to have the Prologue spoken midway through the first scene, so that it would cut through the street-fight and suspend the action; and he also wanted it to be spoken by Romeo. This wouldn't be the same Romeo that we would meet for the first time a few minutes later, however; this would be Romeo after his death, a spectre who could speak the Prologue with all the despair, resignation and even bitterness, of hindsight. As the action on stage was suspended, I could even address some of it to other characters in the play, so the lines

> And the continuance of the parents' rage,
> Which, but their children's end, naught could remove
>
> (lines 10–11)

could be said directly to my father, who was even then in the midst of a sword fight with Capulet. It was a bold choice which, you could say, takes the idea of the Prologue as an alienation device to its logical conclusion. It helped, I think, to confound audience expectation early on – something that we'd always been keen to do. It also helped me to answer my own question. This became Romeo's dream, this vision of himself walking through an all-too-familiar battlefield as a ghost of himself telling a story that would only make partial sense, but warned of a tragedy that would take his life. Indeed, as his story unfolded it would seem that this portent of doom was only becoming ever more inescapable.

So it is a Romeo full of angst, anxiety and little joy that first claps eyes on Juliet. It is probably in these first couple of scenes between Romeo and Juliet that the actors feel the greatest pressure of expectation and history. It is very difficult not to try to play the whole thing at once as you struggle to tell the audience that you *are* 'the greatest lovers of all time'. The solution, of course, is not to think about all that and just play the scenes as they come off the page, but that is easier said than done, particularly in that first scene between the pair which lasts all of eighteen lines, the first fourteen of which famously arrange themselves into a sonnet – ending in the couple's first kiss.

You have a lot of ground to cover in this short scene. By the time they part at the end of it the pair have to have turned their respective lives around to follow each other to the end of time, irrespective of consequences. When Alex Gilbreath and I came to the scene for the first time we tried to tell the story of this huge, life-changing moment with every word. We tried to imbue the scene with every delicate romantic thought we could muster until every word dripped with unspoken meaning – with the result that the scene was absurdly slow and entirely turgid.

We were duly sent off to have a session with Cicely Berry, the RSC's resident verse-speaking guru. Although officially retired, Cis is still very involved with the Company and at hand to help actors through some of the trickier sections of the plays she knows so well. She got us to look at the scene afresh and examine exactly what Shakespeare is doing in the language. So we started again, stripping the whole thing down and dumping the baggage: after all, these two people may be the most famous couple in the English-speaking world, but at this point *they have never met before.*

Their conversation (I.v.93–106) begins with what is, to my mind, a rather brilliant chat-up line from Romeo:

> If I profane with my unworthiest hand
>   This holy shrine, the gentle sin is this.
> My lips, two blushing pilgrims, ready stand
>   To smooth that rough touch with a tender kiss.

I'm quite sure that he's used this line before. It seems far too polished and well constructed to be an extempore remark and it is right up his particular alley of pure obsession. He casts himself as a pilgrim and the object of his love as the holiest of saints. Even if he has tried this line before, however, he has never had the response that he now enjoys:

> Good pilgrim, you do wrong your hand too much,
>   Which mannerly devotion shows in this.
> For saints have hands that pilgrims' hands do touch,
>   And palm to palm is holy palmers' kiss.

And this is where it all starts changing for Romeo. Not only has he been entranced by the physical shape of Juliet from across a crowded dance-floor; now he has met his match intellectually. They are sparring with their wits now. He takes her argument and uses it against her:

> Have not saints lips, and holy palmers too?

But, again, she is too quick for him:

> Ay, pilgrim, lips that they must use in prayer.

Continuing the idea, Romeo appeals to her – as it were 'in character' – and warns her that she is responsible for his immortal soul:

> O, then, dear saint, let lips do what hands do!
>   They pray: grant thou, lest faith turn to despair.

And Juliet, ever his equal, manages to give in, knowing full well where all this is leading, without losing any of her own dignity:

> Saints do not move, though grant for prayers' sake.

And so, on the last line of the sonnet, Romeo and Juliet kiss and their destiny is sealed:

> Then move not while my prayer's effect I take.

We found that if we played the scene as a battle of wits, then the rest of the work was done for us. The innuendo is all in the text, and what can be sexier than two people who are attracted to each other trying to outdo each other – push each other away and at the same time reel each other in? The scene became much quicker and more urgent, with barely a pause for breath until after that first kiss. I realize that it can seem terribly mundane to say that the lesson we learned was simply to play the text, but often it proves more difficult than one would imagine, especially when the familiarity of the text you have to work with transcends its meaning.

There is a point immediately after this scene where Romeo discovers Juliet's identity and it seems that their relationship is finished before it can even begin. I wanted to tell the story of Romeo settling in to the doomed inevitability of it all. He is, after all, the misunderstood poet who can never be happy, and to be in love with the daughter of his father's mortal foe is almost too perfect. If Rosaline, the novice nun, was a bad choice of girlfriend, then Juliet is even more of a disaster. When he wanders into the orchard below Juliet's window, he has no reason to believe that this is anything other than another Rosaline situation where he can protest his unrequited love to an unforgiving world.

> But soft! What light through yonder window breaks?
>
> (II.ii.2)

This is another line that seems beyond reinterpretation, but I tried to play the very real danger of the situation. If Romeo is caught in this orchard, under this window, he will be killed without question, something that Michael was always reminding us of and which would help to power the scene that followed. It is only Romeo's free-wheeling imagination that pulls him back towards the dream of Juliet. The speech which follows is a glorious marriage of the poetic and the earthly – as, indeed, is Romeo and Juliet's entire relationship. He compares Juliet to the sun, and then she is the moon's maid, wearing green livery (a reference to virginity) which he urges her to cast off, and his final thought is 'That I might touch that cheek' (II.ii.25).

She is still a heavenly body to him, but there is a genuine sense of his sexual desire too. He is marrying the idolization of his heart's desire (which we have seen with Rosaline) with very real sexual urges: already their relationship is more real and mature, but it is all still part of Romeo's fancy until he hears Juliet say

> O Romeo, Romeo! – wherefore art thou Romeo?
> Deny thy father and refuse thy name.
> Or, if thou wilt not, be but sworn my love,
> And I'll no longer be a Capulet.   (II.ii.33–6)

And it is only here that Romeo's journey really begins. For the first time his love is reciprocated, for the first time he has found his soul-mate, and from that moment his destiny is set in stone. From that moment he is, as he will later realize, playing straight into the arms of the fates he was so keen to avoid.

Act Two, Scene Two, the 'Balcony Scene', is one that Alex and I always enjoyed playing. For a start, it is the only point in the whole play that Romeo and Juliet actually get to spend any real time together, so everything else that happens springs from this twenty-minute scene. Both the characters speak the most wonderful lines; not only is the text very beautiful, however, it is also very human, and at times, it transpired, very funny. We never set out to 'get laughs' in the balcony scene, but they did happen. All we tried to do was to play the situation and the dialogue as truthfully as we could, and I suppose the act of two people falling in love and getting to know each other is not altogether without its lighter side. Michael certainly guarded against any accusation of sentimentality and kept this scene on a strictly truthful basis by shouting 'Soup!' at us during rehearsal if ever we slipped into the bog of emotional over-indulgence.

There is also a conflict of interest between them in this scene, with Juliet full of the practicalities of the danger Romeo is in and the need for him to get to safety, and Romeo's desire to flout the risks in order to tell her how enchanted he is:

> JULIET If they do see thee, they will murder thee.
> ROMEO Alack, there lies more peril in thine eye
> Than twenty of their swords! Look thou but sweet,
> And I am proof against their enmity.
>
> (II.ii.70–3)

This youthful, idealistic, and completely charming Romeo will develop into something else very quickly. In Act Three, Scene Five, after they have spent their first night together and Romeo must leave before they are discovered, the roles have changed. He is the husband now, and has taken on the responsibility he has for both of them. Then it is Juliet who wants to ignore the truth and Romeo who takes control: 'I must be gone and live, or stay and die' (III.v.11).

Both of them, however, are aware of the gravity of their situation from the beginning. When Juliet proposes the idea of marriage (and the initial idea does come from her: Romeo is slower to grasp the necessity of practical action), he doesn't hesitate to agree. They have to legitimize their relationship if it is to have any chance of surviving in this climate.

14 David Tennant as Romeo with Alexandra Gilbreath as Juliet, *Romeo and Juliet*, Act III, Scene v: 'I must be gone and live, or stay and die.'

Again that sense of violence that pervades their lives defines both of their characters in so many ways. Romeo talks to none of his friends about this most important of life-changes – simply because he can't risk it. The only person he can turn to is the friar.

The friar is one of the most important keys to figuring out who Romeo is. It is the friar who is Romeo's closest *confidant*, it is to him that Romeo takes all his problems, and it is in the friar's cell that Romeo hides out after he has killed Tybalt. Des McAleer provided our production with a brilliant, solid, no-nonsense friar who offered a strong counter to any of Romeo's adolescent extremities. We wanted there to be a familiarity between the pair that was to do with mutual affection and respect. We decided that Romeo, forever in the grip of some existential argument with himself, would be regularly at the friar's cell, picking his brains and quizzing him on the nature of his own beliefs. We felt that the friar (not a conventional priest) would enjoy debating the finer points of theology with his young friend and it made great sense to me that Romeo, in search of some world outwith his own, would need the outlet of someone who considered things on the spiritual plane. It is not always an easy relationship, however. The friar doesn't give Romeo an easy time when he reveals that he has fallen in love with Juliet, and it seems clear that Romeo expects it to be a hard sell as the friar has to force him to get to the point:

> Be plain, good son, and homely in thy drift.
> Riddling confession finds but riddling shrift.
>
> (II.iii.51–2)

But Romeo needs someone to test him like this and the friar provides that for him. It is also the friar who sees Romeo at his most vulnerable.

The scene which closed the first half in our production, Act Three, Scene One, contains a pivotal moment for Romeo. After the unconfined joy of the lightning marriage ceremony, things are beginning to look up for young Montague and for the first time it looks possible that he might just live happily ever after. Running into a vengeful Tybalt in the street is the last thing Romeo had gambled on, and the resulting sword fight which will see Romeo cause Mercutio's death and then kill Tybalt in vengeful rage, destroys any sensation of the hope that Romeo was beginning to feel.

It is a brilliantly written scene, one which we found came to life fairly easily, since each of the characters is so strongly motivated in opposing directions and the stakes are so high: for Tybalt, his own pride and need for revenge; for Mercutio, the need to protect the honour of his friend; and for Romeo, the future of his wife and the safety of both his friend and his new cousin-in-law. Romeo is paralysed by his need to maintain the secrecy of his brand new wife, and it is this paralysis that leads to his ill-advised attempt to stop the fight between Tybalt and Mercutio. The extraordinary stage fight between Adrian Schiller and Keith Dunphy (playing Tybalt), put together by fight-director Terry King, made this very easy to play. The more dangerous the battle looks, the more impotent and terrified Romeo becomes, making his eventual intervention all the more desperate.

These feelings of impotence and fear make Romeo's sense of in-equity – and, more importantly, guilt – at Mercutio's death all the sharper. Adrian's Mercutio showed no forgiveness at his death – he would, after all, be back in the second half to kill me off – and so I was left on stage full of remorse, anger and a sense of bewilderment at what had just occurred. Again Romeo sees it all written in the all-seeing, ever-malicious stars:

127

This day's black fate on more days doth depend.
This but begins the woe others must end.

(III.i.119–20)

It was important to me that when Tybalt reappeared Romeo dispatched him quickly, violently, and with as little sense of honour as possible. We know that Romeo is not, by nature, violent and there is nothing in the text to suggest that he is a particularly good swordsman (Mercutio suggests earlier in the scene that he is no match for Tybalt), so if we are to believe that he could kill Tybalt it has to be a sudden, reckless act done in the blind heat of a moment's pure rage. He is in a miasma of confusion, injustice and terrible, terrible guilt and the presence of Tybalt alive and well with the sight of Mercutio's blood still vivid in Romeo's mind pushes him into a stupor of fury and violence. It is several lines later, with Tybalt dead at his feet and Benvolio pleading with him to make a run for it, before the true gravity of what he has done wakens Romeo out of his reverie of vengeance. With 'O, I am fortune's fool' (III.i.136) Romeo sees his life unravelling before his very eyes. Suddenly he has single-handedly killed his future, his hope, and another human being. One of his closest friends is dead and he has become a murderer. His chances of living happily ever after have evaporated terrifyingly quickly.

The scene in the friar's cell (III.iii) where Romeo learns that he is to be banished from Verona, sees him at his most helpless. Romeo has no one to blame but himself for the death of Tybalt, and consequently the death of his marriage to Tybalt's cousin, and it is the friar who gets the full front of Romeo's rage of helplessness. I didn't want to hold back on this. I felt that Romeo would react like a cornered animal, lashing out at the friar and blaming him for his predicament. Unreasonable and childish though that may be, this is, it seems to me, often how we treat those closest to us. Shakespeare certainly gives Romeo (ever the poet) a rash of words to express himself with. The word *banished* chimes through this scene (and the previous one) like a death-knell and every time it came up I would try to use it to punish the friar, to hurt someone else as I had been hurt. It is Romeo's crisis point, and it is the friar who lifts him out of it. The friar is Romeo's base point, to which he will always come home. They are much more in tune than Romeo and his parents are; indeed father and son is the dynamic of their relationship. It is important that Romeo has an unquestioning trust of the friar – as children often do of their parents – to allow the events at the end of the play to unfold as they do.

When Romeo reappears after being banished to Mantua (and being off stage for the whole of Act Four), I felt he should have matured and moved on. No longer dressed all in black, he's been away from the continual threats and challenges of Veronese life and although he's being denied his Juliet, he seems calm. He's had some time in isolation to think things through and plan the life that he and Juliet may lead together. It is as if he has finally managed to escape the fingers of the fates. Certainly the dream he talks of at the start of Act Five, Scene One is of an optimistic nature (albeit with a morbid flavour) and it seems that he can finally see light at the end of the tunnel. This calmness and state of readiness perhaps explains his reaction to the news that Juliet is dead: 'Is it e'en so? Then I defy you, stars!' (v.i.24). He refuses to be beaten by his own destiny and there are no tears or protestations of grief. In that instant I wanted him to see everything that must happen very clearly. His language is certainly full of practicality and he sees a clear sequence of events. The thought of dying alongside Juliet becomes inevitable and absolutely necessary and no side-issue – emotional or otherwise – must get in the way. He becomes filled with such full-fronted motivation that from that moment until he sees Juliet's body, he slips into another reality altogether. Michael described its being as if he were full of 'toxic energy' and this is the energy that kills Paris and threatens to do away with Balthasar. It is only when he has lifted Juliet out of the grave and is cradling her in his arms that he can breathe again and begin to understand where circumstances have brought him.

I find Romeo's final speech fascinating. There is relatively little self-indulgence or grief. Instead I found there to be a strong sense of someone who has come home. The only thing that seems to damage his resolve to die is Juliet's lack of decay:

> Ah, dear Juliet,
> Why art thou yet so fair? Shall I believe
> That insubstantial death is amorous,
> And that the lean abhorrèd monster keeps
> Thee here in dark to be his paramour?
> For fear of that I still will stay with thee
> And never from this palace of dim night
> Depart again.   (v.iii.101–8)

And then the idea of dying becomes a release:

> Here, here [*repeating the word seems to underline his resolve*] will I remain
> With worms that are thy chambermaids. O here [*again*]
> Will I set up my everlasting rest
> And shake the yoke of inauspicious stars
> From this world-wearied flesh. (v.iii.108–12)

So finally he has beaten the fates that have been pushing him around and forcing this misplaced poet to live in a world that he doesn't fit into, and in death he can finally escape and be with the woman who understood him. In our production Michael had Alex and me walking through the people round the tomb after our death and then walking off the stage and out through the audience so that, indeed, through death, Romeo and Juliet had somehow escaped. The real tragedy is left for those who have to rebuild this ruined society. One suspects that their problems are bigger than a couple of gold statues can mend.

Romeo and Juliet is a much-produced play full of lines more famous than any of the actors who could hope to play them. One could never hope to be definitive in it, but I'm glad to have had the chance to give it a crack and I look forward to seeing it performed again and again in years to come, so that I can see the way it should have been done. And it goes without saying that I shall greatly enjoy terrorizing young actors by telling them how very, *very* tricky it is!

Timon of Athens

MICHAEL PENNINGTON

MICHAEL PENNINGTON played the title role in Gregory Doran's production of *Timon of Athens* at the Royal Shakespeare Theatre in the summer season of 1999, and afterwards at the Barbican Theatre. It was his only part that season. Among his many roles for the Company during the preceding twenty-five years are Hamlet, Angelo, Mercutio, Edgar, Berowne, the Duke in *Measure for Measure*, Hector, Mirabell in *The Way of the World*, and Donal Davoren in *Shadow of a Gunman*. He co-founded and co-directed (with Michael Bogdanov) the English Shakespeare Company and played many major Shakespeare parts with them, including the title roles in *Richard II* and *Henry V* and Prince Hal in 1 and 2 *Henry IV*, which were later filmed for television. An enormous range of stage work includes many leading roles in the West End, at the National Theatre, for the Peter Hall Company at the Old Vic, and, most recently (for English Touring Theatre), the title role in *John Gabriel Borkman*. He has directed Shakespeare in Britain, the United States and Japan, has a long list of television and film credits, and has published books on *Hamlet* and on *Twelfth Night*. His essay on his performance of the title role in the RSC's 1980 production of *Hamlet* was published in *Players of Shakespeare 1*.

It happens that I was in Los Angeles on the night of 9 August 1969, seriously lost in a car in the Hollywood Hills. It was late, and every road seemed to lead mistily up into the mountains and none down to the basin of the city, where I needed to be. It was quite unnerving, especially as none of the houses at which I tentatively knocked for directions responded – not at that time of night, not in that place. They were right: the next morning the news of the Sharon Tate killings broke, and soon after the face of Charles Manson glared out from the police photographs. It had all happened on Cielo Drive that night, a mile or so away from where I was.

This sensational memory came back to me thirty years later, almost to the month, as I was getting ready to do Timon of Athens for the RSC. One of the disturbing things about the whole horrific affair, certainly to those of us sympathetic to the popular culture of the day, was that Manson looked like a hippy – or some iconic rock star from the summer of love, Jim Morrison of the Doors, perhaps. The face seemed to represent both the gentler liberations of the time and the very heart of darkness: a year that had jangled with the apparent benedictions of the Woodstock Festival was presenting to history an exact image of their opposite.

The 1960s were full of polarities, even before Manson: muddled idealism and noble follies, essentially middle-class revolutions easy to mock in hindsight but so much more heartening than the cynicism and violence that could be glimpsed whenever they faltered. Now, it struck me that if I were to re-imagine these extremes into a single personality, I might find a way through the famous difficulty of Shakespeare's Timon – that is, how to make the black misanthropy of the second half, as he crouches snarling in his wilderness, somehow of a piece with the blitheness of the first, when his magnificent altruism knows no bounds. The critical shorthand on Timon, such as it is, is that he is a sort of generous ass who is wasting himself on people who mean him no good, so that he deserves his disillusionment, but not the tragic sympathy of the second half, where he sees himself as some comminatory angel out of William Blake while looking like a curmudgeon on a park bench. His agonized account of himself as a victim rather than a blunderer will always seem a little face-saving; but if his prodigal bounty sprang from some hapless philosophy – and neurotic compulsion – we might be able to follow him more sympathetically from Camelot to cardboard city. In the end it is Apemantus who says it best: 'The middle of humanity thou never knewest, but the extremity of both ends' (IV.iii.302–3). In other words, Timon's vindictiveness is philanthropy with its nap reversed.

The 1960s only showed up in our production in a touch of tie-dye in one of my gowns and a generously long wig; though perhaps Timon's banquet did have the feel of the extravagant parties of those days where anything went, sexually or pharmaceutically. You might not know, or even meet, the host, who could be leading the dance or, just as easily, quietly reading Proust in an upstairs room. It would have limited the play to have nailed it precisely to that period, though we did use a suite written by Duke Ellington for a Canadian production of the play in 1963, brilliantly re-orchestrated by John Woolf and delivered by the RSC's band with the chutzpah of the Ellington All Stars.

Timon of Athens is on its own in the canon, despite the passing shadows of *King Lear*, *Coriolanus* and *Antony and Cleopatra*. It is possible that Shakespeare never finished the play, or never revised it, leaving it in the kind of state that reassures you that he could be as erratic as most writers. In the theatre, directors invariably tidy it up to some degree, conflating the smaller characters and snipping off loose ends of subplot. It is like a collaboration with Shakespeare's perhaps unwilling ghost, or, to put it another way, like discovering a neglected score in a wardrobe and being allowed by the lapse of copyright to do what you like with it. The play is fitfully magnificent but oddly secretive, and by 1999 I thought I knew something about it. I had been a very junior spear-carrier when it was last done on Stratford's main stage in 1965, so I am among the very few actors to revisit it. And like many of us, I have inside me useless spools of Shakespeare turning gently like computer tapes, so that although *Timon* is not as familiar as some, I did have a nodding acquaintance with its turbulent, lyrical flow.

However, as with all great texts that last much longer than you do, you measure up to them in the light of what you have become with time – a light that may or may not be mellower, but will surely be more searching. In 1965 I had predictably supposed that the play was just a matter of a second-rate *Lear* without Lear's full cause of weeping, Timon's reaction to his own unprovoked follies more a massive petulance than a tragic cleansing. It now struck me as a subtly sardonic satire on how people behave under the pressure of indebtedness, its central figure a fascinating study in benevolent neurosis. What accounts for the psychological tension in Timon, his uncertainty of his place in the world? I did a wild survey of my own experience – movie stars, moral cowards and terrified loners I have known. Is his, like some of theirs, a narcissism that holds human contact at bay by wildly parodying it? The play points out how close kind-heartedness lies to its near relation, vanity; it is humanized first by marvellous insight and then, in the more famous second half, by a wintry *tour de force* of language that is almost its own justification.

The part is one of Shakespeare's longest in a play which is one of his shortest; in fact Timon has a full quarter of the lines, so it is obviously taxing and no one else gets much of a look-in, it seems. It's a long time to listen to a passionate fool, if that's all he is – but Shakespeare never lets you take a protagonist at face value. Just as, in *Hamlet*, Fortinbras, Horatio and Laertes embody the Prince's alternative characters and courses of action, the dominant figure of Timon is still part of a cat's cradle, and the light on him shifts with your angle. You could say that the play is about four men, or perhaps four facets of a single man: the prodigal hero; his honest steward Flavius, who, watching his master's fate, might lose faith and become a Timon himself; the professional cynic Apemantus, who claims to have lost faith already but is revealed as something of a poser by his encounter with Timon's blazingly authentic rage; and the man of action, Alcibiades, who turns disillusionment into revenge rather than, like Timon, sulking in a hole. The technique is Shakespeare's way of asking you what you would have done yourself.

Timon is Shakespeare's great loner: no family, no evident sexuality, no relationship except the doubtful compensations of his small circle. Alcibiades at one point offers a (very) small hint that he has been a soldier:

> I have heard, and grieved,
> How cursèd Athens, mindless of thy worth,
> Forgetting thy great deeds, when neighbour states,
> But for thy sword and fortune, trod upon them –
>
> (IV.iii.93–6)

and when Timon finally believes Flavius's warnings about his impending bankruptcy, he seems to feel that Athens owes him something:

> Go you, sir, to the senators,
> Of whom, even to the state's best health, I have
> Deserved this hearing . . .   (II.ii.201–3)

But that's about it. Perhaps, as a wealthy man, he has built the new sports complex on the edge of town; perhaps he has been an unlikely Coriolanus. Shakespeare seems to lose interest in the documentation, and though the vagueness may be a measure of the play's unrevised state, it may be intentional: had he returned to it, he might just as well have cut these references as amplified them.

For in some ways the play's style sways away from documentary towards parable. In the first half, the normal theatre desire for a surprising narrative is often thwarted by a sense of predetermination. The play opens with a prediction of its outcome as pointed as that of *Romeo and Juliet*, and it comes from the poet, not a chorus but a character within the play, though he is symbolically anonymous:

> When Fortune in her shift and change of mood
> Spurns down her late beloved, all his dependants,
> Which laboured after him to the mountain's top
> Even on their knees and hands, let him fall down,
> Not one accompanying his declining foot.
>
> (1.i.87–91)

When he is presented with a portrait a moment later, Timon seems to know his problem too, though he fails to be warned by it:

> Painting is welcome.
> The painting is almost the natural man;
> For since dishonour traffics with man's nature,
> He is but outside; these pencilled figures are
> Even such as they give out . . .   (1.i.160–4)

The conclusion is foregone: the whole interest is to be in the manner how.

Timon has arrived to buy paintings, accept poems, pretend to be discerning with a jeweller, and to sort out the problems of an avaricious Athenian father whose daughter wants to marry a servant of Timon's, whose modest bid for her hand Timon offers to bring to par. It is like surgery hour, except that the doctor seems not quite to concentrate, dispensing his placebos with his mind somewhere else, his satisfaction guaranteed by his patients' approving oohs and aahs. How are we to take these clients of his now filling the stage, who will accept all his gifts and outrageous hospitality only to refuse him, a few scenes later, in his hour of need? Respecting Shakespeare's loathing for flattery, we may want to make his satire as painful as possible by encouraging Timon's friends – Sempronius, Ventidius, Lucullus, and Lucius – to be eminently sincere at all times, so that the audience will be as deeply deceived as he is. It is not only in my own profession that it is hard to distinguish tactical bonhommie from friendship: many fellowships characterized by warmth and idealism are oiled by insincerity. Unconscious insincerity too – it is as if these men would themselves have expected to help their patron and are surprised, at the critical moment, to feel a paralysis of the giving hand on its way to the pocket.

On the other hand there is something didactic about Shakespeare's treatment of these Bad Samaritans: they are a little close to caricature, and it is quite hard to be as fooled as Timon. Lucius, Lucullus and Sempronius are described in the cast list as 'flattering lords' and Ventidius separately as 'one of Timon's false friends' – unusually specific descriptions. The lords seem to be there only as three good reasons for refusing Timon, neat variations on the same theme: in rapid succession, Lucullus somehow blames the social circumstances (the 'time', III.i.42); Lucius claims he is simply out of pocket, having just made a huge purchase; and Sempronius is so insulted to be the last to be approached that as a matter of honour he quite refuses to oblige. Clearly there is a comic impulse here: three is a magic number in comedy as well as parable, which is perhaps why Ventidius's story, essentially the same, is denied a pay-off of its own. It's a hint that a bitter sense of humour, the author's relish for the ordained catastrophe, may be holding the play together and keeping its metaphor from sententiousness. To see these scoundrels punished by being blinded by steam at Timon's final banquet, then secretively returning when he's gone to pick up their expensive cloaks, may be as horribly entertaining as watching Timon knock everyone else's heads together in the second half while sitting on a pile of gold.

For the present, Timon thinks he is leading some kind of philosophical revolution: nowadays we might call him a champagne socialist. He believes, with a kind of whiffly religiosity, that everything should be in common:

> there's none
> Can truly say he gives, if he receives . . .
> (I.ii.9–10)

and he waxes lachrymose as he toasts his guests:

We are born to do benefits . . . O, what a precious comfort 'tis to have so many like brothers commanding one another's fortunes . . . Mine eyes cannot hold out water, methinks. (I.ii.99–104)

But there are moments of solitude and panic in this gregarious man, especially if he thinks the party is dying:

FIRST LORD Where be our men?
SERVANT Here, my lord, in readiness.
SECOND LORD Our horses!

TIMON O my friends,
     I have one word to say to you. Look you, my good lord,
     I must entreat you honour me so much
     As to advance this jewel.

(I.ii.162–8)

The unfinished half-line starting Timon's speech suggests an anxious need to arrest their departure before he has really worked out a way of detaining them; and, left with Apemantus at the end, he would rather be alone than hear good counsel:

APEMANTUS ... thou wilt give away thyself in paper shortly. What needs these
     feasts, pomps, and vainglories?
TIMON Nay, an you begin to rail on society once, I am sworn not to give regard
     to you. Farewell, and come with better music.   *Exit*
APEMANTUS So ... I'll lock thy heaven from thee.

(I.ii.246–52)

Much of the first stage of the character is clear enough: the woozy benevolence of the opening, the neurotic joy of the banquet, a tendency to shoot the messenger – Flavius in particular – when the news is bad. The turning-point comes, of course, when Timon's creditors send their servants to collect payment from him, which he cannot make because his friends have failed to bail him out – and the fact is that Timon has so imprisoned them all in his generosity that they have felt oddly justified. This moment (in Act Three, Scene Four) is not very well delivered by Shakespeare, one of several times when you would like to send the script back for clarification. Timon enters 'in a rage' (III.iv.79), which is all right except that there is a lot of rage to come, and it is quite difficult for the actor to demonstrate that his anger is at the 'Creditors? Devils!' (III.iv.105) who are hounding him, rather than at the flatterers – 'rascals' (III.iv.113) – who have let him down. In his disappointment the two groups get mixed up together in our ear; and the crucial scene is anyway very short, a flimsy hinge for the whole of the second half to hang from.

    Timon's inspiration – to entertain them all with a dinner of stones and hot water, then throw them out and leave the city – is as viciously jovial as his earlier mood was oppressively benign. This final banquet, with its undeserved overtones of the Last Supper, should create a kind of dread in the audience as well as in the guests. His eruption is held back while he delivers an ambiguous oration that parodies his paeon in the earlier banquet, and when it comes, the denunciation has all the impact of delay. His jeremiad outside the walls of the city is an extravagant release; but it is so final, so brutally fascistic, that an audience ignorant of the play will limp to the bar as bewildered as to where Shakespeare can take his apparently completed story as they will later be at the same halfway point in *The Winter's Tale*.

I'm assuming that this is the interval, if for no other reason than that Timon needs to transform himself for life in the wild, seeming to abandon his old identity as completely as his clothes. The little scene (Act Four, Scene Two) with Flavius and Timon's redundant servants gives unexpectedly beautiful notice of the play's shift into an inverted key – or the relative minor, if you like – and it comes more from the servants than from Flavius himself:

> And his poor self,
> A dedicated beggar to the air,
> With his disease of all-shunned poverty,
> Walks, like contempt, alone . . .
>   We must all part
> Into this sea of air.   (IV.11.12–22)

In this exact way the stage is set for the great atmospherics of the second half – probably the reason the actor wanted to do the part. In this marvellous oratorio there will be conflicting images of heat and wind, darkness and desert, but the savagery of the sun is a constant. I thought Timon should be near-naked and defenceless, terribly tender and burned, dehydrated and vocally cracked, though there are also times when he seems to be looking invigorated out across wintry heathland.

The language now is some of the most virulently beautiful Shakespeare ever wrote, for some melancholy reason straight from the heart, I think – a blasted landscape ringing with Timon's wild, inordinate eloquence. His temper seems to tilt and buck, from excoriation to lament, from self-punishment to a kind of pantheistic embrace of the unforgiving nature around him:

> Behold, the earth hath roots;
> Within this mile break forth a hundred springs;
> The oaks bear mast, the briars scarlet hips . . .
>   (IV.iii.419–21)

As if in the shivering fever of sunstroke, he goes on uncontrollable riffs, then lapses into impishness:

APEMANTUS What wouldst thou have to Athens?
TIMON Thee thither in a whirlwind.

(IV.iii.289–90)

The whole half (in effect one long scene) is a series of exemplary interviews with a rather thin narrative (Alcibiades's attack on Athens and the Athenians' reaction to Timon's windfall of gold). The quality of the writing between the great tirades is quite uneven, and it is tempting to rearrange it, as with the throng of tiny parts and blind alleys in the first half. The scene with Alcibiades and the girls is rather too long for what it has to say, the heart-to-heart with Apemantus the best and most searching, the bandits rather feeble, the reunion with Flavius a premature diminuendo, the poet and painter not much better than the bandits. And then there are the senators: they at least have a story, persuading Timon to return to the city, but you know what they're going to get. It's all a bit humpbacked. In 1999, feeling this roughness, we experimented with moving the episodes about, trying to impose a more obvious 'build' – the bandits and the poet and painter earlier, then running in a deepening mood through Alcibiades to Apemantus and Flavius – but some scruple held us back, some sense that the jagged music of Shakespeare's experiment might be more rewarding than our dull editing.

Just as the actor had to find the positive idealism behind Timon's folly, in this great song of defeat it is an underlying sorrow that makes the repetitive fury palatable. If he is alert, he will find valuable touches of the old Timon in his mocking patronage of the poet and painter; images of theft, borrowing and renewal (now applied to the sun and moon as much as to the workaday world) weave obsessively in and out of his language, and there is a sort of splendid regret as he remembers the past:

> But myself –
> Who had the world as my confectionary,
> The mouths, the tongues, the eyes, and hearts of men
> At duty, more than I could frame employment;
> The numberless upon me stuck, as leaves
> Do on the oak, have with one winter's brush

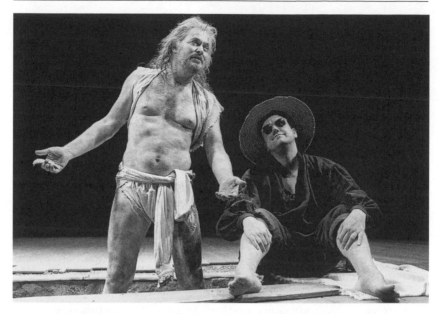

15 Michael Pennington (left) as Timon with Richard McCabe as
Apemantus, *Timon of Athens*, Act IV, Scene iii: 'If thou wert the lion,
the fox would beguile thee . . .'

> Fell from their boughs, and left me open, bare,
> For every storm that blows.   (IV.iii.260–7)

Such precarious beauty is threatened all the time by satirical comedy. Largely this is the doing of Apemantus, who discredited Timon's
'nobility' in the first half, in a sense coming between us and him. Now
he arrives to question any tragic status. For one thing, he suggests the
demeaning possibility that Timon's grandiloquent walk-out has been
pointless since Athens has forgotten all about him and is getting on
with its life:

> Thy flatterers yet wear silk, drink wine, lie soft,
> Hug their diseased perfumes, and have forgot
> That ever Timon was.   (IV.iii.207–9)

The odd thing is that while Apemantus is always there to expose and
diminish him, Timon, whose despair is far deeper, does the same for
him, and their encounter precipitates a most unusual black comedy
that reminds many people of Samuel Beckett. Not to mention Timon's

'root' (distant cousin of Estragon's carrot), there is no great difference between the two of them outdoing each other in insults –

APEMANTUS Thou art the cap of all the fools alive.
TIMON Wouldst thou wert clean enough to spit upon!
APEMANTUS There is no leprosy but what thou speakest.
TIMON If I name thee
      I'll beat thee – but I should infect my hands . . .
APEMANTUS Beast!
TIMON Slave!
APEMANTUS Toad!
TIMON Rogue, rogue, rogue!   (IV.iii.360–76)

– and this, from *Waiting for Godot*:

ESTRAGON That's the idea, let's abuse each other . . .
VLADIMIR Moron!
ESTRAGON Vermin!
VLADIMIR Abortion!
ESTRAGON Morpion!
VLADIMIR Sewer-rat!
ESTRAGON Curate!
VLADIMIR Cretin!
ESTRAGON (*with finality*) Critic!
VLADIMIR Oh!
      (*He wilts, vanquished, and turns away.*)

And, as for Beckett's characters, it is just a little 'canter', a routine led by despair but coming out with the smack of vaudeville. The job is not to let one style disqualify the other: Shakespeare is using Apemantus as a necessary perspective, a little like the fool in *King Lear*, but, unlike the fool, not killing him off early. Timon, meanwhile, can be lucid, precise, and touching, as in his big prose speech about the animals, and viciously obsessed with putrifaction, as with the whores. The sea laps around him and into his language. Like Lear, he has entered a world he has 'ta'en too little care of':

> Common mother, thou,
> Whose womb unmeasurable and infinite breast
> Teems and feeds all; whose self-same mettle,
> Whereof thy proud child, arrogant man, is puffed,
> Engenders the black toad and adder blue,
> The gilded newt and eyeless venomed worm . . .
>   (IV.ii.178–83)

In the end, longing to be free, he rejoices that his

> long sickness
> Of health and living now begins to mend
> And nothing brings me all things.
>
> (v.i.184–6)

His very eloquence drains him of life, and he dies inexplicably. Shakespeare has sustained his metaphor so thoroughly that he doesn't trouble with a cause – beyond, presumably, malnutrition and a superflux of his prevailing emotion. (Something similar happens to the broken-hearted Enobarbus in *Antony and Cleopatra*, written at much the same time.)

It has been the strangest history, but not so very remote from us. Pascal, citing Tacitus, said that there's something annoying about kindness. Ruefully, we can recognize the sort of man who always gives a friend a gift too big for the friendship, and insists on paying for dinner, always, embarrassingly. He will lend before you ask, and won't let you repay the debt. Whose, really, is the pleasure when a gift is more than the recipient could have dreamed of? In an individual or a group, the converse of this energy is extreme, and the redemption rather tiny. Timon drove headlong towards what he most feared, his own company, which for him of all people should have been a nightmare; but in doing so he faced down his demons and, like Richard II in prison, even began to save himself.

Throughout the Jacobean phase of his career, Shakespeare seems to be continually trying to find a way to say goodbye, and at the same time to come home. In my own way I have found a home in Stratford as well, though I've left several times. I was first there in the days when it felt like a market town and the Honeybourne railway line still ran down to Long Marston; disused now, that's the Greenway, where I can practise my lines walking down a precious corridor of walnut and ash trees, with sometimes the skylark, and always the wild flowers that Shakespeare knew: knapweed, cowslip and King Lear's 'rank fumitory'. This was an ideal play to be back with, not only because of 1965, but also because Greg Doran made a production in which we could catch the play's complicit humour as well as its bleakness. When Timon, within moments of starting his new life, was confronted by a pile of gold, the audience loved the dark joke of it, and when, at the end, he laid his final ambush for the Athenians, sweetly recommending an ideal

16 Michael Pennington as Timon, with his epitaph, *Timon of Athens*, Act V,
Scene i: 'Sun, hide thy beams. Timon hath done his reign.'

means for them to hang themselves, I could feel them willing me on.
At this moment I felt that we could be back in Shakespeare's study in
New Place: the author scratches his chin, looks out of the window at
his mulberry tree (of which the present one is a scion) and lifts Timon
away from his craggy shore, where there is no such thing as a garden,
into the world we know:

> I have a tree, which grows here in my close,
> That mine own use invites me to cut down,
> And shortly must I fell it . . .   (v.i.203–5)

A moment later, with his last words, this great threnodist seems, like
Hamlet – 'the rest is silence' – to cancel language altogether:

> Lips, let sour words go by, and language end:
> What is amiss, plague and infection mend!
> Graves only be men's works, and death their gain!
> Sun, hide thy beams. Timon hath done his reign.
> (v.i.218–21)

But, coming from Shakespeare, that is a joke. The one sure thing about *Timon of Athens* is its glorious theatrical language: for all the play's odd quiddity, it is some of his very best, and a great place for an actor to live. I knew that I had always wanted to play this part, but I didn't expect that in Timon's benighted ecstasy I would have felt so exhilarated, so much in touch with the origins of what I do and why I do it.

Hamlet

SIMON RUSSELL BEALE

SIMON RUSSELL BEALE is an Associate Actor of the Royal Shakespeare Company and an Associate Artist of the National Theatre. He
played Hamlet in John Caird's production at the National Theatre's
Lyttleton auditorium, and on a national and international tour, in
2000–1. A long series of earlier Shakespeare roles includes, for the
Royal Shakespeare Company, the Young Shepherd in *The Winter's
Tale*, the King in *Love's Labour's Lost*, Thersites, Edgar, Ariel and
Richard III, and, for the National Theatre, Iago. Among many other
roles at the National he has also played Guildenstern in *Rosencrantz and
Guildenstern are Dead* and Mosca in *Volpone*, and for the RSC the title
role in *Edward II*, several leading roles in Restoration comedy, and those
two 'Hamlet-derivative' parts, Konstantin in *The Seagull* and Oswald
in *Ghosts*. A wide range of work for radio and television, includes, for
television, *A Very Peculiar Practice*, *Persuasion*, and *A Dance to the Music
of Time*; among his films are *Hamlet*, *The Temptation of Franz Schubert*,
and *An Ideal Husband*. At the Donmar Theatre (and later in New York),
he played, for Sam Mendes's final season in 2002–3, Malvolio in *Twelfth
Night* and the title role in *Uncle Vanya*, receiving the Olivier Award for
best actor for the latter. His essay on his performance of Thersites in the
RSC's 1990 production of *Troilus and Cressida* was published in *Players
of Shakespeare 3*.

Soon after accepting the title role in John Caird's production of *Hamlet*
for the National Theatre, I was invited to give the annual lecture in
Stratford-upon-Avon in honour of Shakespeare's birthday. What I wrote
for that occasion under the title 'Hamlet's Hell' was an account of
my response to the role after much thought about it and after many
discussions with John Caird, but some weeks before rehearsals began. I
repeat it here, slightly adapted and abbreviated from the form in which
it was delivered, as a prologue to the rest of this essay, written during
and after the run of the production.

*

In his book about acting, Simon Callow points out that the period between an offer and the first day of rehearsal (in this particular case, nearly a year) is the most exciting in an actor's professional life, a period when there is no limit to the exploration of ideas and when the honour of being allowed to pitch oneself against a great text has not been overshadowed by one's limitations – a period, in short, when a perfect production is still a possibility. I have to say that my elation after the offer did not, in fact, last long. I had been sniffing around Hamlet for a long time, telling anyone who would listen that I would like to play the part, and my bluff had been called. To be honest, I was scared stiff.

In part, this fear manifested itself in rather unhelpful questions that spun in my mind. At thirty-nine, was I too old? Was I too short and – what do they call me? – stout? I had had enormous experience studying Shakespeare's analyses of human hell, in Richard III and Iago and Thersites, but was I capable of exploring a character as full of grace as Hamlet? Was I, even after Richard III and Iago, fit enough? I knew these questions were unhelpful because, apart from keeping fit, there was little I could do about them and, more importantly, because the real reason I was scared was the role of Hamlet itself – its history and its substance.

Its history is there for all to see. No actor can approach the part unaware of who has played it before, and there had been some great recent performances – Fiennes, Rylance, Jennings. When I did Richard III ten years earlier, I remember waking up to the papers on the morning of press night and reading various articles that looked forward to analysing my performance (charitably or uncharitably, it was difficult to say) in the light of those by Sher, McKellen, Holm and Olivier – Olivier, for God's sake! I was completely taken by surprise. Not knowing much about the history of theatre and filled then with a confidence that seems to be dwindling with the years, Richard III felt to me like a part that I could and should do – partly because the director, Sam Mendes, had told me that I could and should do it – and I hadn't fully absorbed the other implications. Such naïveté had its benefits; when it came to Hamlet I could no longer pretend to be unaware of the comparative histories that yet another performance of the role would produce. Unfortunately, such concern for how other actors played Hamlet in the past – or how well they played it – must be set aside, principally because it inhibits one's instincts, but also because such concern is self-important. Pride is not an attractive quality, especially in a proto-Hamlet.

So much for Hamlet's history. More daunting was the problem of tackling the substance of Hamlet. I know that a weakness of mine is a tendency to compare a part that I am currently tackling with one that I have played in the past – although Terry Hands once jokingly (or at least I hope it was jokingly) said that I had a tendency to play any part in the style of the one that I would like to do next. The last Shakespearian character I had studied was Iago, a man whose experience of a personal and loveless hell is acute and all-encompassing and which I found useful in an attempt to define the rather different nature of Hamlet's hell. Iago's final silence is as much about evasion as revelation. We can never really know *why* Iago behaves as he does. The privilege an actor enjoys is a sense of getting near to how it *feels* to behave as he does, a feeling that is like a release of self-hatred. His diabolic motives in the play seem to me to have their source in a desire for others to join him in hell, to experience what he is experiencing, to share his world of worthlessness. Iago has to fail because his self-hatred and his hatred of others produce only a vacuum, a nothingness. There is nothing grand about his life, nothing that makes someone like Richard III (another hell-experiencing Shakespeare character) exciting and attractive.

I never felt a sense of exhilaration in playing Iago. Richard III had been, for me, a distinctly lighter experience than Iago, mentally at least, if not physically. Up until the murder of the princes, Richard is surrounded by men and women who would behave as ruthlessly as he, if only they had his wit and his courage. Richard is simply out-manoeuvring the others in a game that they are all playing. What differentiates him are his wit, his sense of the absurd, and his capacity for ironic analysis of his motives and actions. It is an irony that is, except in a few rather uncharacteristic flashes, entirely missing from Iago, who is a dull and second-rate man, with a plodding, if large, vocabulary, who takes himself very seriously indeed.

Two types of hell, then, seem to be in evidence in a comparison between Richard and Iago, one self-dramatizing and self-mocking, the other small, pedestrian and self-important. What, or where, is Hamlet's hell? I wrote an essay once, as an undergraduate, about *Macbeth*. The central argument proved useful in shaping my preliminary thoughts about *Hamlet*. It seemed to me odd that Macbeth, despite his acknowledgement that his life has become worthless, refuses to give up and never lets go of the will to live. Losing the will to live was something I had been taught is an essential ingredient in the last moments of a tragic hero's life, the wish to die being the price that must be paid for that first fatal flaw. I could see that this rather neat (perhaps over-neat) idea could apply to King Lear, or Othello, or Antony, or Cleopatra, but it seemed to be missing in Macbeth. His punishment is not death but continued life – or, at least, his very human inability to accept death; and, to make matters worse, he is aware of all this. There is something blackly comic about his last moments – as anyone who saw Jonathan Pryce play the part knows. Othello, Cleopatra, Antony, and, subliminally, King Lear all want to die, and in three of these cases take matters into their own hands and kill themselves. There is a sense of resolution in their lives, of responsibility having been accepted, of self-control. Macbeth's life, or the punishment that is his life, is beyond his control. I wonder whether that is why Shakespeare introduces, through the witches, a supernatural element that effectively renders Macbeth's fate inescapable – a supernatural element that is, of course, famously present in *Hamlet*.

In my first meetings with John Caird the ghost of Hamlet's father loomed large. When we first meet him he is, as it were, misinterpreted. Horatio and his companions see a warrior in 'complete steel' (I.iv.52) and presume he has come to speak of some purely political horror. But the ghost, when he finally talks to Hamlet, talks not so much as a king and warrior (as one might have expected), but as a father, husband and brother. Because of who he is, or was, his personal predicament has a political effect, but had he not appeared to Hamlet it seems that Denmark, rotten or not, would continue to do rather well under Claudius's stewardship. The new king certainly knows how to cope with his aggressive neighbours and both his taking of the crown and his new marriage seem to go unchallenged by the courtiers and politicians who surround him. If Hamlet were to ignore his father's request for vengeance, then political chaos would be avoided – even if the price of that is to ignore the murder of a king. Hamlet's first problem is that inaction is, oddly enough, the wisest course – wisest not in the sense of preserving his spiritual well-being, but certainly wisest in a coldly pragmatic sense. Shakespeare does not, of course, allow the possibility that an immoral act can remain contained: the warrior king who talks as a father is a symbol of the fact that the political and the personal are inextricably linked. But, unlike *King Lear*, the tragedy of *Hamlet* is essentially a private, personal, family matter. And the appearance of a *ghost* – whatever his message – is a reminder that, private and personal notwithstanding, Hamlet has no real choice. He has to act. Hamlet's father, in a rather unpaternal fashion, signs his son's death-warrant: the old political dispensations must disappear, and Hamlet must die. The young prince becomes a ghost himself, with a ghost's narrow horizons and loss of personal freedom. The supernatural element, as with the witches in *Macbeth*, takes away the possibility of choice from the central character; and the fact that here the supernatural element is the father of the hero only makes the emotional landscape more cruel.

We have no real idea of the relationship between the son and the father. Hamlet idealizes him as 'so excellent a king' (1.ii.139), but that is about as far as it goes. But to see a father, especially after death, in such pain must be a distressing experience. To be told also that a father's pain is in part due to the actions of one's own mother makes that distress almost unbearable. The destruction of any normal network of family relationships can only mean that Hamlet is suddenly deprived of his sense of identity; and so he must reconstruct it, through thinking and talking – just as, oddly, Iago clings on to his sense of identity through thinking and talking. And just as Iago's actions are in effect a long suicide that ends in silence, so are Hamlet's. The ghost's message is a very cruel one.

I wonder whether this loss of identity – or rather its reconstruction – is behind Hamlet's relationship with Ophelia. It is important that anyone playing Hamlet should invent or construct a series of events that took place before the play began – the good old (and very un-Shakespearian) 'Method'! It is important, for instance, to know what Hamlet's life was like in Wittenberg, studying philosophy and theology, the principal disciplines at an early seventeenth-century university. (Indeed the play is in some sense a demolition, or at least a questioning, of those certainties, intellectual and spiritual, on which Hamlet has, so far, based his life and thought.) It is equally important that all his relationships with other people – Gertrude, Horatio, Claudius, Ophelia – have a history. I have no doubt that Hamlet, before the play opened, was, or believed himself to be, in love with Ophelia. But his father's commission – the suicide note handed to his son – precludes any normal or living connexion with another human being. Part of Hamlet's death-sentence is necessarily the denial of a future, so that he can do no other than deny his love for Ophelia. Perhaps his insistence that she spend the rest of her life in a nunnery can be seen as protective as much as abusive: no one with virtue like Ophelia's can survive in a world as poisoned as that of Denmark.

Which brings us to Gertrude, the centre and focus, however hard Hamlet may try, of his tragedy. She is the first person he mentions after hearing his father's story (I.v.105), although he takes himself by surprise and presses on to curse Claudius instead. She then reappears in the figure of Hecuba, who in turn becomes the source of one of his greatest soliloquies. She figures in the play within the play and, most importantly, is Hamlet's partner in perhaps the most emotionally bruising scene of the play. However hard he tries, he cannot de-personalize his mother, in the way that he does Ophelia, or Claudius, or even Horatio, whose friendship with Hamlet is largely dependent on Horatio's being loyal and unquestioning. Gertrude lies outside the clear, ordained pattern of revenge set down by Hamlet's father and the ghost's instructions that he cause her no pain or indignity are essentially impossible to carry out: he has to hurt her if he is to revenge his father. Indeed, the intensity of the bond between mother and son leads to his *wanting* to hurt her, even if the same bond tells him that that impulse is wrong. In short, Hamlet's relationship with his mother, lying as it does at the centre of the play, confused and unresolved, dominated my preliminary thinking about the role.

Perhaps the relationship should remain a mystery. Hamlet's attitude to other characters is so often clear-cut – his hatred for Claudius and his contempt for Polonius, for example – even if they, in return, find him confusing and dangerous. But if my thoughts about Gertrude were incoherent, my instincts told me that a young man's grief plays a large part in the relationship, as it does (and this is blindingly obvious) in the whole play.

Grief was something that I myself was fully experiencing during that period for the first time in my life: my mother died during this time of preliminary thinking about the role. She was an extraordinary woman, and someone with whom I had a close and unquestioningly loving relationship. I know that I began grieving some months before her death, when she first became ill – a luxury, if that is the right word, that Hamlet cannot enjoy. What was similar, however, was the sense of confusion; and my overriding emotion, at that time, was a frustration that I seemed incapable of feeling enough. Numbness is a term that is too self-aggrandizing, but the inability to locate what one felt was a bitter preparation for playing Hamlet. My performance, I knew, would be dedicated to her – who, as a girl, had switched off the lights in her bedroom and listened to Olivier performing some of Hamlet's great soliloquies – and I regarded it as a privilege that I could explore, with her, the greatest meditations on grief and death ever written.

On a weirder note, a few days before my mother's funeral, I was walking in the churchyard behind our house and met the gravedigger who was preparing her grave. I found myself asking, as Hamlet does (v.i.115), 'Whose grave's this?' – although, I hasten to add, I didn't call him 'sirrah' – and it reminded me that *Hamlet* is a play almost unique in its universality. It is quite simply a play about something we all go through. Other Shakespeare plays deal similarly with grief and death, of course, but all of them debate other themes – kingship, madness, ambition, sexual jealousy – and give them equal weight. *Hamlet* is essentially monothematic, despite its picture of political disturbance, and its theme is the most important any man or woman will encounter: that of their own humanity and mortality.

All the relationships Hamlet enjoys or endures pale into insignificance when we consider the debate he carries on in his own head. In order fully to analyse his own dilemma he ironically seems compelled to nullify any normal, balanced human contact. When put like that, the hell Hamlet goes through, the hell his own father forces him through, is not dissimilar to Iago's. But where Iago is static, Hamlet is active, and the results of his agony, although on the surface depressing, could not be more different.

And the chief result – or at least to my mind the most profoundly moving result – is the play itself. At the end of the play Hamlet says to Horatio

> O God, Horatio, what a wounded name
> Things standing thus unknown, shall I leave behind me!
> If thou didst ever hold me in thy heart,
> Absent thee from felicity awhile,
> And in this harsh world draw thy breath in pain,
> To tell my story. (v.ii.338–43)

It is a great commission – the greatest – to tell the world of one man's struggle to understand his own humanity, of one man's struggle to accept his own death, his struggle to find a value (wherever his thoughts might lead him in the struggle itself), and, most importantly, to tell it to the world, out of love for that one man, in a spirit of compassion. Whatever the moral confusion at the end of the play, whether as an audience we believe that for the hero the rest is indeed silence, whether beyond our little lives there is value, humanity's ability to think and to speak, to make some sense of it all, is of profound importance. Perhaps Horatio, the storyteller, the loving observer, is the unsung hero of *Hamlet*. It is he who finds the way out of Hamlet's hell, and the fact of Hamlet's story being told, and being told so exquisitely, is one of the greatest wonders of all.

*

It was with contemplation of that wonder that I concluded the lecture written before rehearsals began, and which records some of the ideas that we took into the production process. It is interesting that many of them remained intact through that process – the status and function of Horatio, for example, or the potentially loving relationship between Hamlet and Ophelia. In the lecture I had been wary about saying anything about the central 'Closet Scene', and although the pressure of having to speak and inhabit Shakespeare's lines forced Sara Kestelman (Gertrude) and me to make certain clear decisions, the scene changed radically at every performance and the love between mother and son through the length of the play remained essentially indefinable – and perhaps that is as it should be.

Looking back, what strikes me first is that the title I chose for the lecture – 'Hamlet's Hell' – tells barely half the story. Hamlet does experience a type of hell, of course, though even in the darkest times in his life there are moments of joy or revelation. But one of the chief reasons that Hamlet is an extraordinary part to play lies buried somewhere in the last act, when he has returned from his short exile and where the playwright's creation of a man somehow at peace and prepared for his death is frankly miraculous. The hells experienced by Richard III and Iago seem, in comparison, a long way away. An experience of hell is, in Hamlet's case, an early, if important, stage on a journey that ends in peace. But just as it is difficult to define his experience of hell, so it is equally difficult – more difficult, indeed – to locate what he feels and thinks at the end of the play, especially since his conversion from an active misery to calm resignation happens off stage. I may, I know, be accused of sentimentality, but I do not believe that Hamlet is, in any profound sense, brutalized by his experiences – changed, of course, damaged, but not brutalized. I realize that I may be too much in love with him – the 'sweet prince', the 'noble heart' (v.ii.353) – not to find his attitudes to the deaths of Rosencrantz and Guildenstern and his crass attack on Laertes over Ophelia's grave very difficult to accept. (And although he regrets his aggression over the grave towards a man whose father he has killed, Hamlet's astonishing lack of remorse over the deaths of his two school-fellows cannot be ignored.) His final resignation is also necessarily self-centred, but his trust in some 'special providence' (v.ii.213) for all of us, his understanding of a man's place in the universe, conservative though it might be, is deeply moving and very important. Perhaps I should judge him more harshly, or with greater disinterest, but I cannot. The fact is that the Hamlet that emerged from our rehearsal room was sweeter, gentler, perhaps meeker, than I had expected, and I felt I had to stick with him.

I shall come back to the fifth act later in this essay and ought, perhaps, to start with the beginning of our rehearsal process, when the cast and director sat round a large table and cut the text. This took two weeks – a long time in an eight-week rehearsal period. At the end of the process, every actor was happy with the version of the play in front of them, since it had not been presented as a *fait accompli* before our work started; and our knowledge of the text had been immeasurably deepened, since every decision to cut derived from long and detailed discussion. Collectively, too, the cast and director had to decide, now that Fortinbras was no longer in the picture, on the best way to begin and end the play. Using Horatio as storyteller and framing device was the result not only of early discussions between John Caird and me, but also of this lengthy and important collaborative effort to find a version of *Hamlet* that we were all proud of.

Those early days in rehearsal also reminded me that I am not a purist about cutting Shakespeare. Our decision to cut in the first place, and the nature of those cuts (as with many recent productions of the play) provoked some controversy. But the 'full' text is such an extraordinary mixture of different versions – bad quarto, good quarto, folio – that almost every other line presents a choice for the actor and director. Equally, there is at least one section that seems to have been added for reasons above and beyond the story: the discussion of children's acting companies, a subject that is not of enormous interest to the majority of a modern audience. I admit that getting rid of all of one character and his story (in our case Fortinbras) is dodgy, but I have no objection to the *principle* of cutting. A Shakespeare play is not like a Mozart symphony, where cutting, even of repeated sections, is problematic, because words relate to each other in a less precise, or less easily defined, way than notes in music. With Shakespeare, quite simply, doing less than the 'full' text is fine if the production that results has its own internal coherence.

I have divided what follows into three parts, the first covering Act One, the second Acts Two, Three, and Four, and the third Act Five. This reflects what I see as the distinctive shape of Hamlet's journey, although I hope I shall be forgiven if I jump backwards and forwards in the story – and if I am incoherent, it is because there is simply too much to say.

ACT ONE

Having decided that we did not want the Fortinbras sub-plot, the first scene became, for the most part, irrelevant. Indeed, during the first day of discussion, John and the cast floated the idea that we could dispense with it altogether, leaving the first mention of the ghost until the moment when Horatio tells Hamlet of his frightening experience. This idea, despite eventually being abandoned, had its strengths. If an audience member with no previous experience of *Hamlet* – and they do exist – came to a production that started with the *second* scene, then news of a ghost's appearance would come, as it were, out of the blue, with Horatio's 'My lord, I think I saw him yesternight' (i.ii.189). The same audience member would then share directly Hamlet's confusion, excitement and scepticism. At one point in rehearsal I tentatively suggested that, if we were to keep the first scene we could perhaps cut at Marcellus's 'Look where it comes again' (i.i.40), thus revealing that something strange is about to happen on the battlements, but not its precise nature.

In the end we kept with more of the first scene than we had originally planned. This was partly for sentimental reasons – the first line of the play (indeed the whole scene) is too famous to be dropped – but it was also felt that opening the play with Claudius's first elaborate speech might be alienating; that, with a reduced cast, we wanted to establish Marcellus and Barnardo as defined characters and therefore needed the time the first scene gave us; that presenting Horatio at the beginning as a central figure in the play helped with our concept of him as the storyteller; and, finally, that the tension created by an opening scene of frightened whispers was too precious to abandon. So the first famous confrontation with the ghost had to stay.

Nevertheless we cut two-thirds of the scene, paring it down to its bare storytelling essentials. The long description of Denmark's frantic preparation for war had to go and this allowed us to present Horatio as a man with little knowledge of Scandinavian politics, who might not be Danish, might not spend the greater part of his time at Elsinore, and, most importantly, might not know Hamlet very well. I know it is dangerous to smooth over Shakespeare's apparent inconsistencies, but, in this particular case, it seemed to help. I was pleased, however, that we kept the first three of Horatio's four demands to the ghost (I.i.129–39) which show a highly educated but conventional man coping with an extraordinary and unforeseen experience. That Hamlet's response is similar, but essentially broader based – 'I doubt some foul play' (I.ii.256) – reveals the difference between two men similarly educated but worlds apart in imaginative scope.

Horatio's demands are a reason why, although we got rid of the ghost being dressed in full armour, with 'his beaver up' (I.ii.230), we had him holding a dagger. This dagger was to have great significance later in our story, but originally it allowed for Horatio's conventional response and for Hamlet's later worries. I had an early idea of Hamlet's father as a scholar-king, a man very like his son, a man not given to unnecessary displays of aggression; so the dagger became a symbol, not of war, but of some unusual violence that young Hamlet finds disturbing. Interpreting the ghost is a problem to both Hamlet and Horatio, and the dagger is the first and simplest sign that 'foul deeds will rise' (I.ii.257).

I shall return later to a more precise description of what I feel is Hamlet's initial reaction to Horatio's news of the ghost. Before that turning-point in the story, the first problem in rehearsal was locating both the nature of Hamlet's misery and its manifestation. His silence at the beginning of Act One, Scene Two is interesting, given that, elsewhere, talking, putting his thoughts into words, is something for which he has a great facility. Is his silence not only the result of his not wishing to invest his time and energies in this new smooth-talking court – he could, after all, say goodbye to Laertes, whom he later describes as a 'brother' (v.ii.238), a man he has known and loved for a long time – but also the result of his not knowing what precisely he is thinking and feeling?

When he finally talks, his first two lines are witticisms. The first is an aside – 'A little more than kin, and less than kind' – and the second a reply to Claudius – 'Not so, my lord. I am too much in the sun' (I.ii.265, 267). Hamlet's sense of humour, his sense of the ridiculous, never leaves him, of course, even when he is dying, and these two lines are a sign of that. The fact that they are witty is also, it seems to me, a pointer to his being self-protective. This humorous self-protection need not be overtly aggressive. The reply to Claudius could be a joke that Hamlet is willing to share with his uncle – a man that even Hamlet, as yet, cannot accuse of having done anything criminal, however distasteful his speedy marriage to Gertrude may be. Sharing a joke with Claudius (or, at least, the attempt both to disguise and reveal a sense of distress through a witticism) developed from a notion of John Caird's that Claudius is a man who wanted his brother's crown, wife, *and* son. The need in his uncle to preserve, as much as possible, the *status quo ante* is something that Hamlet is acute enough to recognize and, perhaps, play up to, although this, in turn, does not preclude a desire in him to be convinced by Claudius. Equally, Claudius's long speech to his nephew about old Hamlet's inevitable death is couched in terms that would appeal to a young scholar: Hamlet's grief shows an 'understanding simple and unschooled' and is 'to reason most absurd' (I.ii.97,103). I felt that, in his confusion, his inability to locate precisely what is troubling him, Hamlet is, despite himself, looking to Claudius to provide a solution. Like anyone suffering a new grief, he would like things to be as they were.

This is also the scene in which we first see Hamlet with his mother. Her attempts to comfort her son are, inevitably perhaps, clumsy, especially her statement that death is 'common' and that her son's grief 'seems . . . particular' (I.ii.72, 75). Hamlet's reply, in the speech beginning ' "Seems", madam?' (I.ii.76–86) is both heartfelt and self-conscious. The language is elaborate and courtly, a response not only to the formality of the occasion, but also, perhaps, a wry comment on that formality. Late in the run I wondered aloud to Sara Kestelman whether perhaps 'windy suspiration of forced breath' (I.ii.79), or indeed the whole speech, could be played as if in joking code, as if Hamlet is trying to include his mother in an analysis of the situation that only they, given their close and loving relationship, can understand. It would then be up to Gertrude whether she accepts the invitation to enter such a harmless conspiracy. However the speech is played, it is unquestionably the only substantial sequence of thought that Hamlet presents before the king, queen and court disappear, and that, of course, is significant.

The release and the confusion of Hamlet's first soliloquy are glaringly obvious. I decided early in rehearsal that I would try to address the audience, as directly as I could, as if Hamlet is asking for help. This serves to make him, I hope, less irritating and self-obsessed and also highlights the fact that when he stops using soliloquy, in Act Five, he has, in some way, come to a resolution, and thus no longer has to rely on the audience for support and encouragement. Here, at the beginning of the play, he needs friends and has to appeal to those who will listen rather than advise – although, throughout his story, his desperate loneliness is unrelieved.

Thoughts of suicide are a result, of course, of his grief, but the immediate impetus for the first lines of the soliloquy seems to be Claudius's (and Gertrude's) foolish, though understandable, decision to keep him in Denmark. I've always thought that had Hamlet been allowed to go back to Wittenberg, back to the security of his friends and his scholarship, things might have worked out. After all, Hamlet shows precious little interest in being king (and Claudius's taking the crown seems to have the support of the court and, at least until the last act, of the country), and I suspect that, given the comfort he evidently finds in his academic work, an abdication of political responsibility would be welcome.

It is interesting that Shakespeare creates a central character who is not only a prince, but also a university student – a combination that was, I presume, a rarity in the early seventeenth century. Presumably Wittenberg was not chosen lightly: Hamlet no doubt studies scholastic – radical or not – theology. So much of the play is, in effect, Hamlet's debate with his god, and the appearance of the ghost overturns or challenges his deeply held convictions (after all, evil, and evil acts, are always a problem theologically). Before meeting the spirit of his father, Hamlet can use a conventional church-centred argument against suicide – 'Or that the Everlasting had not fixed / His canon 'gainst self-slaughter' (I.ii.131–2) – which is glossed in a more radical way in 'To be or not to be' (III.i.56–88), where a general fear of an afterlife is a more powerful deterrent than a dread of doing something wrong in the eyes of the church. His famous statement to Horatio –

There are more things in heaven and earth, Horatio,
Than are dreamt of in your philosophy   (I.i.166–7)

– which is spoken in the excitement of having just talked to the ghost
of his father, could come as a surprise to Hamlet, as it does to Horatio.
Faced with Horatio's intellectual certainties and limitations, he knows
instinctively that he himself must start again. What reads as an admo-
nition to a colleague could equally well be a frightened recognition that
previously held convictions are no longer tenable.

The venomous attacks directed against his mother – against all
women, indeed – in the first soliloquy reveal both Hamlet's sense of
betrayal and his innocence. Despite his undoubted intellectual abilities, it is, of course, a mistake to assume that Hamlet knows anything
about sex – or, at least, sex with women. His disgust with women is, in a
sense, a convention of the time, but later, in the scene with his mother,
he shows, above and beyond that conventional set of assumptions, a
puerile understanding of the nature of sexual desire:

Refrain tonight,
And that shall lend a kind of easiness
To the next abstinence; the next more easy.
(III.iv.166–8)

As a recipe for the cure of sexual obsession, or even desire, this seems
to me a disaster. Perhaps I am being cynical, but I cannot imagine
Gertrude taking Hamlet's advice seriously – or, at least, she would
recognize that the price of such a sudden abstinence would be heavy.
In fact, by the time Hamlet says this it would appear that the marriage
of Gertrude and Claudius is already under strain (she must know now,
for certain, that he is a murderer), but this does not make Hamlet's
words less crass. The fact that he compounds his offence by insisting
that people over a certain age cannot experience overwhelming sexual
desire only heightens our sense of his insensitivity and inexperience.

We know, too, that the relationship between Ophelia and Hamlet
is highly problematic and, to our ears, underwritten. It appears that
Hamlet cannot discard the received wisdom that all women, even
Ophelia, are essentially both sinful and the occasion of sin. This is
difficult for the two actors who play Ophelia and Hamlet in a modern
production, and although ways can be found out of the problem (I felt,
for instance, that Hamlet, for as long as he can, believes in Ophelia's

essential *innocence*), Shakespeare is of little help in that he gives no indication of what the relationship between Ophelia and Hamlet was like before the play started. What we know, from the first soliloquy, is that Hamlet distrusts women: 'Frailty, thy name is woman' (I.ii.146).

Technically, the first soliloquy is hard – more demanding, perhaps, than any of the others. Hamlet finds it hard to settle: he keeps interrupting himself, and although what he wishes to say to the audience is clear enough, his distress muddles him. It is only with the arrival of Horatio and the news of the ghost that he can move on.

We decided, with the help of the cuts we had made in the first scene, that Hamlet and Horatio do not know each other very well. Although this idea is, perhaps, partly contradicted by Hamlet's later statement of respect for Horatio – 'my dear soul . . . hath sealed thee for herself'(III.ii.73–5) – a distance between the two men, a formality, was useful at this stage of the play. It explained why, despite being present at old Hamlet's funeral, Horatio had made no contact with Hamlet, and it thus allowed the actor playing Horatio (Simon Day) to explore and play a deep sense of unease in the telling of potentially distressing news to someone he respects but does not know well.

In fact it happened that Hamlet, in our production, feels a kind of exhilaration on hearing that his father's spirit has appeared. This took me by surprise, but it made unexpected sense. Given his previous confusions, Hamlet can now *do* something – he can talk to the ghost. It is important to realize, too, that the exact nature of the spirit is unknown to those who see him: as Hamlet says later, it 'may be a devil' (II.ii.597), 'a spirit of health or goblin damned' (I.iv.40). The appearance of a ghost does not seem in itself surprising to him. It is the reason for its appearance, the news that it might bring, that is both frightening and exhilarating. The necessary secrecy is also part of that exhilaration, a temporary cure for his loneliness and the first step towards a closer relationship with Horatio – a relationship that will survive the horrors later in the story.

The meeting with the ghost – and I think other Hamlets might agree – is the most intensely exhausting part of the play for the actor playing Hamlet. The significance of the ghost's appearance is recognized by all four men, although their fear of making direct contact, of speaking to the ghost, is counteracted by Hamlet's courage, a courage that stems from his realization that a conversation, or a contact, is the only means of resolving his sense of aimlessness: 'My fate cries out . . .' (I.iv.81).

17 Simon Russell Beale as Hamlet, *Hamlet*, Act i, Scene iv: 'Angels and ministers of grace defend us.'

It is odd that, despite the scene with his father's ghost being tiring, Hamlet is so passive. He risks few questions, merely accepting the information given him; listening requires all his energy. He has to cope, too, with the demands of reassessing his relationship with his dead father. As with other areas of the play, this relationship has to be, in a sense, invented by the two actors playing father and son, for Shakespeare gives few clues. I felt strongly that the love Hamlet has for his father should be deep and unquestioning. This helped in making the ghost's story (and his description of purgatory) more painful and his departure, as dawn begins to break, unbearable. Unbearable, too, is the fact that Hamlet is forced to watch his father in great pain and hear him admit to past sins. Even for a relatively sophisticated student of theology, this admission must be profoundly distressing, as Hamlet makes clear in a later soliloquy:

> 'A took my father grossly, full of bread,
> With all his crimes broad blown, as flush as May;
> And how his audit stands, who knows save heaven?
> But in our circumstance and course of thought,
> 'Tis heavy with him. (III.iii.80–4)

Most importantly, the ghost of old Hamlet seems to have great faith in his son's ability to carry out his instructions. Hamlet, indeed, plays up to his father's expectations, rushing, when he hears the news of murder, to say

> Haste me to know't, that I, with wings as swift
> As meditation or the thoughts of love,
> May sweep to my revenge. (I.v.29–31)

– to which the ghost replies 'I find thee apt' (I.v.31). I wonder, in other words, whether young Hamlet is *playing* the part, perhaps unconsciously, which his father expects of him – a part of noble single-mindedness.

I have already remarked that the ghost's commission is effectively a death-sentence. Whether Hamlet knows this at the time is doubtful, and certainly his response, after the ghost disappears, is surprising. In his soliloquy he abandons, or so it seems, all his previous learning, focuses on his mother in an unexpected and significantly short line – 'O most pernicious woman' (I.v.105) – and effectively reinterprets his commission. That may be too harsh a judgement on him, but it is, I think, important that the idea of revenge is not directly mentioned in this soliloquy. Rather, Hamlet repeats his father's last emotional instruction:

> Now to my word:
> It is 'Adieu, adieu, remember me'.
> (I.v.110–11)

I am not saying that Hamlet is unaware that he has to revenge his father's murder, that he has to *do* something. In his mind, though, the demand to kill his uncle (and, more problematically, to avoid harming his mother) is less important than the gentler request to remember his dead father.

It is an odd speech in other ways. Despite dismissing all he has learnt hitherto, the scholar in Hamlet does not disappear: his first instinct is to write his thoughts down in his 'tables' (I.v.107) – a strange, almost bathetic moment. In our production, old Hamlet gave his son a dagger, a terrible and constant reminder of what young Hamlet is required to do, but the implication of which he is, at this moment, trying to ignore. What he knows or feels now is that his grief has a focus – forgetting his father would now be, accurately rather than sentimentally, a betrayal – and that makes him, in a sense, happy.

The pressure of meeting his father's ghost produces an hysteria in Hamlet, so that his reaction to the ghost's reappearance as a disembodied voice feels, in playing the scene, like laughing at a funeral. It represents the beginning of one of the most frightening journeys he has to make: this hysteria is the first indication that Hamlet might descend into madness. At this moment, the possibility of going mad is something of which he is only dimly aware. He warns his friends that he might appear 'strange or odd', that he might adopt 'an antic disposition' (I.v.170, 172) – almost predictable behaviour, given the pressures that he is under. What he cannot know is where this will lead; how, above all, it will be analysed by those around him. Uppermost in his mind at the end of this act is, rather, an overwhelming sense of his own inadequacy:

> The time is out of joint. O, cursèd spite,
> That ever I was born to set it right!
> (I.v.188–9)

ACTS TWO, THREE, AND FOUR

When we next see Hamlet, in Act Two, Scene Two, he has been offi-cially designated as mad – or, rather, he is regarded as mad by Polo-nius, a man whose understanding of human nature is not particularly acute. This is, I think, important – although Polonius, to be fair, has good reason to doubt Hamlet's sanity. If he is worried about Hamlet as the play starts (and certainly others seem to be), then his fears can only be strengthened by Ophelia's strange tale in Act Two, Scene One.

I happened to be in the rehearsal room when Denis Quilley (Polonius) and Cathryn Bradshaw (Ophelia) were rehearsing this scene in which Ophelia, distraught, tells her father of Hamlet's odd behaviour in her closet. Since I was around, John Caird asked me to mime the actions as Cathryn told Ophelia's story. These actions are precisely and, for all we know, accurately, described: the taking of Ophelia's arm by the wrist, the extension of Hamlet's arm, the shaking, the sigh 'so piteous and profound' (II.i.94). As it was re-enacted in rehearsal, it looked as if Hamlet was miming (perhaps experiencing) masturbation and or-gasm. I can promise that this is not what I had expected, but there is a grim potency in the idea that Hamlet might abuse Ophelia in this clumsy way – especially if the relationship between them is, up until this point, not a sexual one, frustration and incomprehension on both sides being dominant emotions. Polonius's reaction to Ophelia's story is predictable and understandable. He describes it as 'the very ecstasy of love' (II.i.102) and it is a short step from this appalled analysis to a confident declaration to the king and queen, in the next scene, that their son is mad.

What I am leading to is the idea that it is others who are convinced that Hamlet is losing his mind; he remains, essentially, aloof and lonely, though he may be aware that he is being spoken of in this way. His lack of engagement is famously present in the odd encounter with Polonius in Act Two, Scene Two. It is odd because, at no other point in the play does Hamlet behave in quite this way; his meeting with Claudius in Act Four has a similar feel, but Hamlet's intentions there are aggres-sively clear, less remote, and informed by the fact that both he and the king share the knowledge that the latter is a murderer. In the earlier scene it is very difficult to pin down precisely what Hamlet means by his verbal games – although it seems obvious that he doesn't really want to talk. Once drawn into conversation, he launches a predictable attack on old men – the supposed subject matter of his reading – and later cannot pretend that he is unhappy to see Polonius go. It is important that he wants to be left alone, despite the fact that his mind is so unsettled that even reading is uncomfortable: he describes the book at first as 'words, words, words' (II.ii.193), a phrase that can be played in a multitude of ways, but seems to me to imply weariness and dissatisfaction. This tension between the wish to be alone and a fear of one's own unbridled thoughts is important and a major element in the soliloquy that ends this long scene.

One element of the scene that began to interest me in the early days of rehearsal was Hamlet's two direct references to his own life and death. Given that he *may* be aware of others' analyses of his behaviour, a paranoia would be perfectly natural, and his deliberate misreading of Polonius's question 'Will you walk out of the air, my lord?', and his answer 'Into my grave?' (II.ii.206–7), could, I thought, be the result of his fear, his desire to find out how he is to be dealt with, now that the diagnosis of madness has been accepted, and also, as always with Hamlet (complementary and almost contradictory emotions in this case), a desire to be reassured that he is safe, and an appeal for help. This many-layered response proved useful in the thrice-repeated 'except my life' (II.ii.216) at the end of the conversation, and the playing of these lines, except that it elicited no easily readable response from Polonius, changed every night.

Hamlet's need for security is answered by the arrival of Rosencrantz and Guildenstern, old friends, in our production, with whom he feels immediately comfortable – as is shown by his quickly falling into the rhythm of university banter. This familiarity, perhaps even love, provides a useful contrast to the formal start of the on-stage relationship between Hamlet and Horatio, in that it allows the actors playing Rosencrantz, Guildenstern and Horatio to experiment with ideas of resentment, jealousy, loyalty and embarrassment as one friendship strengthens and the other deteriorates.

The deterioration starts early. Rosencrantz's easy assumption that Hamlet is upset because of frustrated ambition is a sign that the friendship is perhaps more shallow than it appears – that is if the word 'ambition' (II.ii.251) does not have a broader meaning. As I said earlier, desire for the throne never seems to be a hugely important part of Hamlet's make-up, something a sensitive friend might be aware of. Despite the sincerity of Hamlet's reply, the lack of understanding in Rosencrantz's quick analysis of his misery obviously sticks in his mind. Much later in the play, when the friendship between the three men is on its last legs, Hamlet's response to another of Rosencrantz's displays of apparent solicitude is what I would read as a brush-off, an answer that Rosencrantz would readily understand and that allows Hamlet to get him off his back:

ROSENCRANTZ Good my lord, what is your cause of distemper? . . .
HAMLET Sir, I lack advancement.

(III.ii.344–7)

The reply is so brusque that I cannot believe it to show anything but irritation on Hamlet's part, an urgent desire to get rid of a man who is now merely a pest. It is true that, to give him his due, Rosencrantz keeps trying to get to the bottom of Hamlet's problem long after Guildenstern has lost patience. What the motive for such concern might be is difficult to define – although the line 'My lord, you once did love me' (III.ii.342) might be a clue. I enjoy the idea (supported by nothing in the text) that Rosencrantz and Guildenstern are undergraduates of that not uncommon type who have, despite their innocence, a shrewd eye on their future careers, students for whom their studies are not an end in themselves. In other words, they could not be more different from Hamlet. Despite the easy sense of relief, and fun, in their first meeting, there is an unbridgeable gap between Hamlet and his friends, shown most clearly in their response to his extraordinary speech 'I have of late . . .' (II.ii.295–310). This is a pivotal expression of desolation and a devastating exposure of private pain; in reply, Rosencrantz can only smile. He and Guildenstern see that Hamlet is suffering, but cannot come near to understanding and helping him.

This is not to say, of course, that the friendship is not real and valued as far as it goes, or that it is not based on affection and respect. All three enjoy meeting again. The banter is deliberately formulaic, the logic-chopping game ludicrous. (In passing, it is delightful that Hamlet, of all people, cannot keep up: 'Shall we to th'court? For, by my fay, I cannot reason' (II.ii.263–4).) But the pleasure is sullied by an act of betrayal – apparently small or, at least, not hugely significant at the time, but with unforeseen and enormous consequences – the admission that they have been 'sent for' (II.ii.274), to spy on him. In rehearsal the moment when this is admitted by Guildenstern (and the fact that Hamlet may have guessed a few seconds earlier does not make the shock any less) became enormously important, and it remained so in performance. (I have a habit of pausing too often, and I was allowed by our stage manager only two pauses in *Hamlet* – one here and one with Ophelia, though I confess to not always keeping to that.) Much of this play is about trust that is betrayed and love that is destroyed and it is no accident that this evidence that those around him are not what they seem spurs Hamlet into his desolate expression of his loss of faith in the beauty of man. Something I realized later, in performance, is that here with Rosencrantz and Guildenstern, and later with Ophelia, Hamlet's sense of betrayal springs not only from his being lied to, but also from his being spied on, which is an affront to his dignity. He cannot, and will not, explain to others (even, I suspect, Horatio) the full extent of his misery, and those that love him, or apparently love him, are mistaken in their assumption that catching him out in unguarded conversation will reveal anything of real value. Hamlet's pain lies too deep to be exposed by a trick.

Nevertheless, after a momentary, if important, hiccup, things seem to return to normal. They might not understand Hamlet in any profound sense, but Rosencrantz and Guildenstern know that he loves the theatre, and actors. Rosencrantz is on relatively safe ground when he tries to lighten Hamlet's mood by telling him that his favourite troupe has arrived in town. The mere mention of players cheers Hamlet and, a moment before they arrive, he can reiterate his welcome to his friends. This was, in our production, genuine, leading to a mutual desire to start again, and it leads to another revelation: 'But my uncle-father and aunt-mother are deceived. . . . I am but mad north-north-west' (II.ii.374–77) – a statement that confirms both that Hamlet knows that the word 'mad' is being used by the court to describe his behaviour, and that his ability to analyse his situation in an ironic, even dispassionate, way has not deserted him.

I do not think we ever see Hamlet happier than when he is with the players. There is an innocence and a gaiety about his enthusiasm for them and their work and the pressures he is under seem momentarily to disappear when they arrive. The experience of grief has been likened to suffering a series of muggings. Things seem just fine and then suddenly, when it is least expected, the familiar sense of loss returns with a force that is almost overwhelming. In this joyful scene with the players, the mugger is a long way away and Hamlet feels, for a moment, safe. There is delight in the actors' skill and their creative energy; but, more importantly, they are a breath of fresh air, a reminder of a living, breathing, healthy world outside Elsinore. I loved John Caird's idea that one of the actresses in the group should be pregnant and that Hamlet, despite his earlier miserable analysis of humanity, should take a great delight in this.

Hamlet, then, is a fan, and a fan who is also a prince can insist that the players perform immediately, without the chance to settle into their lodgings or to wash the dust off their faces. He loses no time, not only in insisting on a performance of his favourite speech, but also in indulging in a little exhibition by trying to act the speech himself. I was keen that Hamlet, despite his teasing of the First Player – 'If it live in your memory, begin at this line' (II.ii.446) – and his confidence in his own abilities, should find himself momentarily out of his depth after only one line. Indeed, in our version, the First Player had to prompt Hamlet – with some glee. For a split second, the prince looks foolish: not an intellectual super-star, but an ordinary man underestimating a craft which should *look* effortless and true to life, but which requires some nerve and skill.

It is, of course, the behaviour of Pyrrhus that is important in Hamlet's choice of scene:

> For lo! his sword,
> Which was declining on the milky head
> Of reverend Priam, seemed i'th'air to stick.
> So as a painted tyrant Pyrrhus stood,
> And like a neutral to his will and matter
> Did nothing. (II.ii.475–80)

Whether the choice of a situation in which a man is rendered impotent in battle is conscious or not does matter, of course, but is not easily resolved. I suspect that Hamlet, when he affectionately remembers the play and the speech, has, for the moment, forgotten how the story of Pyrrhus develops. I am sure, however, that the description of Pyrrhus doing 'nothing' has a tremendous impact. The mugger is back. Later, in the soliloquy that ends the scene, Hamlet says

> Yet I,
> A dull and muddy-mettled rascal, peak
> Like John-a-dreams, unpregnant of my cause,
> And can say nothing . . .   (II.ii.563–6)

and every time I came to it in performance, the still-fresh memory of Pyrrhus's inaction resurfaced.

The soliloquy, needless to say, is magnificent – and, at first, worryingly long. It does have, however, a clear narrative line, a structured argument divided into three, perhaps four, distinct sections. Hamlet is here ordering his thoughts in a way that could not be more different from the barely suppressed hysteria of his first moments alone.

In my mind (and I know this sounds vague), each soliloquy in *Hamlet* has its own distinct flavour or colour – a flavour or colour that did not change over the run, even if the details of thought, emotion, or presentation did. This may sound non-sensical, but, especially in this speech, I knew at the outset if I was in the right frame of mind to deliver it as best I could – and, of course, there were too many times when I was not. At the end of an act that has seen Hamlet, passive as he often is, responding to a tumbling series of new stimuli, he starts the soliloquy with 'Now I am alone' (II.ii.546).

I never knew, as I said this, precisely whether Hamlet was frightened or relieved to be by himself – or, indeed, both. Whatever it is he is feeling leads, however, to a careful presentation of what he is thinking and, with that, an appeal for the support of his listeners. There are so many moments in the speech seeming to require a response of some sort – 'Am I a coward?', 'Why, what an ass am I!', 'The spirit that I have seen / May be a devil' (II.ii.568, 580, 596–7), for example – that Hamlet appears instinctively to know that only by promoting his argument clearly, with opportunities for disagreement, can he hope to retain the support of one of his few allies, the audience.

This mode of direct address, coupled with the fact that a decision is made within the speech and that Hamlet is active in furthering the plot (a rare thing), means that his introspection, and near suicidal apathy, come as a great surprise when we next see him. It feels, in the playing, like a step backwards. We played around, indeed, with the idea of moving 'To be or not to be' back into the previous act, before the arrival of Rosencrantz and Guildenstern, when Hamlet is thinking directly about his life and death. It was an idea that had the value of consistency: surely, having decided to put on a play, Hamlet would not fall back into his former, suicidal state of mind. But, somehow, the inconsistency was exciting. Hamlet should not be expected to develop in a simple linear way; and, in any case, the speech is far greater, far wider in its implications, than a simple debate on one man's suicide.

I have to admit that, before I played Hamlet, I never quite knew what all the fuss was about 'To be or not to be'. It seemed to me that the argument was simple and conventional, with none of the more obvious excitements of the previous soliloquies. I was right in one limited sense, in that the argument *is* simple, but the power of the speech lies in the statement of something that is absolutely and inescapably universal. The power and skill that Shakespeare shows in breaking effortlessly beyond the limitations of structure and of story to present the unanswerable question of human existence is surely what makes this short speech the most famous in world drama. And, at its best, playing it requires and produces – 'acquires and begets', in Hamlet's words (II.ii.7) – a strange balance of unassailable introspection and the sense of common and shared humanity. In my experience of Shakespeare, that is unique.

It is no accident that the next scene should involve the only person in the play who (probably) commits suicide; and, indeed, in our production Ophelia stayed on stage for Hamlet's soliloquy – a sad and ironic touch that I liked, but which some found distracting. In rehearsing the confrontation between Ophelia and Hamlet I tried to locate those moments when aggression was unavoidable, to explore the possibility that Hamlet might, at some level, want to help or advise Ophelia, rather than terrorize her. He knows that the possibility of a loving relationship has gone (a result both of the demands of his situation and of his complex emotional response to it), and, perhaps, the suggestion that Ophelia go into a nunnery is the only way he can see of protecting and preserving the virtue of the one person in his life who is not corrupted by those who surround her. What provokes Hamlet's aggression – and aggression is ultimately unavoidable – is his inability to interpret the motives behind her return of his letters and, of course, the lie she tells about her father's whereabouts. This betrayal unleashes a stream of conventional misogyny that shows Hamlet at his worst – although I found that this same expression of irrational loathing might produce a sudden fear in him that he could really be going insane: 'Go to, I'll no more on't. It hath made me mad' (III.i.147–8). These are lines that remind me of

King Lear's heart-breaking appeal, 'O let me not be mad, not mad, sweet heaven! / Keep me in temper; I would not be mad'(I.v.43–4), a fact that encouraged me to play Hamlet's lines as equally genuine and vulnerable. This required him to drop his voice, so as not to be heard by Polonius (and Claudius), since any distress at the real possibility of insanity must be kept from them.

It is almost as if this scene is written in code, a code so impenetrable that Ophelia cannot understand what Hamlet is trying to tell her. Indeed, what Hamlet would really like to say is now hidden so well that the pain is evident, even if the reasons for it are not. I found this useful. The building pressure of keeping so much dangerous information hidden, even from those he loves, must sometimes be unbearable, although, of course, he does tell Horatio about the manner of his father's death. Hamlet, I'm sure, must feel tempted to drop hints, to scatter a few clues.

The need for concealment disappears with the presentation of the play within the play, and once the information that Hamlet has (or believes he has) is out in the open, the pressures on the court and the king change. Whether the accusation is true or not, Hamlet must, in some way, be disposed of; and, equally clearly, Hamlet now has nothing to lose. This does not mean, however, that he stops talking in code. As the king storms out of the performance of *The Mousetrap*, Hamlet utters a mysterious little verse:

> Why, let the stricken deer go weep,
> > The hart ungallèd play.
> For some must watch, while some must sleep.
> > Thus runs the world away. (III.ii.280–3)

In our version of the play, I spoke these lines directly to, or at, the Queen. Just as *The Mousetrap* itself is a code – simple enough, in this case, to break – so is this short rhyme. Since Gertrude knows precisely what he means, and what he meant to say in putting on the play, the confrontation between mother and son in the former's closet can be, in very fundamental and important ways, about something other than the accusation of murder. One code is dropped to be replaced by another.

Once the play within the play is over, the nature of his relationship with his mother becomes, for Hamlet, his overriding concern. I think, frankly, that he is frightened – both of her, perhaps, and certainly of hurting her and losing her love and support. He does not race to see her when she summons him; he knows any meeting will be difficult and he procrastinates – and in our production this procrastination was supported by John Caird's decision to place the interval just after the play, when Hamlet asks for music. His procrastination is part of the larger situation in which, his suspicions having been confirmed, he can still do nothing about the task that has been set for him. The music becomes, therefore, not a celebration but a distraction, while he waits for the king, the queen, Polonius, to react.

The great scene between mother and son became, not so much a discussion about Hamlet's accusation, or, indeed, a violent release of tension (I was keen to avoid any physical abuse), but rather an attempt by both of them to find a *modus vivendi*, to make a new contract based on love and respect. This contract involves, too, an observance of Christian procedures – repentance, confession, absolution. I have said earlier that, despite the challenge to his beliefs, Hamlet is ultimately conservative in his response: even in the last act, his fatalism springs from a faith in a benevolent god. After the initial and understandable aggression – when he calls Claudius a 'murderer and a villain' (III.iv.97) – an aggression that Gertrude recognizes as unproductive, Hamlet moves on to a series of recommendations that he feels his mother should take up – avoiding Claudius's bed, coupled with confession 'to heaven' (III.iv.150).

We found that the catalyst for change from futile anger to something more constructive was the reappearance of the ghost. Although Hamlet's initial reaction to this unexpected visit is fearful, there was something to be said for the idea that he finds the presence of his father comforting. The family unit – father, mother, son – has, for a moment, been re-established. Although Hamlet might delight in this – at one point in our production both father and mother touched him simultaneously on each shoulder and the tensions in him, and in the scene, melted away – it is also a reminder that his longing for things to be as they were can never be satisfied, and that it is essential for the love here displayed between the three of them to be preserved and developed in a new relationship between the surviving mother and son.

The scene in the closet does not start well. Hamlet is wilfully, ostentatiously difficult, his first question being essentially puerile: 'Now, mother, what's the matter?' (III.iv.9). This sulkiness does not necessarily come as a surprise, despite the fact that Hamlet has, in the preceding scene, shown a real strength of purpose. He displays, with Rosencrantz

18 Simon Russell Beale as Hamlet with Sara Kestelman as Gertrude and
Sylvester Morand as the ghost of old Hamlet, *Hamlet*, Act III, Scene iv:
'Nothing but ourselves . . .'

and Guildenstern, and then with Polonius (who, irritatingly, has come
to deliver the same message as Hamlet has just received from his fellow
students), both arrogance and waspishness. This is, moreover, one of
the few occasions when he uses as a weapon the fact that he is a prince,
deploying, with Rosencrantz and Guildenstern, the royal plural – 'Have
you any further trade with us?' (III.ii.341) – and forcing Polonius to ac-
quiesce in a ridiculous game that achieves nothing beyond reminding
the old man that Hamlet, and only Hamlet, will decide when to visit
his mother in her closet. This new and grim attitude leads to a black
statement of intent – 'Now could I drink hot blood' (III.ii.397) – and,
indeed, in this apparently decisive mood, it is not surprising that he
comes very near to killing Claudius as the king is praying. What stops
Hamlet is, characteristically, a theological argument.

This tension between a firm, almost amoral, resolve and a concern over the requirements of his faith is now almost unbearable and brings about, inevitably, the killing of Polonius. This supremely clumsy murder changes the course of Hamlet's life, and throughout the scene with his mother the corpse of Polonius serves as a reminder that he has failed, that, through a momentary and uncharacteristic loss of self-control, he has become a man no better than those around him, a killer like Claudius. The fact that, in our production, the dagger used to murder Polonius was the one given to Hamlet by his father's ghost (and therefore a profoundly precious thing) merely intensifies his recognition that not only has he failed, but also that he is, in a fundamental and perhaps irredeemable way, sullied.

As Polonius falls to the floor, Gertrude's terrified reaction and Hamlet's hysterical cascade of accusatory words are only to be expected. But, as I implied earlier, it is after the ghost's reappearance and departure that things change in ways that are unanticipated both by the two characters and by the audience.

As we rehearsed this scene, Sara Kestelman (Gertrude) became convinced that it is at this point that Gertrude realizes that her first loyalty is to her son and not to her husband – a conviction supported by the happy reunion of the dead father and his family. This rediscovered sense of priorities is never put into words, but it is something that Hamlet, too, understands – indeed, perhaps unconsciously, such an affirmation is what he has been looking for in his mother. We found that, by the end of a scene in which an important relationship could have been destroyed, precisely the opposite has happened. Gertrude and Hamlet begin to enjoy each other's company again, and although this does not preclude extreme distress, it allows Hamlet to move forward towards an admission that he is incapable of carrying out his task of killing Claudius, and Gertrude to accept that her new marriage is essentially unworkable.

Deliciously, too, Hamlet's sense of humour returns. I found it useful to share both his description of Rosencrantz and Guildenstern – 'Whom I will trust as I will adders fanged' (III.ii.204) – and his final rhyming couplet (with its grim pun on the word 'grave' (II.iv.215)), with his mother. A sense of misery being shared and understood comes as a relief.

And this black levity continues into his meeting with Claudius – the first and only time we see the king and his stepson without the intermediary presence of Gertrude. Hamlet knows now that he has lost the game: his friendship with Rosencrantz and Guildenstern is beyond repair and Claudius, still in power, and knowing that Hamlet wishes him dead, will do anything to be rid of him. Consequently I decided that Hamlet should make one last feeble effort to kill Claudius with the dagger given him by his father, now no longer a precious thing, but something shameful. The fact that Hamlet finally gives the dagger to the king and that he accepts his banishment to England with res-ignation – even with contentment – is an indication that he has fully taken responsibility for his inadequacy. This is the lowest point of his story.

Ironically, though, he is now free. He can leave Denmark and start again:

> KING Therefore prepare thyself . . .
>   For England.
> HAMLET For England?
> KING Ay, Hamlet.
> HAMLET Good.
>
> (IV.iii.42–8)

ACT FIVE

It is difficult for me to write anything remotely coherent about the last act of *Hamlet*. It is, especially from the viewpoint of the central character (or, more accurately, of the actor playing him), a mystery that is insoluble. I cannot, therefore, *precisely* express my thoughts and feelings in playing it.

Something profoundly important happens to Hamlet during his exile from Denmark – we can know that, at least – but what this change in him consists of, and how and why it came about, is difficult to say. I cannot decide whether it is a stroke of genius that Shakespeare allows the most important development in Hamlet's character and attitudes to happen off-stage, or whether it is a missed opportunity; the fact that we (audience and reader) are told so little certainly has a strange and provocative impact. It is as if the character we have grown to know, and perhaps to love, is slipping away – is, in effect, dying.

This sense of Hamlet's slow disappearance is important. At the end of the fourth act (in our reduced version of the play) we see him destroyed and in despair, though if we had kept the great soliloquy 'How all occasions do inform against me' (IV.iv.33–66), our last sight of him would have been as a man with a new sense of purpose:

> O, from this time forth,
> My thoughts be bloody, or be nothing worth!
> (IV.iv.65–6)

When Hamlet appears in the graveyard, however, he shows neither acute despair or self-hatred nor that the desire for action is in the forefront of his mind. It is sad that, given the possibility that Hamlet may have discovered a new resolve, the final series of deaths should be such an unpredictable muddle. In other words, something else has happened, something that allows Hamlet to accept, fully and calmly, the inescapable fact of his own (imminent) death.

I can only compare this sense of acceptance to that experienced by some people who suffer a long and fatal illness. I have witnessed that series of moments when, despite being alive, a human being consciously grows to a decision to accept (and accept fully) his or her death. It is this that comes to my mind in one of Hamlet's last speeches:

> I am dead, Horatio . . .
> . . . Horatio, I am dead.
> Thou livest. (V.ii.327–33)

When I came to the rehearsal of Hamlet's death, I said at the time that I wanted him to die 'standing up' – meaning only that I thought his last wonderful words should be spoken with a simplicity and a clarity unspoiled by my having to writhe around on the floor. Actually, the truth is that, in one sense, the whole of the last act shows Hamlet dying 'standing up'.

Hamlet not only cuts himself off from the audience (consciously or unconsciously), but also from other characters in the play. He says little of importance to Gertrude or Claudius, and his apology to Laertes is there only for the precise reason that he has insulted him in an uncharacteristic and careless manner. Indeed the 'new' Hamlet takes himself by surprise, I think, with the vehemence of his attack (a memory of a former life, perhaps) and by the unthinking whine behind the line 'What is the reason that you use me thus?' (v.i.285) – a question to which Hamlet cannot fail to know the answer. It is interesting to note, too, that Hamlet's apology to Laertes (v.ii.220–38) is very largely couched in the third person – a weird device and a sign, perhaps, that he is not fully engaged.

Even in his friendship with Horatio, now secure and unquestioned, there is a sense that, for all his desire to tell his story to his friend and later for his friend to tell the world, Hamlet is oddly remote. As an example, Horatio's entirely sensible wish to postpone the fencing-match elicits a response from Hamlet which, although in some ways comforting for Horatio (spoken, indeed, to comfort him), is essentially the thoughts of a man who has closed in on himself. It is also, by the by, the one speech that I am sure most other Hamlets would agree is the moment when the actor has to strip away any sense of display, or contrivance, or self-consciousness:

There is a special providence in the fall of a sparrow. If it be now, 'tis not to come. If it be not to come, it will be now. If it be not now, yet it will come. The readiness is all. Since no man knows of aught he leaves, what is't to leave betimes? Let be. (v.ii.213–18)

This fatalism is repeated at the end of the play when, despite a longing for his story to be told and his life to have some real significance, Hamlet finally lets go. John Caird asked me to talk directly to the audience at this point – an inspired idea, I think:

> You . . .
> That are but mutes or audience to this act,
> Had I but time . . . O, I could tell you –
> But let it be.   (v.ii.328–33)

Hamlet's story is told, of course, and is still being told. Horatio accepts the commission from his friend, despite knowing that it will be hard, that 'in this harsh world' he must 'draw [his] breath in pain' (v.ii.342). And that, in our version, is where we left the play, as Horatio goes out into another world, haunted by his own ghosts.

*

Looking back over this essay, I am acutely aware that almost everything I have written can and should be contradicted, both by other people, of course, but also within my own performance. That's the trouble with writing about *Hamlet*. The play is, quite simply, both too big and too hospitable. I was going to say, in addition, that the character of Hamlet himself is elusive, but that would imply that there is something to catch, to get hold of, to get *right*. But, more than any other character I have ever played, the person called Hamlet does not exist. There is only a series of actors' responses to, and reactions with, the part. It is as if anyone could play him and produce something right and true. And that is what makes the experience thrilling.

King Lear

NIGEL HAWTHORNE

THE LATE SIR NIGEL HAWTHORNE played King Lear in a production directed for the RSC by Yukio Ninagawa. It opened in Tokyo in
the autumn of 1999 and was then seen in London (at the Barbican),
and later at Stratford, where Sir Nigel was making his début, his only
other performances for the RSC (as Orgon in *Tartuffe* and Major Flack
in *Privates on Parade*) having been in London. King Lear was Nigel
Hawthorne's last stage role at the end of a distinguished fifty-year career
as a stage, film and television actor. Among numerous theatre awards
were an Olivier for best actor for the *The Madness of George III* at the
National Theatre (a performance he repeated on film) and a Tony for
his performance in *Shadowlands* on Broadway. His earlier Shakespearian roles on stage included (among much else) Macbeth and Falstaff
(both given at the Sheffield Crucible) and on film Malvolio in Trevor
Nunn's *Twelfth Night*. Among his many other films were *The Clandestine
Marriage*, *The Winslow Boy* and *Amistad*, while a long list of television
credits included *Mapp and Lucia* and *The Barchester Chronicles* as well
as *Yes, Minister* and *Yes, Prime Minister*.

Within the space of a year, Shakespeare wrote two of the greatest plays
in the English language, *Macbeth* and *King Lear*, remarkable for their
insight and imagery, the epic nature of their construction, and their
extraordinary perception of the frailties of man. He was forty-two. Both
of the men about whom he wrote were leaders at the turning point in
their lives: the younger man, Macbeth, a general in 'the day of success'
(I.v.I); the older a monarch whom we meet at the point of retirement.
Both men are dominated by strong women. Was this choice merely a
device to make good drama, I wonder, or was there more to it?

Lear is often played as a tyrant who is transformed by his deteriorating
mental state into a man both loving and compassionate. Of the monster
I could find no evidence – if one disregards his treatment of Cordelia.
There is, however, evidence that he commands affection: he is loved

19 Nigel Hawthorne as King Lear with Robin Weaver as Cordelia, *King Lear*,
Act I, Scene i: 'Come not between the dragon and his wrath.'

by the fool; Cordelia, despite the way he has behaved, loves him too;
Gloucester is blinded because he contrives to save the king's life; and
why should Kent, after so violent an altercation, risk death by returning
in a dangerously penetrable disguise to serve him? It doesn't smack of
'tyrant' to me. Yet he does fly off the handle at his favourite daughter
when all she has done is to be honest. This is certainly one of the
dilemmas facing any actor taking on the role.

Well, to begin at the beginning – not the beginning of the play, which
I shall come to shortly, but how I came to be involved in this particular
production. People refer to *King Lear* as 'the Mountain', and there are
no nursery slopes. If you take it on, you have to do it the hard way.
The Artistic Director of the RSC, Adrian Noble, rang from New York:
would I like to climb it? I had been asked once before, shortly after I had
finished the run at the National Theatre of Alan Bennett's *The Madness
of George III*. At the time I had felt it might not be wise to attempt in
quick succession two kings who went potty, but now that several years
had gone by, perhaps this was the right moment – before I left it too
late.

It was August. I had celebrated my seventieth birthday in April. My memory was still reliable provided I began learning the lines early enough. How about my stamina? – pretty good for my age. I swim every day, play tennis and garden: no problem with carrying Cordelia on at the end. But did I really *want* to do it? Theatre is impossibly demanding. Each day that there's a performance the actor has to prepare in readiness. The need for massive concentration and commitment would be total. Eighteen months of my life devoted to one of the 'great' parts, and I would be compared and contrasted with those who had gone before – Wolfit, Gielgud, Olivier, Scofield, Hordern, Howard and Holm: a nasty little shiver was running up my spine. Did I need all that stress in my life – and at the sort of money the RSC would pay me?

Aware of my hesitation – after all, he was paying for the call – Adrian chimed in: 'It's to be a major production of arguably Shakespeare's greatest play, rehearsing and opening in Tokyo for ten weeks, Yukio Ninagawa directing; then coming to the Barbican for a straight run of four weeks – only one performance a day – and ending up in Stratford. You've never played Stratford, have you? And playing over the Millennium, to finish on 26 February 2000.' His words of encouragement just seemed to tumble out. I took a deep breath: 'All right. I'll have a go' – unaware at that stage that this *Lear* mountain had twin peaks, the other peak being Mount Fuji. I was soon to discover that our director didn't speak English.

Ninagawa was coming to London so that I would have the opportunity of meeting him. His production of *Hamlet* in Japanese was opening at the Barbican with a thirty-eight-year-old martial arts expert, Hiroyuki Sanada, in the lead. I enjoyed the production very much. Ninagawa has a wonderful visual imagination and, most importantly, the narrative line was clear and uncluttered. Sanada was splendid and I clocked his vulnerability, which prompted me to suggest him for the fool. It might be the perfect bridge between East and West. I spoke about it to Ninagawa, who nodded and smiled. 'After all', I elaborated, 'the fool is an outsider, someone at the court who has the ear of the king and can speak to him frankly and wisely.' He said he would think about it. He seemed open to ideas, which was encouraging, and was extremely likeable. I had the feeling that we'd get along well. Bursting with curiosity, I asked how he was going to interpret the play – the storm scene, for instance, how did he visualize that? There was some to-ing and fro-ing with the interpreter before she came back with 'Stones will fall from above.' 'Stones?', I repeated, 'how big will these stones be?' 'Rocks', came back the answer, 'there will be rocks'. Unaware of how accurate a direction my mind was pursuing, I asked 'Supposing they bounce?' Ninagawa-san smiled toothily.

When pressed about any further ideas, he was not forthcoming: a delightful man, very charming and approachable, but I came away none the wiser about how he would be interpreting the play. We didn't even mention the leading character. The following morning Ninagawa-san returned to Japan and I was left alone with my thoughts. After all, I reassured myself, there was a whole year before we began rehearsals.

That meant that there wasn't a moment to lose. I had to know the play inside out before we began. If I couldn't discuss problems of interpretation with my director beforehand – fine, I'd make notes and store them up until I got to Japan. But at least I would be prepared. I bought every edition of *King Lear* that I could lay my hands on and started to read essays on the play and accounts of other actors' performances, including Granville Barker's notes to John Gielgud. I even read Nahum Tate's absurd reworking, which held the stage for a hundred and fifty years as the original text was declared unactable – even unwatchable. Shakespeare had based *King Lear* on an earlier uncredited play, much praised by Tolstoy but dismissed by just about everybody else, called *The True Chronicle History of King Leir*, which was published in the summer of 1605. Shakespeare's version contains many characteristics of the older play, and some of the names – 'Gonorill', 'Ragan', and 'Cordella', for example – have a familiar ring. At the beginning there is the same competition as in *King Lear* to determine which of the daughters loves her father most, though in *King Leir* it is rather different – a device to trick Cordella into marriage.

It was that very competition in Shakespeare's play that provided me with my first stumbling block:

> Which of you shall we say doth love us most,
> That we our largest bounty may extend
> Where nature doth with merit challenge.
>
> (I.i.51–3)

So says the king, who then invites Goneril, as the eldest, to speak first. No sooner have the last words of her eulogy left her lips than Lear, without waiting to hear whether her sisters' declarations of affection might be even more acceptable, apportions a generous third to Goneril and makes it official. Regan is next and he does the same to her, so that, whatever Cordelia might say, she's stuck with what's left. So what was the point of having a competition when it was a stitch-up anyway? Hmmm . . . was there beginning to be a faint glimmer of light at the end of a very dark tunnel? Perhaps the 'madness' of the king began earlier than most of the editors suggested. Generally speaking, it seemed that they believed that it began with the entrance of Poor Tom in Act Three, Scene Four. But supposing, just supposing, that some irregularities were already starting to disconcert those who knew him well as early as this first scene. And if that was the case, what was the cause of these irregularities?

'Three daughters by one loving wife' is part of a line from the earlier *Leir* play. When I came across it, it set me thinking about Lear's queen. Supposing (again) that she had died only recently and that Lear's first appearance is as part of a funeral procession in which her coffin is brought onto the stage – just supposing. The mood sombre; everyone in black: where would that take us? Well, the king could be apart from the others, lost in his grief; the fool watching from behind a pillar, or at Cordelia's side, comforting her. Let the king begin his first speech slowly, the pain and stress showing in his face, the court standing respectfully by, not daring to protest at his intention to abdicate and divide the kingdom –

> while we
> Unburdened crawl toward death.
> (I.i.40–I)

– the king's line given a special significance here. It all begins to go wrong during the competition, when it is Cordelia's turn to speak, and the resultant row takes place over the coffin. At least this would provide a springboard to the first scene, as well as giving the audience a clear reason for the king's uncharacteristic behaviour. My mind was working overtime. It was maddening not having the director at the end of a phone, at the very least. I spoke to David Hunt, the bright young associate director, showing him the passage in Shakespeare's play where Lear's queen is mentioned:

REGAN I am glad to see your highness.
LEAR   Regan, I think you are. I know what reason
        I have to think so. If thou shouldst not be glad,
        I would divorce me from thy mother's tomb,
        Sepulchring an adult'ress.

                                        (II.iv.123–7)

David's reply was instantaneous, and it was no. He felt strongly that the play should open with a celebration; it was, after all, an occasion to mark the betrothal of the king's youngest daughter. A sombre mood would not be appropriate. It would also mean that, in the structure of the role, I would have no peak from which to fall. In any case, he wasn't at all sure that the fool should appear so early on. So we dropped the idea there and then and, once again, I was left with the problem of the first scene.

I felt passionately that if I could crack that bloody scene, the rest of the play would slip miraculously into place. I returned to my old friend the competition. Could this be the clue to the cause of Lear's rage? I went through the next scene, and the next, and so on, marking moments where I thought the king might falter, signals he might give of the impending 'madness'. I knew from having played George III that people were often classified as 'mad' in days gone by when there was something else the matter with them. King George was incarcerated when it is now believed that he was ill – an illness which only later descended into madness. Was King Lear similarly not mad to begin with, but ailing? Was he suffering from a form of senile dementia, perhaps? Once again I felt frustrated at not being able to discuss these matters with the director. It is true that I could have written them down and posted them to him in Japan, but, by the time they had been translated into Japanese, and Ninagawa had thought about them, then had his decisions translated into English and posted back to me in England, an awful lot of time would have been wasted. I put my imaginative forces to bed for the time being, and concentrated on learning the lines.

The trouble with learning so far in advance is that there is no immediate need to remember, so the mind hangs about, dwelling on interpretation rather than concentrating on the tedious business of cramming quantities of words into an extremely reluctant head. But I persevered. I learned my lines. Even on holiday, I startled people idling along the beach with a burst of Shakespeare. Each day I learned a little more about the man, though, as yet, I hadn't the foggiest idea of how to play him. Of one thing I was certain: I wasn't going to boom. I'm not a boomy sort of actor anyway. I've sat through an awful lot of boomers when I've prayed for Gloucester to come on again, because I've been so bored with the Lear. All that ranting and raving may show you that the actor in question is jolly good at holding the stage, but you find out very little about the man he's supposed to be playing. The storm scene is a case in point. I had been much encouraged during my reading to come across a line spoken by an anonymous gentleman about the king in the storm, who

> Strives in his little world of man to out-storm
> The to-and-fro conflicting wind and rain.
>
> (III.i.10–11)

That's it: the king doesn't dominate the storm; it dominates him. Donald Wolfit, I'm told, used to duck into the prompt corner just before the storm scene and get them to turn up the volume so that he could outblast the elements. But isn't the impotence of the king at being unable to drown the thunder more touching. I became more determined than ever to find the Real Person. I suspected that I'd hit on something with the first scene; now I painstakingly worked through the play making sure that I was being consistent. Sadly, I have several friends who suffer from Alzheimer's disease. I know how the moods of sufferers from this distressing complaint can fluctuate: bewilderment changes in a flash to anger, to self-pity, to forgetfulness and repetition; lucidity comes and goes. I began to find places where I could work these moods into my performance.

The days slipped by into weeks and then into months. I sent away my passport for the Japanese visa and started to grow a beard. Word about some of the casting was leaked to me by Thelma Holt, who was the associate producer on the project and a close friend for almost forty years. John Carlisle as Gloucester: what a good choice – a kind, gentle man with a beautiful voice. Perfect. My old friend Christopher Benjamin as Kent, another excellent choice. Michael Maloney as Edgar – his mad streak ideal for Poor Tom! I didn't know the girls, Siân Thomas, Anna Chancellor, and Robin Weaver, but their reputations were first class. All of a sudden it was August. The year was up. It was time to meet them.

The Barbican is not the most actor-friendly complex in the world. It is a large and very ugly building built of that hideous rain-stained concrete that was so mistakenly popular in the 1960s and seventies. Backstage one enters a mineshaft, for both stages housed in the building, as well as the rehearsal rooms, are underground. In order to buoy up flagging spirits, some bright spark had painted the walls and ceilings of each of the five descending floors in garish colours – purple, yellow, scarlet – in gloss. In the rehearsal room we were allotted, deep down in the bowels of the Barbican, Jessie Norman, the opera diva, for some reason that I can no longer remember, had instructed that one of the walls be painted bright blue. It helped, but not much. With an exit at each end, the room looked and felt like a corridor. The formalities began. We had a welcoming chat from Adrian Noble and one from Thelma; then I was called upon to say a few words. I introduced Sanada-san to the company. He was looking green with terror; it didn't look too good against the blue wall. I couldn't check my own colouring because there was no mirror, but I could guess. Over the next three days we read the play. Various theories were brought up from time to time, but I didn't get involved. I wanted, as far as was humanly possible, to keep an open mind until we got to Japan. At least it was reassuring to find that I knew all my lines.

The Saitama Arts Centre was about forty minutes from our hotel in the Ikebukuro district of Tokyo. The flight had been a long one, and when we arrived at the complex to begin rehearsing we were all tired and jet-lagged. But there were speeches. The Japanese love to make speeches, and they are seldom short; particularly when they have to be translated, sentence by sentence. And this gives time to think of more to say. But at last they were over, and Ninagawa-san invited us to follow him into the theatre. We processed down a long linoleum corridor. The Arts Centre is very modern and spotlessly clean. The corridor was being highly polished by a team of cleaners, identically dressed. As we walked, I glanced up at the high ceiling. I was reminded of the inside of a prison, though I tried not to let that impression colour my excitement. Whatever I might have been expecting, it was very far from what greeted me when the doors were thrown open. The auditorium was large, square, and very modern, more like a huge lecture hall than a theatre, with massive batteries of lights. But there, on the stage, was one of the most chilling sights I have ever seen in my fifty years as an actor.

The scenery was up, and ready for the first night; it was lit; the huge stage crew was standing by all dressed in black; the music had been composed and recorded; the sound effects were all ready; there were rehearsal clothes for us all to wear; and my wig had arrived from London. It was as though Ninagawa-san was saying: 'All right. You've come over here to do *King Lear*. We're all ready for you. Get up there and do it!'

At that moment I felt real terror and I would be very surprised had every single member of our company not felt as I did. Rehearsals began haltingly, with some of the shock waves lingering; and, as we began the most difficult scene in the play, my old friend the first scene, I don't think I've ever felt quite so inadequate. I had done a substantial amount of preparation, that was true, and, in due time, I was hopeful that it would benefit me. I knew, too, that a great deal was expected of me: I was, after all, the leader of the company, and it was up to me to lead by example. But how to *begin*? Very shortly, I pulled myself together and began to assess the situation. Ninagawa-san was really an opera director. In other words, he expected you to know the arias. His job was to shunt you around and make you look good. For the entire time I worked with him on Lear, I never had a single note, never had a single discussion with him about the character I was playing. That, it appeared, was not the way things were done in Japan. I was a senior actor visiting the country to play a major role. I was expected to know what I was doing.

Rehearsals were tense and scratchy from the outset, with some of the company feeling sorry they'd agreed to do it in the first place. I tried manfully to make suggestions as to how scenes should be staged, and met with stubborn resistance and quite a little hostility for at least the first ten days: as if things weren't difficult enough, I was now Public Enemy Number One! After that, I think people started to see that all I was trying to do was to get the creative juices working. Ninagawa-san was not going to be a huge amount of help. For one thing, his working script had Japanese on one side and English on the other and most of the time, while we were speaking the lines in English, he was following us in Japanese. It was, therefore, up to David Hunt, the Associate Director, to help us out. Yet there was a problem there too. David felt that Ninagawa-san was excluding him. The Japanese creative team seemed to be making decisions among themselves in their own language. Discussions between the director and the British actors about the staging, and the performances themselves, inevitably had to be conducted

20 Nigel Hawthorne as King Lear with Hiroyuki Sanada as the fool, *King Lear*, Act III, Scene ii: 'A poor, infirm, weak, and despised old man.'

via the interpreter. Yuriko-san was working her socks off, and we all admired her enormously, but I have to say that communication wasn't easy. Back at the hotel, a lot of sake was drunk.

On top of all this, Sanada-san was having problems with his English. There wasn't a single moment in the whole of our association that I didn't admire this young man for his courage and his professionalism. I never heard him complain. He was always punctual, as well as being the perfect company member. He was much loved by all of us who worked with him. Each day, David and I would find time to help him with his lines. Each day he became just that bit more confident. The fool is a difficult enough part for an Englishman. The 'rocks' for the storm scene turned out to be huge lumps of wood covered with lead foil. Sanada-san, Christopher Benjamin, and I, therefore, approached the storm scene with more than usual trepidation. They were dropped from the grid and landed with the most almighty crash. I knew that if one of the stage-hands was incorrectly cued, or wasn't paying attention, just one of those 'rocks' was heavy enough to crush the living daylights out of me. At the dress rehearsal, to prove the point, Christopher, as

Kent, came on with a plastic bucket over his head! Ninagawa-san went through the scene with me to mark the moments –

> Blow, winds, and crack your cheeks! [*rock*] Rage! Blow! [*rock*]
> You cataracts and hurricanoes, spout [*rock*]
> Till you have drenched our steeples, drowned the cocks! [*rock*]
>
> (III.ii.1–3)

– and so on. Sometimes a cue would be changed and I would have to wait for the wretched rock to land before continuing. There was considerable competition. The whole theatre shook. I couldn't help feeling from time to time that the storm scene was difficult enough without 'rocks' to contend with. A wag called it 'The Rocky Horror Show'. Occasionally a fearsome-looking specimen would roll into the audience, provoking squeals of alarm. That didn't help matters either, or inspire confidence.

The feeling of panic that had almost annihilated the company on the first day never totally left us. It hovered. It was easy to see where Ninagawa-san's strengths lay: the show looked fantastic. The costumes were spectacular, and Harada-san is one of the best lighting designers in the world. We were going to look absolutely great. But what about the play – how was that shaping? Were we ready for the first night, which was almost upon us?

Well, I wasn't. That was for sure. There were great stretches of the play in which I embarrassed myself deeply. It was almost as though I'd never, ever done any acting in my life. My self-esteem was non-existent. I wished to God that I'd kept my big mouth shut when Adrian phoned from New York, stayed at home, done some gardening, and walked the dogs. I toyed with sneaking out of the hotel before anyone got up, getting a cab to the airport, and catching the first plane home. It didn't help matters when management people from the RSC paid a flying visit, saw the show, and never mentioned it – talked instead about the weather. Adrian Noble himself came to Saitama and gave me three or four notes of such deceptive simplicity that I wanted to hug him. Never before had I been so desperate for help and so grateful to receive it.

We sold out every performance in Japan. Unexpectedly, as we'd been warned that the audiences would be very reserved, they rose to their feet at the curtain calls and cheered. Word had filtered through that the Barbican season was sold out too and that tickets at Stratford were selling fantastically well. Encouraging though that was, it didn't dispel the feeling deep down in the pit of my stomach that we could be a lot better than we were – well, *I* could.

One of the reasons for this was that the audience in Japan didn't react at all until it was all over. It was almost as though they weren't there. They were hearing the play translated into their own language through headphones. I thought I'd discovered places where laughs were legitimate, but in Tokyo there was silence. It wasn't until the previews began in London and there was some response that I could see whether they worked or not. We ended our Tokyo season on a high note, with scores of little gifts and huge bouquets, while fireworks were let off on the stage behind us. Saying goodbye to all the friends we had met in Japan wasn't easy.

The rest of the story, from Japan on, is tinged with disappointment. Although the production was sold out for the entire run, a number of the daily critics were spiteful about it, and about me in particular. They had a field-day: they felt I didn't rant and rave enough; that I was too mild. Well, I had made the decisions myself. Nobody else was to blame if the choices were wrong. Set against that, I am the proud possessor of a huge file of letters, mostly from people whom I've never met, saying that it was the critics who were wrong; how moved they'd been; that it was the first production of *King Lear* that they'd ever really understood, the first time they'd found something genuinely funny and touching, the first time they'd been able to hear the words in the storm scene. I'm inordinately proud to have been sent those letters, and feel that some of those critics had arrived with a preconception. With regard to my own performance, I did what I did because it was right for me. I was truthful to the play, didn't cheat, and knew where I was going, every inch of the way. It was just as well I did, as there was little or no guidance. Well, so what? For centuries before directors were invented actors made their own decisions, so if I wasn't going to have notes from our director, then I'd give myself some. Here are ten of them:

(1) *Act One, Scene One* Take the first scene slowly. Make the court wait. Come in with huge energy and speed, sit on the throne, watch them all kneeling in front of you – enjoy the power. 'Give me the map there' (1.i.37) – speaking to servants. When Goneril finishes her declaration of love, and curtseys, forget she's there for a moment, then turn and applaud perfunctorily. Take Cordelia by the hand, seat her on the throne – then be hit in the stomach when she replies

'Nothing, my lord' (I.i.87). Give her five chances to recant, then go ballistic. When Kent goes into exile, watch him go. Then watch Cordelia. Regret.

(2) *Act One, Scene Four* Delight at seeing the fool. When he gets abusive, be hurt rather than angry – like a spurned lover. Then forgive him. Hug him. It is a very tactile relationship. Watch him for guidance. A pupil with his teacher – Lear the pupil.

(3) *Act One, Scene Five* In front of Albany's castle, seething with indignation at Goneril's ingratitude. Yet suddenly revealingly open and honest when he says to the fool of Cordelia 'I did her wrong' (I.v.24). When he speaks to the gods he has a hot-line. One friend to another: 'O let me not be mad, not mad, sweet heaven' (I.v.43) – quiet and personal. Deeply felt.

(4) *Act Two, Scene Four* The daughters, with their newly acquired wealth and status, take over. Find the humour in Lear's impotence as they cat-and-mouse with him. How many knights – a hundred, fifty, twenty-five? Have fun in the 'O reason not the need' speech (II.iv.259 ff.) – Lear trying to think of ways of revenging himself on them. Then hug the fool in anguish and stumble off with him into the storm.

(5) *Act Three, Scene Two* The storm scene. Avoid the rocks!

(6) *Act Three, Scene Four* Carry the fool on my back; perhaps he's twisted an ankle. Thoughtful and gentle with him, understanding his discomfort. When Poor Tom arrives, find the comedy: 'What, has his daughters brought him to this pass?' (III.iv.60). Begin to replace the fool. Sit next to Edgar on the wet ground. Reach out to touch his bare shoulder. Find him fascinating.

(7) *Act Four, Scene Six* Dover. Think Becket. Find the silences. Just sit, watch, and listen. When Gloucester has difficulty pulling off Lear's boots, laugh with him: two old men united on a pebbled beach. Embrace him suddenly and unexpectedly. Comfort him like an older brother. Cry with him at what life has done to them both.

(8) *Act Four, Scene Seven* Restoration. 'You do me wrong to take me out o'the grave' (IV.vii.45) – not angry. No reproof. Rather sad and mystified. He is in hell; Cordelia is in heaven. A gentle scene, full of forgiveness and frailty.

(9) *Act Five, Scene Three* Don't play the beauty of the speech, play the reconciliation with his beloved daughter. At his happiest, despite the chains of imprisonment.

(10) *Act Five, Scene Three* Carry Cordelia on to display her to the assembled crowd. The absurdity of asking a group of soldiers for a
looking-glass. Then see the feather on the ground. Time stands
still as Lear holds it beneath her nostrils, knowing, as we all know,
that there's no point. When Albany says of Lear 'He knows not
what he says' (v.iii.291), Albany is wrong. Lear knows exactly what
he's saying. He knows his sanity comes and goes. He knows that
Cordelia is dead: 'And my poor fool is hanged' (v.iii.303) – an animal cry. 'Thou'lt come no more' (v.iii.305): lay her gently down
and begin to rise. Take each 'never' to a different person. Confront
them with the reality that there's no return. Final. With a terrible
stab of pain on the last 'never', Lear clutches his left shoulder. The
heart has finally rebelled. Fumble with button to ease his breathing. Edgar helps. 'Do you see this . . .?' (v.iii.308): try to shock the
onlookers into reacting. Then crash like a felled tree.

The voyage of discovery had been a perilous one, but, by the time we
opened in London we were a strong, fine company, working together
with confidence, energy and dedication. I believe that we gave our audiences something very special. It may not have been everybody's cup
of tea, but those that it pleased will never forget it. I certainly never
shall. The last performance in Stratford was my farewell to the stage as
an actor. It came and went without any fuss. That's the way I wanted
it. I'm proud to have been a part of Ninagawa-san's gloriously rich and
spectacular production, and feel deeply honoured to have been chosen
to play King Lear on this unique occasion.

Iago in
Othello

RICHARD McCABE

RICHARD MCCABE is an Associate Actor of the Royal Shakespeare
Company. He played Iago in Michael Attenborough's production of
Othello at the Royal Shakespeare Theatre in the summer season of
1999, and later at the Barbican Theatre. His other part that season was
Apemantus in *Timon of Athens*. His numerous earlier roles for the RSC
include Chiron in *Titus Andronicus*, Puck, Tranio, Autolycus, Thersites,
Truewit in *The Silent Woman*, Flamineo in *The White Devil*, and
Christopher Marlowe in *The School of Night*. In a wide range of other the-
atre work he has played Caliban, Hamlet and Malvolio at Birmingham
Repertory Theatre and Ford in *The Merry Wives of Windsor* and Fainall
in *The Way of the World* at the National Theatre. His television appearances include *Bramwell*, *A Prince Among Men* and *Persuasion*, and his
films *Notting Hill*. He has also composed music for a number of theatre productions. His essay on his performance of Autolycus in the
RSC's 1992 production of *The Winter's Tale* was published in *Players of
Shakespeare 4*.

There is traditionally a perceived problem with the motivation of Iago.
There is textual evidence for his discontent, the most obvious and immediate cause being his lack of preferment. But this is not in itself a
convincing argument for what follows: to destroy a man in the way Iago
destroys Othello for want of promotion is altogether disproportionate
to the offence, and stretches credibility in the character. Cassio's promotion may well provide a catalyst for subsequent events, but Iago's
psychosis runs far deeper than mere ambition. The play is concerned
primarily with the effects and consequences of sexual jealousy on the
human mind and it is here that the true root of Iago's problem lies; in
other words, it is the inner psychology of the character that is fundamental to understanding him, to discovering his core, and any external
motivation is purely contributory. So much of what we term evil is an
inability to understand, on a psychological level, behaviour that exists

on its own terms. A dysfunctional background, or dissatisfaction with life, may appear superficially a convincing motive for murder, but not everyone with a grudge against life goes on to take life. Ultimately social conditioning and upbringing cannot always convincingly explain illogical behaviour. And so it is with Iago. Here is a man consumed by professional and personal jealousy to the point of destruction; such a degree of mental imbalance will always remain a mystery because it exists outside our experience.

The play's setting is very important. Although it would be fifty years after Shakespeare's death before the first recognizable modern army appeared, providing a familiar military framework for a production immeasurably helps one of the play's central motives of appearance versus reality, as well as supplying a strong visual identity and a coherent world. The date decided upon for Michael Attenborough's production, 1911, represents a time of relative complacency and self-satisfaction before the world was plunged into chaos with the advent of the First World War. To anchor the play too far in the past loses points of connexion with the audience; equally, a modern-day interpretation would be unsustainable as the idea of the exotic outsider is largely redundant in today's multi-cultural society. A setting in 1911 was considered to be far enough removed for credibility, but not so distant in time as to lose recognition. It is no accident that the last three major productions of this play have all been set within thirty years of one another.

The play opens in mid conversation, which gives a sense of immediacy and forward momentum. Iago is aggrieved over Cassio's appointment as lieutenant to Othello. It is a position he feels himself more entitled to, by virtue of his practical experience in the field of battle, compared with the theoretical and 'bookish' Cassio (I.i.24). This is an argument never enlarged upon in the play. Why was Iago overlooked? There is no evidence that he was snubbed for professional incompetence or personal inadequacy. How conscious was Othello of Iago's ambition? He is aware enough to appoint him as his lieutenant at the end of Act Three, Scene Three (which, motivationally, doesn't have any effect on Iago's behaviour). Did 'three great ones of the city' (I.i.8) really plead Iago's case? There is no other textual evidence for it. It could be suggested in performance that Cassio's background and bearing make him more suitable as officer material, but this would make Othello guilty of class-consciousness, which clearly he is not. Iago refers to himself as 'ancient' (I.i.33, etc.), which (as well as being the familar and accepted corruption of 'ensign') has an archaic meaning of personal assistant, or, in a military sense, as an aide-de-camp – so, a very particular and individual job. It seemed to me that perhaps Iago suffered by being just too good in this capacity, and that it was judged to be harder to fill this place effectively than to find a suitable lieutenant. Whatever the true reason, it is clear that Iago sees it as favouritism – 'preferment goes by letter and affection' (I.i.36) – and hints obliquely that, motivated by this grievance, he is best placed to use his position against Othello. It is unfortunate that the prime catalyst for Iago's actions should be revealed so early in the play, when an audience is still attuning its ear to the richness of Shakespeare's language.

Roderigo is in love with Desdemona, and is paying Iago to act as intermediary between them. But we soon discover where the balance of power lies in the relationship: Roderigo may hold the purse-strings, but Iago holds the purse. Roderigo is no fool, however, but a young man in the throes of a desperate infatuation. It is this vulnerability that makes him so pliable, and compliant to Iago's increasing demands as the play goes on. We see this manipulation in practice now, in the play's opening moments, as Iago uses Roderigo to rouse Brabantio. Roderigo's conciliatory tone contrasts sharply with Iago's overtly racist and sexual imagery. Iago sees all human life as essentially bestial and for him, therefore, love is reduced to carnal desire. The obsession with sexuality that colours so much of his language, and his frequent employment of innuendo, become a formidable weapon throughout the play. It is this language that finally brings around the incredulous Brabantio, who reveals himself to be as vicious a racist as Iago. Although these two are the only manifest racists in *Othello* – Roderigo's 'thick-lips' (I.i.67) seeming forced and unnatural – there is a persistent unvoiced sense of racial tension that frequently colours the mood of the play. At this early stage, Iago's intention is no more than to have Othello's covert marriage to Desdemona discovered and annulled.

The first scene Iago has with Othello shows the marked difference between the play's two protagonists: Iago's insinuating pettiness contrasts markedly with Othello's dignified authority, a contrast that intensifies as the drama unfolds. It is clear that Iago not only knows of the marriage between Desdemona and Othello, but also where they are to be found. This indicates the close working relationship between the two men, for it seems that not even Cassio is privy to such information, as is shown by his appearance with the search-party: ''Tis well I am found by you' and 'Ancient, what makes he here?' (I.ii.47, 49). We had Cassio conduct his exchange with Othello out of Iago's hearing, to highlight the status of the officers, further compounded in the way they address each other. From Brabantio's storming entrance into the scene Iago is silent until after the senate. With such a voluble character as Iago, this reserve is significant: it allows him to maintain neutrality while being professionally aligned to Othello against Brabantio.

In the senate scene, instead of ordering a more appropriate formal guard to collect Desdemona, Othello tellingly sends Iago off to fetch her. Likewise it is into Iago's care that Othello assigns Desdemona at the end of the scene. This indicates the degree of confidence Othello has in Iago as a completely trustworthy man. This is central to any realization of the character. An examination of the text reveals numerous references to Iago's honesty. We had to remove several of them in performance, for fear of overstating the point. But Shakespeare's intention is absolutely clear: that there should be no sense that Iago is perceived as anything other than he appears, a trustworthy, honest soldier.

The Duke finds in favour of Othello and the cheerless Brabantio exits on a line laden with proleptic irony: 'She has deceived her father, and may thee' (I.iii.290). This will be recalled later by Iago (III.iii.204), who now busies himself with rallying the disconsolate Roderigo, as well as exposing something of himself. Iago reduces Roderigo's love for Desdemona to mere lust that can and must, he says, be controlled by reason: 'But we have reason to cool our raging motions, our carnal stings, our unbitted lusts' (I.iii.327–8). This is remarkably revealing of Iago's own Janus-faced quality – the placid exterior hiding a torrent of feeling – and indicates a degree of self-awareness. Ironically, it is the assurance of Roderigo's eventual sexual conquest of Desdemona that finally wins him over. The repeated use of the phrase 'put money in thy purse' (I.iii.336, 339, 342, etc.) has a hypnotic, mantra-like quality which, apart from its practical call to raise money, also takes on an equally important implication of 'count your blessings'. After agreeing to go to Cyprus, Roderigo exits, leaving Iago alone on stage for the first time.

In the soliloquy that follows we have our first encounter with Iago without his mask, and get nearer to the heart of his grievance. After explaining his interest in Roderigo, which at this stage is purely financial, he then startles us with the abruptness of 'I hate the Moor' (I.iii.380). The use of the conjunction 'and' that follows is brilliantly effective: Iago

21 Richard McCabe (left) as Iago with Aidan McArdle as Roderigo, *Othello*,
Act I, Scene iii: 'Put money in thy purse.'

hates Othello *and* here is an active reason, indicating that his prejudice
against Othello was prior to, and independent of, any motive. He tells
us that it is public knowledge that Othello has been sexually intimate
with his own wife, Emilia. Whether this is true is unclear. Certainly
the allegation of adultery is unfounded. I believe his fear of its public
revelation shows the extent and intensity of Iago's paranoia. There is
an irrational compulsion in the jealous mind to obsess unnaturally over
its subject. And the truth of the suspicion is immaterial. As Emilia tells
us later:

> Jealous souls will not be answered so;
> They are not ever jealous for the cause,
> But jealous for they're jealous. It is a monster
> Begot upon itself, born on itself. (III.iv.155–8)

The power of this emotion in Iago is such that he is prepared to destroy
Othello on a 'mere suspicion' of its 'surety' (I.iii.383–4). What should
be dismissed rationally by Iago as spurious has taken root in his mind
as a possibility. It is this uncertainty that is more damaging to him psychologically than having absolute proof – as we find out later by seeing

the effect the same insinuation has on Othello. Ultimately, irrational jealousy turns indeterminate suspicion into certain truth. The bare bones of a plan are laid, with Iago appropriately choosing to revenge himself by igniting in Othello the same jealousy that he himself has experienced *because* of Othello. It must be remembered, however, that at this stage it is no more than an idea: it is only 'engendered' (I.iii.397).

The threat of the Turkish fleet is used dramatically to shift the location to the more appropriately exotic, and hotter, climes of Cyprus, and the rest of the action takes place in a time of military inactivity. The presence of the two displaced women is juxtaposed with the formal, military, male world, creating underlying sexual tension. In our production we arrived at the shoreline wet from the sea-crossing and busied ourselves in drying down while waiting for the ship carrying Othello to arrive. The scene shows Cassio being relaxed and familiar with the ladies and Desdemona acknowledging a bawdy joke. It is also the only time in the play when we see Iago and Emilia in anything resembling a playful mood, although his contempt for her is only barely disguised. We presented a glimpse of Iago's intense sexual jealousy at this point by means of Cassio's innocent kiss of greeting to Emilia (II.i.99), which froze Iago momentarily before being released as a laugh. This would later translate itself into real concern with the line 'For I fear Cassio with my night-cap too' (II.i.298). This theme was further highlighted in the group exit from the scene: Cassio proffered his arm to Emilia and as the pair walked off together I flicked her with the towel I had been using while giving a look of dire warning not to exceed the familiarity. With such little stage time together, it is important to give their relationship as much substance as possible.

The following conversation with Roderigo shows a significant advance in Iago's plotting, with all the essential ingredients now in place. It is interesting to note how Iago, from reducing Roderigo's love for Desdemona to mere lust in the last scene, now tries to convince him that the outwardly virtuous Desdemona is secretly a wanton, citing the innocent paddling of palms (II.i.247) between her and Cassio as evidence of their sexual conspiracy. Cassio is equally attacked for duplicity in a character description that is more suited to Iago himself.

Once alone, Iago reviews the situation. He admits an attraction to Desdemona, but primarily as a tool for revenge. For much of the play she is purely functional, the pawn that is used to destroy Othello. The soliloquy also shows the strongest evidence in the play of Iago's essential motivation:

> For that I do suspect the lusty Moor
> Hath leaped into my seat, the thought whereof
> Doth, like a poisonous mineral, gnaw my inwards.
>
> (II.i.286–8)

This is a man devoured by sexual jealousy to the point of physical pain. What makes this confession all the more significant for me is its brevity, as he only lets us glimpse his vulnerability momentarily. To enlarge on it would reveal too much of himself to us. But retaining Iago's enigmatic quality should not blind us to the fact that there is believable motivation within him. His persecution complex even extends to fearing cuckoldry from Cassio, but he recovers himself through the anticipation of his success in practising upon Othello's 'peace and quiet, / Even to madness' (II.i.301–2) – ironically, *his* madness.

The dialogue with Cassio in Act Two, Scene Three is a brilliant example of Iago working on more than one level. Apart from his obvious goal of trying to get Cassio drunk, Iago's banter hides an equally damaging objective. His innuendo relating to Desdemona seems designed to get Cassio to admit to sexual awareness of her. This could then be used against him to Othello, as evidence of his lust for her. But Iago fails in this, Cassio successfully invalidating each of Iago's insinuations. This dialogue is reflected later in Iago's highlighting of their markedly different qualities:

> He hath a daily beauty in his life
> That makes me ugly. (v.i.19–20)

The scene that followed was presented as a barrack-room bacchanal, with 'Let me the canakin clink' (II.iii.64 ff.) being delivered as a regimental drinking contest. Every officer filled a glass and stood in line, in parody of the parade ground. Iago then produced a flask of particularly strong alcohol. This was the forfeit for the loser. The song was sung in unison and at the conclusion of the second line everyone, with the exception of Iago who assumed master-of-ceremonies status throughout the scene, raced to empty their tumblers, the slowest being deemed the loser. Cassio's reluctance – 'I have very poor and unhappy brains for drinking' (II.iii.30–1) – ensured that he was obliged to pay the forfeit.

Another drinking bout with Montano – 'To the health of our General' (II.iii.80) – followed quickly, by which time Cassio was becoming quarrelsome. 'King Stephen' (II.iii.84 ff.), led by Iago on accordion, began in melancholy vein, focusing on the isolation felt by the men deprived of female company. This soon descended into bawdy behaviour culminating in a soldier, representing a woman, performing mock fellatio on a champagne bottle. The mood was cut by Cassio's outraged 'I hold him to be unworthy of his place that does those things' (II.iii.96–7) and order was restored. Cassio's provocative 'the Lieutenant is to be saved before the Ancient' (II.iii.104–5) was delivered with a hearty slap to my chest which caused a frisson of tension between us. This was broken by a joint laugh, but when Cassio turned his back, my broad smile turned instantly to a look of contempt.

The plotting here is so breathtakingly good that it is often too easy to miss some of the subtler felicities in the writing. When Iago reacts to the bell being sounded during the brawl, his exclamation that the town will rise, although ostensibly an expression of exasperation, is also an invitation for the town *to* rise. Iago's defence of Cassio is superb in both clearing himself of any involvement as well as firmly implicating Cassio while appearing to defend him. The following section of the scene sees Iago rubbishing reputation, which in reality is extremely important to him and will form the foundation of his enticement of Othello. It also confirms Cassio's ignorance of his assailant while forwarding the plot considerably in suggesting Desdemona's intervention on his behalf. It is an astonishing quality of the writing that almost every scene and episode, while revealing greater depth of characterization, also manages seamlessly to further the narrative.

The following soliloquy was a particular favourite of mine. By this time the audience was becoming aware of how dangerous Iago could be. It begins beautifully, with the actor commenting on his role: 'And what's he then that says I play the villain' (II.iii.326). This was always guaranteed to raise a laugh – which brings me to what I consider to be one of the most useless and damaging misconceptions in theatre: 'Shakespeare's tragedies are not funny.' This could not be further from the truth: they are often very funny. Shakespeare deliberately and consistently puts humour into *Othello* to temper the seriousness of the subject. It is a theatrical device used to highlight the intensity of the tragedy by releasing tension. There are many so-called 'problem plays' where the mixture of the weighty and the frivolous creates an uneasy blend of styles for modern audiences. But this is our problem: as human life encompasses every emotion, so too do Shakespeare's plays embrace far more than the confines of the definition ascribed to them. To play Iago without the humour that Shakespeare imbues him with is to withhold the quality that makes him so believably human. Shakespeare's genius is to have us seduced by this man, to laugh along with him – and then watch the screw turn and be incapable of doing anything about it; to feel guilty, indeed, for having laughed in the first place. It is brilliant psychology and to deny it would reduce Iago to a two-dimensional melodramatic villain and seriously diminish the character's credibility. Iago's danger lies in his apparent ordinariness. This is not a devil sprouting horns, but an average man consumed by his fears to an excessive degree. In P. D. Ouspensky's *A New Model of the Universe* this demonic aspect of human nature is explored: 'The devil is vulgarity and triviality embodied. Everything he says is mean and vile; it is scandal, filthy insinuation, the desire to play upon the most repulsive sides of human nature.' This is the banality of evil and by the end of the soliloquy we should be chilled by his revelation of it.

We were keen to give a sense of continuous action – Shakespeare being notoriously vague about time-schemes – and so at the end of Iago's scene with Roderigo (in which I lovingly applied the stinging iodine to his fresh wounds) reveille was trumpeted to indicate the heralding of the morning. A large basin of water was brought in which would feature prominently later, in Act Three, Scene Three. While washing my face and checking my hair (appearance being of absolute importance to Iago), I smugly contrasted my looks with Cassio's dishevelled state – 'You have not been abed then?' (III.i.30) – while reassuring him of my further aid. Physical appearance was a very important factor in creating the character. I felt there was a strong sense in Iago that everything was being held together by his military bearing. This gave him an almost painful ramrod erectness. I wore five-pound ankle weights on each foot to root me to the ground and gained nearly thirty pounds in weight to contrast my appearance with Othello's muscular physique. This incongruity in our looks fed the jealousy theme wonderfully well.

I consider Act Three, Scene Three of *Othello* to be one of the greatest achievements in the history of drama. The plotting is spectacularly good. At the beginning of the scene Othello is at his most secure with Desdemona:

> Perdition catch my soul
> But I do love thee! (III.iii.90–1)

By the end of the scene he is plotting her demise:

> I will withdraw
> To furnish me with some swift means of death
> For the fair devil. (III.iii.473–5)

On entering the scene Iago's almost throwaway 'Ha! I like not that' (III.iii.35) alerts Othello to an unease which will be enlarged on later. Desdemona pleads Cassio's cause as Iago had instructed and the ladies leave.

The whole history of what follows has its root in one casual enquiry from Iago:

> Did Michael Cassio,
> When you wooed my lady, know of your love?
> (III.iii.92–3)

This seemingly innocuous question arouses Othello's curiosity and it is he who takes up the questioning. Iago's calculated reluctance to elaborate only has the effect of intensifying Othello's interest. We performed this dialogue while attending to mundane paperwork. At the natural conclusion of the section – 'Why, then, I think Cassio's an honest man' (III.iii.128) – I crossed the stage and took to polishing Othello's ceremonial sword as a displacement activity. This continual deflection of the topic eventually prompted Othello to come and snatch the sword from me, at which point the jealousy theme was introduced. This is a completely new idea that Iago presents to Othello, planting the seed of doubt in him when he is at his most receptive:

> O, beware, my lord, of jealousy!
> It is the green-eyed monster, which doth mock
> The meat it feeds on. (III.iii.163–5)

Iago speaks here as the man of experience. As with the reputation dialogue earlier, we see again the difference between appearance and reality, Iago in this instance putting himself above susceptibility to jealousy while secretly being victim to it.

Othello, assuring Iago of his trusting nature, asserts that he is comfortable with the personal freedom Desdemona enjoys. In doing this he unwittingly gives Iago the opening he needs. Othello says that he will

22 Richard McCabe as Iago with Ray Fearon as Othello, *Othello*, Act III,
Scene iii: 'She did deceive her father, marrying you.'

only doubt Desdemona upon absolute proof of her infidelity (III.iii.188).
(It is interesting to note that Iago's insinuations, all completely false, will
have become 'proofs' by the end of the scene.) Iago is now able to hint
at an intimacy between Desdemona and Cassio. He plays on Othello's
lack of experience with the female sex. Othello has already told us that
his life prior to Desdemona has been all 'broil and battle' (I.iii.87) and
Iago uses this, contrasting Othello's unfamiliarity with womankind with
his own supposed knowledge of the subtleties of sophisticated Venetian
women.

This is followed by what I think are the most devastating lines in the
play:

> She did deceive her father, marrying you,
> And when she seemed to shake, and fear your looks,
> She loved them most. (III.iii.204–6)

Iago not only recalls Brabantio's parting warning (I.iii.290), but immeasurably increases its significance by pointing out that, even before Othello's courtship, Desdemona's modest looks concealed her true

feelings towards him. This is undeniable, and becomes the first sign of Othello's questioning his faith in her. Iago almost overplays his hand with inherent racism when he reminds Othello of Brabantio's accusation of witchcraft, but pulls back just in time, pleading honest love for Othello as the reason for his runaway tongue. The line that follows is another example of Shakespeare relieving the tension momentarily through humour. After the intensity of the exchange that has preceded it, 'I see this hath a little dashed your spirits' (III.iii.212) completely undercuts the mood, as does Othello's equally unconvincing reply: 'Not a jot'.

Having sown the seed of doubt in Othello's mind, Iago lets his insinuation work. A half-hearted defence of Desdemona's honesty is concluded by a beautifully subtle line from Iago: 'Long live she so! And long live you to think so!' (III.iii.224). Clearly confident, and sensing Othello's growing doubt, Iago again nearly overreaches himself in his racism by accusing Desdemona of being perverse in nature in going against her own kind, and adding that her natural instincts may lead her toward rejecting Othello in the future. This is clearly too much for Othello, who dismisses Iago with a peremptory 'Farewell, farewell' (III.iii.236, the split line indicating its abruptness), adding as an afterthought that Iago should use his own wife to observe Desdemona's future conduct. Shakespeare doesn't give Iago an exit for Othello's aside, but we found it worked best dramatically to have him leave the stage only to re-enter almost immediately, interrupting Othello's thought process and further unbalancing him. Iago's speech is brilliant psychology. Any defence of Cassio by Desdemona will be perceived as evidence of her guilt, and imploring Othello not to worry unduly about the matter only reinforces his growing concern – 'fear not my government' (III.iii.254) – which is compounded in Othello's soliloquy that follows.

Desdemona enters and soothes Othello's brow with a handkerchief, which is inadvertently dropped as they exit the scene. Certain previous productions of the play have taken the interval at this point. This seems wrong, not only dramatically, since the whole thrust of the narrative reaches its apotheosis in the bonding of the two men at the end of the scene, but also in attributing a special significance to the handkerchief, an object that, at this stage in the play, should hold none. Further, it makes Othello's emotional journey in the second half of the play extraordinarily difficult to achieve convincingly, requiring, as it does, a gestation period in the character which taking the interval at the end of the scene supplies.

The exchange between Iago and Emilia is important not only in furthering the plot through the transfer of the handkerchief to him, but also in showing the state of their relationship. People have questioned Emilia's later reluctance to tell Desdemona the whereabouts of the handkerchief. Apart from the obvious admission of deceit, it is clear that until the fifth act her marriage to Iago is more important to her than the newer relationship with Desdemona, to whom she is a relative stranger. Emilia uses the handkerchief as a bargaining tool with Iago. It gives her power over him and guarantees his attention. We had Iago trick it from her with a kiss. Such a rare display of affection caused Emilia to drop her guard, during which time the handkerchief was snatched. I tried to convey the impression that Iago achieved the kiss only by the mightiest effort of will. Emilia's following line, 'Give't me again' (III.iii.314), with clear sexual need, was accompanied by an embrace from which I would recoil in disgust, the pretence of affection now redundant. Turning on her I would raise my fist as if to strike, only just recovering enough to say, as much in sorrow as in disgust, 'Go, leave me' (III.iii.317). This physical threat evolved as a direct correlation to Emilia's later suggestion of physical violence: 'or say they strike us' (IV.iii.89). To Iago the notion of his wife's infidelity is central to his being, a theme which we consistently reinforced wherever possible.

The short soliloquy that follows shows Iago at his most demonic, relishing the effect his allegations have had on Othello. I would spit out 'burn like the mines of sulphur' (III.iii.326) and stare contemptuously at the audience, no longer the jocular, affable man of earlier. The notion that it is better to be ignorant of adultery than to be racked with doubt and suspicion is well explored by Othello, with Iago all the while trying to pacify the increasingly distraught man. It is interesting to note how Othello and Iago continually veer to extremes in their attitude to Desdemona's suspected infidelity. When Othello is defensive, Iago is accusatory; when Othello becomes combative, Iago turns conciliatory. This characteristic is most evident in Act Four, Scene One.

We now arrive at one of the most important psychological turning points in Act Three, Scene Three. Iago is seemingly about to turn his back and leave Othello during 'O grace! O heaven defend me!' (III.iii.370 ff.). What would cause him to do this? It would appear to be prompted by some physical interaction during Othello's preceding speech, warning Iago to be certain of his accusations. It would have to be strong enough to provoke Iago's resignation – 'take mine office' (III.iii.372) – as well as matching the expansive quality of the language. We used the water basin that had been introduced earlier, with Iago being dragged over to it on 'Villain, be sure thou prove my love a whore' (III.iii.356), then ducked in the water and only able to resurface for 'My noble lord' (III.iii.364). This worked spectacularly well and raised the pitch of the scene to a new level. We now find ourselves in a situation where Othello is almost begging Iago to confirm, with proof, his worst fears. Othello's use of the word 'satisfied' (III.iii.387) in this context is perverted by Iago with his repeated use of it in a voyeuristic sexual sense; indeed it has the effect of acting as a verbal foreplay for the great improvisation of Cassio's dream that follows.

This speech has been cited as evidence of a latent homosexuality in Iago. This seems altogether too glib a suggestion. It must be remembered that the speech is a means to an end: Othello has demanded proof of Desdemona's infidelity, and a third-hand account would not be enough to satisfy him. Iago therefore puts himself right in the centre of his contrivance. It is a lie that perfectly illustrates Cassio's supposed love of Desdemona while also being an entirely believable scenario for Othello, given the exclusively male world they inhabit. The undeniable, distasteful relish with which Iago relates the tale might be interpreted as denial of his own homosexuality; but in the absence of any overt textual evidence I cannot be convinced of its possibility. Such ideas are not harmful, however, and can add considerably to the richness of the characters in performance. There is an indeterminable quality in Shakespeare's writing that can accommodate such interpretation (as well as all the latest developments in human thought), while at the same time allowing itself to be read in a more direct manner.

Iago, the great improviser, is thinking on his feet as well as taking a huge personal gamble in relating the tale. We played the scene with me standing behind the kneeling Othello, massaging his shoulders gently, as if to soften the horror of the blow that I was delivering him. By the time the show got to London, I had developed the courage to whisper the whole speech, to intensify the experience of it. Having roused Othello's wrath, Iago once more takes the antithetical view, trying to appease the raging Othello with his purposefully lame 'Nay, this was but his dream' and 'She may be honest yet' in response to Othello's 'O monstrous! Monstrous!' and 'I'll tear her all to pieces' (III.iii.424–30).

As the coup-de-grace of the scene, and of the supreme brilliance of Shakespeare's plotting, Iago introduces the handkerchief, and all the insinuations become proofs. Iago's 'Patience, I say' (III.iii.449) acts as a prompt in the guise of an appeasement, and Othello is finally resolved, vowing vengeance in the most inflated language, with which Iago unites, referring to his lord in the personal pronoun for the first time. Just before the end of the scene Iago acknowledges Othello's request to kill Cassio with an appeal to Othello to spare Desdemona (III.iii.471). This is a stunning piece of suggestion on Iago's part, introducing a completely new idea. But given the heightened emotional state of the characters, it is one that is immediately adopted by Othello:

> I will withdraw
> To furnish me with some swift means of death
> For the fair devil. (III.iii.473–5)

We rounded off the scene with a ritualistic blood-bonding: I produced a knife and cut the length of my palm, offering the dagger for Othello to do likewise. Facing the audience, and both kneeling from our vow earlier, Othello appointed me his lieutenant and with the climactic 'I am your own for ever' (III.iii.476), we turned towards one another, clasped hands, and touched foreheads. Othello and Iago had effectively become a single whole.

I have explored this scene at length not only to illustrate its diverse twists and turns, but to counter the commonly held view that Othello is in some way gullible. A careful examination of the text reveals quite the opposite and shows just how hard, and with what delicacy, Iago has to work to convince Othello of his insinuations. It is a miracle of the writing that in less than five hundred lines Iago convincingly transforms a trusting, confident, noble man into the suspicious, violent, tortured human being that he remains for the rest of the play.

After completely dominating the first three acts, Iago takes a much less active role for the remainder of the play. Othello's language now loses much of its heroic grandeur and is replaced by the more prosaic use of Iago's bestial imagery. Act Four, Scene One opens with Iago trying to pacify an out-of-control Othello. The mislaid handkerchief has assumed prime importance for him, so Iago can take on the role of appeaser, making light of its loss. Iago's initial insinuation in Act Three, Scene Three has now grown to become an actual confession from Cassio of his adultery with Desdemona. The speed and intensity in the development of this idea highlights the inevitability of its tragic conclusion. Whatever seizure Othello is struck by – the Folio stage-direction calls it a 'trance' while Iago describes it variously as an 'epilepsy', a 'lethargy', and, most tellingly, to Othello's face, as his 'ecstasy' (IV.i.43, 50, 53, 79) – it is clear that we are witnessing something dangerous and new. It is a mental overload for Othello. Recalling Iago's near-drowning earlier, I always played this moment shocked at what I was witnessing, while at the same time reaching for my dagger lest Othello's attack should turn itself upon me. Observing Othello descending into a state of unconsciousness, I always felt that there was something moralizing about Iago's 'Thus credulous fools are caught' (IV.i.45).

The conversation with Cassio that follows is a huge personal gamble for Iago in contriving to have Othello eavesdrop on Cassio in the mistaken belief that he is talking about Desdemona. This is a difficult scene to stage, requiring, as it does, that Othello overhear some, but not all, of the dialogue between the two men. What Iago can't have allowed for is Bianca's arrival. This is a critical intervention for Iago, but fortunately Bianca's natural jealousy only reaffirms Othello's conviction of Cassio's guilt; and, if further proof were needed, Othello sees his handkerchief in Cassio's hand.

The following exchange between Othello and Iago is the last time we see them alone together. Having arrived at this state of mental instability in the face of seemingly overwhelming evidence, Othello's re-entry into the scene with 'How shall I murder him?' (IV.i.169) represents a peak of achievement for Iago. But Othello still needs to be prompted. The antithetical stance of the two characters in their view of Desdemona that we have seen before is now expressed solely by Othello, changing his opinion of her continually from line to line and even within single lines (IV.i.178–92). It is interesting to note that it is only the threat of public humiliation – 'give her patent to offend' (IV.i.196) – the same fear that informs so much of Iago's behaviour, that stiffens Othello's resolve to murder. The intensity of the build-up to this point was such that I was never in any doubt that Iago truly believed his own lies. I tried, however, to dissemble a deep sorrow at the irrevocable decision to kill Desdemona, while at the same time offering Othello a more appropriately physical method of execution than his stock poisoning.

Desdemona now arrives, and his subsequent striking of her was always a shocking moment. Following close on his fit, here was public proof of Othello's instability, and it was always hard to resist

Desdemona's pitiful 'I have not deserved this' (IV.i.241). The exit after the exchange with Lodovico, played with genuine concern, is an example of how my performance developed during the run. All the soldiers on stage would 'about turn' to leave in formation, but at the last I would spin on my heel to give the audience a knowing, satisfied look. In time this changed to become a dead-pan, cold stare which, apart from being more chilling, also registered the inevitability of what was happening. There was no going back.

Coming on during Act Four, Scene Two, in the aftermath of the desperate scene between Othello and Desdemona, revealed a new depth of callousness in Iago's character. I played the whole scene tenderly, holding Desdemona in a compassionate paternal embrace while stroking her hair and caressing her face. Here was Iago in what amounted to abuse, and the more I played the sympathetic uncle figure, the more repulsive it became. Such apparent concern for Desdemona earned me a tender kiss on the cheek for my trouble, which drew parallels with Iago's earlier desire to 'make the Moor thank me, love me, and reward me' (II.i.299). Iago's profound fear of his wife's infidelity is casually dismissed by her in a totally unexpected reference to it:

> Some such squire he was
> That turned your wit the seamy side without
> And made you to suspect me with the Moor.
> (IV.ii.144–6)

The public statement of this in front of Desdemona highlights its absurdity while also being a totally accurate reading of the situation by Emilia. The effect on my Iago, though, was devastating. I would spin round on her in shock and anger and have difficulty speaking, faltering over my words. On the ladies' exit, Emilia, having witnessed my apparent kindness to Desdemona, but being wary of physical intimacy, used her hand to transfer a grateful kiss between us, leaving me alone on stage.

I thought it would be a powerful moment to see a man momentarily at odds with himself. I wanted to hint at the possibility of a conscience in Iago, after his witnessing at first hand the effects of his plotting on Desdemona. Many killers prefer not to think of their victims as real human beings as this can trigger a moral sense within them. So I let out a gasp, contorted my body from its customary ramrod erectness, and turned upstage as if to hide the effect my internal conflict was revealing – at which point I was met by Roderigo's knife at my throat, which instantly snapped me back into the present to deal with him. Roderigo's threat to make himself known to Desdemona is his downfall, signalled by Iago's chilling 'You have said now' (IV.ii.201). After having assured Othello of Cassio's death earlier, Iago now cleverly suggests that Roderigo might perform it. But not even Shakespeare's genius can convince us that Roderigo could, or should, murder Cassio, and so he wisely has Iago take him off-stage to hear 'further reason for this' (IV.ii.242).

The third scene of Act Four presents the situation from a wholly female perspective, as well as providing a relative oasis before the on-slaught of Act Five. We also discover more about Emilia, who comes into her own as a character from this point on. She provides the nearest thing to a justification of Iago's fears by revealing herself as being capable of adultery, albeit at a supreme price. Her speech 'But I do think it is their husbands' faults / If wives do fall' (IV.iii.85 ff.), so often taken out of context and played archly, was in our production delivered so beautifully and affectingly by Rachel Joyce that I had to avoid listening to it as I stood in the wings, for fear of being moved by its sentiment. It tells obliquely of her marriage to Iago and is, regrettably, as true of many relationships today as when it was written four hundred years ago.

Act Five, Scene One is one of those breathtaking scenes where every-thing moves so fast and with such surety of purpose that it is easy to overlook the fact that it is all done with supreme economy of language. Bearing in mind that it usually takes twice as many words as the original to paraphrase Shakespeare, such was his succinctness, this achievement is all the more remarkable. Roderigo assures us that Iago has given him satisfying reasons to kill Cassio, but he is now prevented from doing this by the 'coat' of 'proof' (v.i.25–6) that Cassio wears. This protects his upper body and ensures that even Iago, seconding Roderigo's attempt, can only maim him in the chaos. Othello, mistakenly believing that Cassio has been despatched, now goes off to kill Desdemona, and it is at this point that Roderigo is murdered by Iago: in complete negation of their apparent friendship throughout the play, I cut Roderigo's throat with impersonal, ruthless efficiency. Implicating Bianca is a master-stroke – Iago having learnt earlier (IV.i.163–4) that Cassio would be dining with her that night – and sending Emilia off to tell Othello the news ensures the earliest discovery of Desdemona's murder. Covering so many bases simultaneously does not allow for complete control of the situation, which is reflected in Iago's resolved, but uncertain, exit line:

> This is the night
> That either makes me, or fordoes me quite.
> (v.i.128–9)

Although the death of Desdemona in Act Five, Scene Two is the ultimate realization of Iago's plotting, I would display a sense of disappointment on my entry into the scene, my satisfaction being tempered by an anti-climactic awareness of completion. The speed of events has taken an appreciable toll on Iago, who now crumbles before the accusatory Emilia. It is ironic that her intervention should be Iago's eventual undoing. Emilia emerges as a true heroine, a woman who, although unwittingly responsible in some part for the tragedy, is now redeemed by her selfless sacrifice. Iago is unravelling, and he lashes out wildly and ineffectively at her, thereby exposing his guilt. The man who has used his considerable verbal skill to such devastating effect throughout the play is reduced to spitting lame insults at his wife. I determined that Emilia's death should be as vicious and appropriate as possible, so I lifted her bodily from behind, thrusting my dagger up between her legs. This was an idea we had used in a production of *Titus Andronicus* years ago, and I remembered the shocking effect of it.

I think Iago's last utterance is one of his finest: prior to informing the world that he will never speak again – an extraordinary claim from such a character – he tells Othello to 'Demand me nothing; what you know, you know' (v.ii.300). This is the seal on Othello's guilt: at no point in the play did Othello have to believe Iago's insinuations; perversely, he almost wanted to believe them. Ultimately Othello didn't control his irrational jealousy and is therefore every bit as guilty as Iago. It is a chilling realization, as well as a moral warning to us all. It provides the final impetus for Othello's suicide, which I greeted with some pain. There is nothing left now for Iago, and this begs the question of whether his achievement was worth the cost.

Our production ended in a tableau, with the three dead bodies in the foreground and myself at the rear of the stage, heavily guarded and with my back to the audience. As the lights went down, I would turn slowly and regard the bodies in profile, with a deliberately neutral expression on my face. This, as I discovered through the run, was regarded variously as being sorrowful, triumphant, bewildered or empty – which shows how an audience will supply any ambiguity with an interpretation. It presented an effective closing image to a monumental play, a play that, in exploring the extremes of heroism and nihilism in the human psyche, remains a relevant, contemporary view of the beauty and the fragility of human relationships.

Cleopatra in
Antony and Cleopatra

FRANCES DE LA TOUR

FRANCES DE LA TOUR played Cleopatra in Steven Pimlott's production of *Antony and Cleopatra* at the Royal Shakespeare Theatre in the summer season of 1999 and later at the Barbican Theatre. It was her only role that season. Previous work for the RSC (in the 1960s and early 1970s) had included Audrey in *As You Like It* and Helena in Peter Brook's production of *A Midsummer Night's Dream*. For the National Theatre her many parts include the title role in *St Joan*. A wide range of theatre work in the provinces and in London (at the Almeida, the Royal Court and in the West End) has included performances of Rosalind and of Hamlet and has brought her many awards, including two Olivier Awards for best actress. Among her many television appearances are *Tom Jones, Downwardly Mobile, Duet for One* and *Rising Damp* and her films include *Rising Damp* and *The Cherry Orchard*.

I had wanted to play Cleopatra for years before the part came my way, more or less since I'd played Helena in Peter Brook's famous RSC production of *A Midsummer Night's Dream* in the early 1970s. Cleopatra is the greatest of Shakespearian tragic roles for a woman, but also funny and sexy – a wonderful combination. I had to wait for a long time, however (as one often does in British theatre), for the ambition to be realized. The notion of doing the part with Steven Pimlott as director came up when we worked together at the Old Vic at the beginning of the 1990s, and we thought at once of Alan Bates as Antony, for getting the right partner in a role like Cleopatra is obviously crucial. It was a great disappointment to learn from Alan (when we were filming together in Bulgaria) that he had been offered the part (opposite Helen Mirren) at the National Theatre. As it transpired, Alan had to withdraw from that production because of an injury and a few months later Steven Pimlott was able to take the chance that fate thus seemed to have offered, and cast us opposite each other in the title roles for the RSC. I couldn't have been more blessed: Alan brought to the role of Antony everything I hoped, and knew, he would – and more.

Apart from watching Elizabeth Taylor and Richard Burton, both looking amazing and sexy in equal measure, in the film, I knew the play in performance only from the National Theatre production, in which I had admired Helen Mirren's performance but felt (as most people did) that the relationship between her and her Antony had not really worked. The play is really Antony's tragedy: this is a man who is always on the front foot, amazed and devastated at his own loss and defeat. The actor must never suggest that he is aware of his own doom or of the futility of his attempts to save his own position. He would have ruled the Roman Empire, but for his meeting with this woman. The play tells the amazing story of the downfall of an immensely powerful man – and it is wonderful to play the cause of that downfall.

As soon as I knew that I was to play the part, I took myself off on my own to a hotel in Tenerife and started reading about the historical Cleopatra. Ninety-nine per cent of people wrongly assume that she was Egyptian. My discovery that she came from Macedonia, which is where my maternal grandfather was born, gave me an extra sense of possessiveness about her. The more I read, the more I was impressed: this was a woman of incredible political astuteness and great learning. She spoke an extraordinary range of languages, had studied physics and mathematics and learned to play the seven-string lyre, and could, apparently, seduce at will any man she chose to, though she was not a classic beauty in the Greek (and certainly not in the Egyptian) sense. To be where she was at the time of her meeting with Antony she had overcome some astonishing obstacles and been through some extraordinary experiences – including having had various people killed, some of them members of her own family. Yet so much is lost, so much unknown and enigmatic, about her – rather like Shakespeare himself, perhaps. There is one surviving little coin with her image on it, with her curly red hair, but that is about all. I enjoyed all this preliminary reading, but having done it I had largely to set it aside, for what Shakespeare didn't write about can only be of latent usefulness, touched on, perhaps, from time to time, in a line, or even in a word; but it is the text of the play that is all that really matters.

We saw a model of the set created by our wonderful designer Yolanda Sonnabend not, as usual, on the first day of rehearsals, but a few days before they began. It did not place the play in any particular time: we weren't modern, or Ancient Roman. I liked the basic idea of the set and of the costumes very much. One had to feel free with it, with its great mirrors that made it clear that these were narcissistic people, living continually within their own reflexions. I liked also the fact that it was clear that we were on a stage, in a theatre (our version of Shakespeare's 'wooden O'), and that the audience were part of that, perhaps even seeing themselves in the mirrors. I was less sure about some aspects of the costume designs, and asked for a few adaptations to the shape of some of mine, a process that Yolanda was very generous about. The changes I wanted, interestingly, were always to make Cleopatra seem more fluid; but it would have been impossible to have improved on the colours, especially the magnificent Egyptian blues, that Yolanda chose for Cleopatra's costumes. I had bought some ornamental ceramics in the same Egyptian blue whilst I was in Tenerife and the brilliant props department at Stratford had them made into a wonderful bracelet for me.

To play Cleopatra is to play a queen who seems to have regarded herself, at times, as a kind of goddess. Octavius, for example, refers at one point to her dressing up as Isis:

> She
> In th'habiliments of the goddess Isis
> That day appeared, and oft before gave audience,
> As 'tis reported, so. (III.vi.16–19)

Yet most of Cleopatra's scenes are purely domestic, and though she frequently swears by Isis, it is usually jokingly. In the last act, however, this undertone comes out, and it was very important to me to try to realize the powerful sense of ritual Egyptianness of that ending. Earlier, however, I did not feel that her queenliness should come from costumes: she may appear in a bath-robe, perhaps, or even naked, but her courtiers will go down on their knees to her as queen, whatever she wears. The play doesn't give her a sequence of scenes in which she receives other heads of state (as she frequently did – learning Persian, or whatever, for the occasion); until the last act her scenes are intimate and the regality needs to come from the way she is treated by those around her. One needs to distinguish, as Shakespeare himself shows, the difference between the authority of monarchy, of the 'divine right of kings' in the English sense, and that of the divine right of the gods, that is the pharaohs, which she embodies.

Queenliness, though, is only part of it. How does one attempt to play what Enobarbus calls her 'infinite variety' (II.ii.241); where does one look for a 'through-line'? For me, I suppose that the 'through-line' became the variety itself. With any part, even one that seems to demand something as limitless and immeasurable as 'infinite variety', one only has oneself to express what the author has provided; your access to what you are trying to convey is through your own physicality, your own thoughts, your own history, experience, appearance, sexuality. That's your base-line, and with it you have to show her turning on sixpence, charming and gracious, cruel and sharp, within a line, then sexy and involving in the next, and straight afterwards simply annihilating. The infinite variety is in the lines themselves, and one tries to bring one's own physicality to that, to show, for example, the 'glamorous' veering towards the 'tarty'. I used to spray myself with loads of perfume (the front rows must have been knocked back!) and vary the redness of my hair from scene to scene, and alter my make-up. She is one thing one moment and it's gone the next, because it's ceased to be interesting to her in the new moment: what's interesting *now* is not what I'm going to say next, nor what I've just said or how I look; or that I'm beguiling you with my scent, or that I'm touching you. It's this sense of the moment itself, and of the moment-to-moment quality of the woman, that is important: her unpredictability. She isn't contained within her own beauty, which is what a classically structured face will give you: she creates her own beauty – then breaks it. She moulds her own body, almost like plasticine, to turn herself into what the occasion, or her own inclination, demands.

Her first word in the play is 'If' – 'If it be love indeed, tell me how much' (I.i.14), so the question of the degree of confidence in Antony's love inevitably arises. I decided that she is confident that he is caught, that he has fallen for her. Any woman knows when a man has fallen; keeping him is a far bigger issue. She knows, in these circumstances (and she must have known it from the start), that the cost of wanting to keep him, and of Antony wanting to stay, will be the fall of countries, the crashing of empires – and, more particularly, the threat to her ability to keep her own empire. The growth and success of the Roman Empire is of interest to Cleopatra only if she is to become queen of it, so one has to wonder if that is her ultimate ambition. Or is her aim to prevent the Roman Empire from growing too far so that she can have her own, adjacent, empire of Egypt, Africa and the East, ruling in tandem with

Antony in the West. To play the role one needs to ask these questions, though the play provides no answers. Certainly half of her appeal to him is her power, her possessions – just as half his appeal to her is as a warrior and a ruler. It is who they are in the world that provides the mutual attraction; then comes the test of what they are like in bed.

Their mutual physical attraction to each other is both explicit and implicit throughout the play. And Antony remains capable of making decisions entirely for his own political expediency (such as marrying Octavia) which justifies her need constantly to test his commitment. As for *her* commitment to him, I never had the slightest doubt about it, though Steven Pimlott, the director (like many men in the production), was always questioning it. I'm sure that any woman would look at Cleopatra and say that this is a woman deeply, deeply in love, passionately crazy about this man. The fact that, within such a situation, she can still order her political affairs is simply what women do; they run the house, get the children to school, rule the roost – but these things do not lessen their love. A man will observe all these things getting done and conclude that love must be secondary, but this is not so; a woman knows that if she doesn't run the house – or, in Cleopatra's case, her empire – it will fail, and the man will leave. And in the end, of course, her very first utterance, 'If it be love indeed', is answered by that eternal question 'What will you do to prove your love to me? Will you die for me?' And Antony provides the ultimate answer by doing just that, though by doing so he must desert her too. Thus he leaves her in every conceivable kind of defeat, political and personal: a prisoner of war, her lover lost, her children to be taken from her. It is striking that she does not question his abandonment of her in death, but uses it as a means to be reunited with him eternally. That is the challenge of the play's final movement, to which I shall return.

As the play begins, Antony and Cleopatra are notably public in their love-making, and this was particularly so in our production. My feeling was that this was driven by him, that he needed the public demonstration, the open defiance: 'I've got these rights, these bedroom rights, these sitting-room rights, these kitchen rights, this intimacy, to do what I like with the Queen of Egypt, and I want to show it off.' She is only going along with that, making public her welcome of his affection so that her subjects will welcome him too, touch his garment in the market-place as if to say 'Our Queen loves you, so we will love you too.' The news that he is leaving, returning to Rome, sets her off in a direction

23 Frances de la Tour as Cleopatra with Alan Bates as Antony, *Antony and Cleopatra*, Act I, Scene i: 'If it be love indeed, tell me how much.'

that becomes familiar, 'quickly ill and well' (I.iii.72), luring audiences into constant wondering about when she's pretending and when she isn't. But 'I'm ill' . . . 'I'm well' mean just that: for the moment she is one, and then the other, and it is the audience that is left to do the guessing; and Antony too, of course, who is driven virtually mad by her – which is her fascination and her mystery. Shakespeare transforms Plutarch's very personal description of her excessiveness into 'infinite variety', which Enobarbus describes so vividly:

> Age cannot wither her, nor custom stale
> Her infinite variety. Other women cloy
> The appetites they feed, but she makes hungry
> Where most she satisfies; for vilest things
> Become themselves in her, that the holy priests
> Bless her when she is riggish.   (II.ii.240–5)

Antony, of course, does go to Rome. With pain, and with profound concern, Cleopatra has to let him go. The play gives no clear sense of how long he is absent: it might be just a few days, perhaps a few weeks (to give time for the marriage to Octavia), but surely not the four years that it was in history. When Antony left Cleopatra she was, in fact, pregnant; when he returned, there were four-year-old twins to greet him. Cleopatra's concern comes from not knowing how long he will be gone and from dreading a long absence. She reveals her feeling to the messengers, and although the gifts (the pearl and so on) are a partial consolation in making it clear that he is thinking of her, what is more important to her than any pearl is how he looked when he was sending it, the expression on his face. She is listless in this section of the play, unable to find anything – fishing, billiards, whatever – that engages her while the energy of action is elsewhere, in Rome, or on Pompey's galley.

Cleopatra, in short, is politically sidelined for a while, and I found that this rather extends to the way one feels as the player of the role: I remember feeling jealous, annoyed and angry with all those chaps enjoying themselves in the galley scene. The response, of course, is to become very intimate with your household, which I did. I was blessed with lovely actors here, and could play with them like toys, to hit or to kiss, trying to get through the great gulf of Antony's absence. She misses him, desperately. I used to wish that Shakespeare had followed history and written her pregnant, which would at least have given me a bit more to act, something more defined than mere frustration – and yet what stronger motivation could the actor playing Cleopatra require than the absence of the object of her desire?

The tone of the two scenes with the messenger who brings news of Antony's marriage to Octavia wasn't at all easy to find. These scenes are there for light relief in juxtaposition to the politics of Antony's life in Rome. And yet these domestic insights into Cleopatra's life in Egypt, deserted by her Antony, reveal more vividly than anything else in the play her capacity to instil terror. If the messenger does not show constant awareness of this, the scene is lost – for she is, after all, however childishly she is here behaving, still Queen of Egypt. In a sense the laughter in these scenes is at Cleopatra's expense, and though the audience is also laughing at the messenger's predicament, the actor playing the messenger cannot for one second allow him to be aware that he is funny. He must be terrified – petrified, indeed – and imagining himself being tarred and feathered and his head coming off as he desperately tries to think of what he can say to please her. Cleopatra, throughout the episode, is at her most unpredictable, promising him reward one moment, savage punishment the next. She remains in control: we may laugh at her when she learns that Octavia is thirty, but she always retains the upper hand, the ability to allow people to laugh right at her and then, suddenly, to turn the tables on them, slicing through the laughter as if to say 'this isn't funny'. That is power; that is control. Of course she is also vulnerable (which is the other side of control) and desperate to hang on, but her brilliance is revealed in the way she uses that vulnerability (which is indisputably there for all to witness) and how she conquers it – and then moves on. It is all part of the infinite variety.

Before the play moves to the great battle sequence, there is Octavius's description of Antony and Cleopatra being crowned in Alexandria:

> I'th'market-place on a tribunal silvered,
> Cleopatra and himself in chairs of gold
> Were publicly enthroned; at their feet sat
> Caesarion, whom they call my father's son,
> And all the unlawful issue that their lust
> Since then hath made between them. Unto her
> He gave the stablishment of Egypt, made her
> Of lower Syria, Cyprus, Lydia,
> Absolute queen.   (III.vi.3–11)

This is a scene of Egyptian ritual seen through Roman eyes. The speech seems to me one of the most important in the play. At one time I wanted Antony and Cleopatra to appear on the stage, behind the mirrors, so that the audience would see us thus enthroned. Guy Henry, who played Octavius, used to do the speech extremely well; it's not very long, yet it seems to me to describe something absolutely crucial for Cleopatra. This is what Antony has done for her: he has left Octavia, come back to Egypt, and here, in public, has placed himself and her on golden thrones, with all their children, and made Cleopatra queen over all those countries. As I listened to the speech over the tannoy I used to think 'that's her – *that's* Cleopatra'. I used to long to try to present that on stage – as, indeed, I think they had done in the preceding RSC production of the play. Instead the two of them are given what seems quite a casual, low-key scene, without any sense of reunion after long separation, let alone golden-throned ritual; just a brief, but nevertheless crucial, meeting with Enobarbus. One can only play, after all, what is written, and here, once more, is the dramatist surprising us – and his characters again showing themselves to be unpredictable. I remember, during one of the rehearsals, that I came on for that entrance with a doll wrapped up in a blanket to suggest her as mother (to Antony's children), but Alan (Antony) and Steven (our director) just stopped dead; their jaws dropped and they burst out laughing – and then gently reminded me that the scene takes place on a battlefield and that, anyway, Shakespeare didn't write that.

No matter how much we talked about the decision to fight at sea at Actium, no matter how much I had read about it, the question of why Cleopatra wants a naval battle remained unanswered. Enobarbus, always sensible and reliable, knows perfectly well that Antony's strength is on land – and says so. Could Cleopatra really have thought that her fleet, without the fleets of her other kingdoms, was powerful enough: 'I have sixty sails, Caesar none better' (III.vii.49)? But if one cannot answer the question of why she wants to fight at sea, no more can one know why she flees in the middle of the battle. Is it simply fear, the realization that she is not winning and that she needs to get out before she is killed – and, with that, a regret that she ever started it in the first place? The play, enigmatic as it so often is, does not allow us to answer these questions – and, historically, then and now, they remain unanswered. Perhaps Shakespeare is simply wanting to present again her wilfulness, Antony's growing dependence on her, and Enobarbus's astuteness. Whatever the explanation, what we see is her making the wrong decision and Antony making things far worse by following her. Through such mistakes are wars, and empires, won and lost.

The humiliation, however, produces a wonderful scene as they come together in defeat:

> Fall not a tear, I say; one of them rates
> All that is won and lost. Give me a kiss.
> Even this repays me.   (III.x.69–71)

In our production we discovered through rehearsal an exit for the two of them in which Antony three-quarters carried, one quarter dragged me off stage in a sort of clumsy piggy-back. It was, at once, an image both of ruin and of mutual interdependence. The scene again shows her wonderful power, and her completeness. What she says is so brief, and so simple:

> O my lord, my lord,
> Forgive my fearful sails! I little thought
> You would have followed . . . O, my pardon!
>   (III.x.54–6, 61)

That's all it is, but it takes bigness to say something like that, for a person in power just to apologize, without trying to invent excuses. Can you imagine any modern politician saying 'I'm terribly sorry, but I got that completely wrong'? Her apology also makes it plain that she does not know what to do without him – that she does not know what to do at all – and from his acceptance of it we know that he doesn't either. 'What do we do now? Well, we'll try to pick ourselves up . . .':

> Some wine, within there, and our viands! Fortune knows
> We scorn her most when most she offers blows.
>   (III.x.73–4)

And like a couple of old turtles who have lost their way, heading inland instead of back down the beach to the sea, they go off directionless. But defeat has made no difference to their love – something I always found interesting in relation to those comments that imply that Cleopatra has taken Antony as her lover solely because of his political power. Here, at this turning point, she knows, and the audience knows, that she loves him – loves him perhaps even more – in defeat. And that clumsy and awkward exit that we found, that image of love, and defeat, and mutual commitment, that image of two broken souls, days of wine and roses over, that turning point in their relationship, marked the interval in our production.

Cleopatra's next scene is with Caesar's messenger Thidias. She may be genuinely interested in doing a deal with him, or just testing the water, or merely pretending in order to buy time – and, as ever with Cleopatra, these are not necessarily mutually exclusive choices. In a sense she's flirting with Thidias, and interested in a deal with Caesar, not at all because she doesn't love Antony, but because it's possible that a deal might save them both. She certainly needs to know whether she can get access to Caesar, how much ground there is for her to play on, how much of her own power she may be allowed to keep. Might there be a chance, given their almost (but not quite) complete defeat, of her being allowed to go to live quietly with Antony somewhere in exile? She knows, right from the time of Actium, that they are in fact finished, militarily and politically, but she needs to know how far she can go with Caesar and what place in the scheme of things there may be for her, and for Antony. The question we don't know the answer to is what she would do if Caesar offered terms acceptable to her but not to Antony, which is what Caesar is getting at when he says

> For Antony
> I have no ears to his request. The Queen
> Of audience nor desire shall fail, so she
> From Egypt drive her all-disgracèd friend.
> (III.xii.19–22)

Would she make some sort of suicide pact with Antony (which is basically what emerges, perhaps partly by accident, at the end), or is she going to safeguard herself for her posterity and her children? As usual in playing the role I felt that to answer the question too definitively was inappropriate: she is, as usual, playing it for the moment. Thidias arrives, bringing Caesar's respects, including kissing her hand. She allows him that intimacy, of course – in order to find out what she wants, and needs, to know. I think she would sleep with Caesar if it was necessary to her political and personal future. But the question of precisely what she wants from Caesar remains unanswered.

Antony's challenge, however, provokes a very clear response from her. He tells her what he understands to be Caesar's terms:

> To the boy Caesar send this grizzled head,
> And he will fill thy wishes to the brim
> With principalities.   (III.xiii.17–19)

It always seemed to me that her reply expressed complete incomprehension and incredulity: '*That* head, my lord?' – 'you really didn't ever think I could have done that . . . or *did* you?', she seems to me to say, 'when you are me and we are one'. And after Antony's rage at Thidias she asks that wonderful question: 'Not know me yet?' (III.xiii.157). Is she knowable? 'Do you really think', she might be asking him, 'that whatever I do – which might include sleeping with Caesar if that would produce some political advantage for us – that I could ever betray you?' And the answer, I was sure, from start to finish of the run of our production, is 'never, never, never'. But the men in our acting company, including Alan and Steven, were never so sure.

The episode of the 'sad captains' (III.xiii.183) marks another stage on the journey to the end. But still it doesn't necessarily mean that the end is inevitably death. Cleopatra and Antony might still be allowed to live privately together somewhere, and even as late as the Proculeius scene she is talking about keeping Egypt for her son, though it is to be under the dominion of Rome (v.ii.18–21). There is a strong sense in Cleopatra of the significance of her own heritage, of her responsibility for preserving the inheritance of the Ptolemies. She sees herself absolutely as a subject of the Egyptian gods, given power by them to rule as Egypt's queen. 'You lie, up to the hearing of the gods', she says to Dolabella (v.ii.95) when he denies the existence of the Antony she has dreamt of; and she means it, literally. These things are of enormous significance to her, and though the play provides only a line or two here and there to present them, I believe they are immensely significant and powerful.

During this scene of the farewell to the captains, Enobarbus and I used to exchange a look as Antony told them

> Thou hast been rightly honest. So hast thou;
> Thou, and thou, and thou. You have served me well,
> And kings have been your fellows.   (IV.ii.11–13)

The text offers two very similar asides from Cleopatra to Enobarbus; 'What means this?' and 'What does he mean?' (IV.ii.13, 23). We cut the first, but somehow the question was there in the look that I gave Enobarbus. Malcolm Storry, who played Enobarbus, would just stand there, looking awkward, seeming to be well aware of the act of treachery that he was about to commit, and I would look at him, knowing the answer to the unspoken 'What means this?' That unspoken moment was very important for the two of us, a sort of farewell from me to Enobarbus, sensing his betrayal, though how well it read in the vast spaces of the RST and the Barbican Theatre I do not know. We needed close-up at this point, Malcolm and I, but that's a lame excuse. There might have been a movement away, perhaps, something to indicate her premonition; but it is to Antony that attention must go – and that's the brilliance of the scene. Antony does all the talking and is almost girlish in his sweetness to his servants at this moment of sharing with them the loss of his power and command, while Enobarbus and Cleopatra remain more or less silent, watching him as he seems to be losing his manhood before her eyes.

For the last movement of the play Cleopatra withdraws to her monument. The scene-change worked perfectly for me in our production. We rehearsed the play more or less in sequence, so it was late in the process before we reached these scenes. I immediately found myself loving the music that accompanied the walls' going up, and the creation of desolation that preceded this sequence. There were moments when I wished that the carpet we'd been playing on for so long would disappear too, but that's the sort of luxury that can only happen when you're on film. That Cleopatra should have a candle was an idea that came to me one day in rehearsal: of course there must be an eternal flame in this monument. Sand, too, seemed important. Cleopatra, I had read, had her own private beach, which on one occasion she had dyed violet in accordance with her whim – the extraordinary imagination of the woman never ceased to amaze me. And so flame, and sand, seemed to be important symbols for this last movement of the play. I wanted everything to come together here: the gods, the pharaohs, Isis, a lost civilization, ancient Egypt crumbling before the new world order of Rome. Of course I couldn't have a violet beach, but I could have a bowl of sand which I could sprinkle in a circle, symbolizing the desert sands, the pyramids, the images of Egypt we all have. The circle represented the circle of life, so important in ancient Egyptian rituals of Isis, and

24 Frances de la Tour as Cleopatra with Rachel Joyce (left) as Charmian and
Hermione Gulliford (right) as Iras, *Antony and Cleopatra*, Act v, Scene ii:
'And it is great / To do that thing that ends all other deeds.'

the candle-flame I thought of as Antony incarnate. At the beginning
of the scene I was without make-up and wore a stocking-top over my
hair, the image of despair and desolation completed by an old brown
dressing-gown of a robe, like something from a Buddhist monastery. I
felt the need for an action that was ritualistic, but intimate and gentle,
to set the tone for this scene, so water and a sponge came into the rehearsal. I wasn't sure what I was going to do with them, or, at that stage,
with the sand, but they came like moments of truth, and we used them,
with Charmian and Iras kneeling beside me within the circle of sand,
and bending over so that I could bathe, or anoint, the backs of their
necks, a ritual that became preparatory to my making up. 'Show me,
my women, like a queen', she says (v.ii.227), and it's no good looking
like a queen at the beginning, when she's desolate.

But later she needs to get her face on – and who, in all history, have
been more famous for make-up than the ancient Egyptians? Some years
before I'd had to do a make-up without a mirror on stage looking out at
the audience as if they were the mirror and applying a sort of Japanese

warrior make-up. It's frightening, but I knew it could be done, and here it seemed absolutely right that the audience should see an actress making up in front of them on stage, representing the Queen of Egypt making herself look like the Queen of Egypt again. 'Show me, my women, like a queen': she's going to dress up to the nines for the arrival of Caesar, so that when he finds her dead, she'll be looking like a million dollars. Those moments of putting on the Egyptian eye make-up, gold powder, and so on, were played in complete silence; but a minute and a half of complete silence is a long time in the theatre, so I had to do it as quickly as I could and sometimes the effect was a little skew-whiff. But I think audiences were impressed by the stillness and by the ritual dignity, especially coming after the distinctly undignified death of Antony.

At Stratford we played much of the scene of Antony's death with Cleopatra sitting on his lap, like a little girl with her daddy. At the Barbican we played it lying down on stage together. A number of other things had developed by the time we moved to London. The opening scene at Stratford was very intimate, and may even have been shocking for some people. In London it was more ritualistic and formal; and yet at the very end of the play I was completely naked for the briefest of moments before the golden robe was put on:

> Give me my robe; put on my crown; I have
> Immortal longings in me.   (v.ii.279–80)

This sharpest of contrasts was important to me: Cleopatra as a woman, mortal in every sense, on the one hand, and on the other Cleopatra immortalized as an icon and a legend.

In his death-scene Antony wants Cleopatra to remember him in more dignified moments:

> The miserable change now at my end
> Lament nor sorrow at, but please your thoughts
> In feeding them with those my former fortunes
> Wherein I lived; the greatest prince o'th'world,
> The noblest . . .   (IV.xv.51–5)

But all this coughing and slow dying, this 'of many thousand kisses the poor last' (IV.xv.20), this glass of wine – the poor last of many too, the way we played it – could hardly be less glorious or less dignified. Cleopatra's decision, at the end of the scene, to die 'after the high Roman fashion' (IV.xv.86) embraces Roman attitudes to suicide that were quite contrary to those of ancient Egypt; but it is a decision that evinces also, of course, a determination to die in 'high' style, in contrast to the way Antony has just met his end. In this moment of deepest desolation she decides – and I believe it's a decision made here suddenly, on the spur of the moment – on a death-scene for herself that will be absolutely ritualistic. We know how fond she was of being Queen of Egypt: her death is going to provide a final ritual affirmation of that, and she is going to be in absolute control of it.

Before we get there, she has her meeting with Dolabella, Caesar's envoy. The question of what she is still seeking politically here, just before the end, is fascinatingly elusive. Colin Mace, who played Dolabella, responded wonderfully to my speech about Antony, seeming, through his listening, to be saying 'how wonderful that there is a woman who can so daringly describe the man of her dreams in this way – how attractive, how enticing!'. His response to my description of Antony's 'delights' being 'dolphin-like' (v.ii.88–9) – which always seemed to me to allude to him in bed, showing his back above the element – was to suggest that I was telling him something altogether too personal. The audience is here lulled both by the beauty of Cleopatra's description of Antony and by the enormous intimacy of this exchange:

> Think you there was, or might be such a man
> As this I dreamt of? (v.ii.93–4)

Cleopatra asks; to which Dolabella replies 'Gentle madam, no.' And then, suddenly, she breaks the mood with 'You lie, up to the hearing of the gods' (v.ii.95) – her unpredictability again. She flirts with him, revealing her very soul, and as if on cue he then lets her know that she is breaking his heart:

> Would I might never
> O'ertake pursued success but I do feel,
> By the rebound of yours, a grief that smites
> My very heart at root. (v.ii.102–5)

And that is exactly what she wanted. Then, when she knows she's got him, she asks what Caesar is going to do with her: 'He'll lead me, then, in triumph?', and he's caught now, and can't escape telling her: 'Madam, he will. I know't' (v.ii.109–10).

227

I sometimes wondered if audiences realized the full horror and degradation implied by being led in chains, in shackles, through the streets of Rome, with her children, hers and Antony's children, in a Roman triumph, so I used to burst into tears at that point to indicate her desperation. This is something she cannot accept; her life may be saved, but there will be nothing for her son and the line of the Ptolemies will be wiped out. With deep sexual disgust she imagines the 'saucy lictors' catching at her body (v.ii.214) and the joke about the 'squeaking Cleopatra' (v.ii.220) is a splendidly Shakespearian risk at this point – but is also simply true, for she was indeed portrayed as a whore for God knows how many centuries. And then one goes back to the very beginning, and to 'If it be love indeed' (i.i.14), and asks what she is choosing here: to die in order to avoid being captured and humiliated, or to die in order to be with Antony in an afterlife. Perhaps it is both, and perhaps that is how all questions about her are finally to be answered.

With Caesar's arrival the questions continue, above all in the wonderfully enigmatic episode of Seleucos the treasurer: is she in collusion with him, he putting on an act of tripping her up so that Caesar will be misled into supposing that there's obviously no suicide plot; or is this a genuine moment of disloyalty for Seleucos and exposure for her? We thought about this a lot, and made a conscious decision not to be emphatic either way, but to play the truth of the lines – the apparent truth, that is – emphatically. Andrew Bone, who played Seleucos, actually came to my dressing room one evening to ask whether we really ought not to make up our minds, and I just replied 'But who *knows* which it is?' I think, however, that there was probably always a look in my eyes that hinted 'maybe we planned this' as I yelled at him in front of Caesar:

> O slave, of no more trust
> Than love that's hired! What, goest thou back? Thou shalt
> Go back, I warrant thee; but I'll catch thine eyes,
> Though they had wings.   (v.ii.154–7)

The episode is yet another example of that 'infinite variety' that has dominated this essay and our treatment of it was just one more of the things that made us utterly committed to every moment – and in this play it's absolutely essential that things are contradicted from moment to moment. And why should Caesar understand Egypt anyway – for 'Egypt' is who and what Cleopatra is: 'I am dying, Egypt, dying' (IV.xv.41). Her meeting with Caesar is conducted with all the superficial courtesies, but when he has gone Cleopatra describes the event brilliantly: 'He words me, girls, he words me' (v.ii.191). She sees plainly that he's been trying to pull the wool over her eyes, that he's been sweet-talking her, but (like all politicians) the more polite, the more ingratiating, he was, the more he dodged all the questions and the less he was to be trusted.

The death-scene itself begins with the audience anticipating something solemn: 'Now from head to foot / I am marble constant', she says (v.ii.239–40), and this is where we expect the aria, the big speech that is going to make her a legend, an icon. And just as the handkerchiefs are coming out in preparation, Shakespeare wrong-foots us all again, and on comes the clown to take over the scene with all his smutty jokes in response to her worries about whether it will hurt or not. Even after that, and after the solemn dressing-up for death, we aren't allowed to settle into the anticipated moment of solemnity, for Iras's death sends Cleopatra off into a fit of jealous anxiety:

> If she first meet the curlèd Antony,
> He'll make demand of her, and spend that kiss
> Which is my heaven to have. (v.ii.300–2)

Our laughter (and it's inevitable) at this moment is even more extraordinary than our earlier laughter at the clown; and then, just ten lines before her death, we are yet again invited to laugh – and *at* her rather than with her – as she desperately grabs the asp to try to catch up with Iras:

> Come, thou mortal wretch,
> With thy sharp teeth this knot intrinsicate
> Of life at once untie. (v.ii.303–5)

This is brilliant writing. Of course Shakespeare could have conducted the audience through a vale of tears to a predictable conclusion; but the manipulation is much cleverer than that, with the audience, wrong-footed, being swung between emotional extremes all the way to the end. If it is not played with all the energy and commitment that it demands, then we cannot understand Antony's downfall: for this is, after all, the story of Antony – and Cleopatra.

At the very end of the play the audience is finally invited, it seems to me, to give their unequivocal sympathy to Cleopatra. They may, and probably do, think that she is impossible, but they cannot but salute her for the joy, and the sadness, that she has given them, and the vast range of feelings that she has revealed. So many women who came to see the play told me how surprised they had been by the fact that Shakespeare should show us a woman behaving like that, how astounded they were by the wonderful outrageousness of the role. It isn't sympathy so much that the part demands; it's celebration. The source of that celebration, of course, is our awareness of its inspiration in Antony; if we were simply shown a passionate woman it would mean nothing, but we are given the source and inspiration of her passion, and that alters everything, allowing us to understand it. I think this is why the word 'husband' waits until the very end:

> Husband, I come.
> Now to that name my courage prove my title!
> (v.ii.286–7)

The audience, I'm convinced, is left knowing why she loved this man, and how much; and why, at the last, she understood how much he loved her. That is why we salute her, and celebrate her love. And perhaps that is what finally annoys historians, for historians need to insist that there are rebellions, and governments, and empires to deal with, and although Shakespeare put his play in that context, overall he seems to want us to concentrate on the love affair. The whole course of history, and the division between East and West and all that it still means in today's world, might have been totally different but for the Battle of Actium and the eastward spread of the Roman Empire; but Shakespeare, when all is said, is writing a love story. The 'time of universal peace' (IV.vi.5) may be near, but 'Husband, I come' is finally where he wants our focus and our fascination to lie. 'This is', Shakespeare seems to have said to himself, 'one of the greatest love stories ever told, and I am one of the greatest writers – so I'll tell it!'

Production credits

Productions are listed in the order of essays in this volume. Dates are those of the first preview performance, with the press performance usually a week or so later. Seven of the productions (*The Comedy of Errors*, *A Midsummer Night's Dream*, *Twelfth Night*, *Romeo and Juliet*, *Timon of Athens*, *Othello*, and *Antony and Cleopatra*) were part of RSC summer seasons in Stratford, playing there in repertoire during the summer before moving for a short run in Newcastle-upon-Tyne and thence to a season at the Barbican in London; *A Midsummer Night's Dream* later played also at the Brooklyn Academy of Music in New York. Of the other five productions, *Hamlet* was a National Theatre production, opening at the Lyttleton Theatre and returning there again for an extended period in repertoire between playing a series of national and international touring venues; *The Tempest* was one of the RSC's regular regional touring productions, opening at the Pit Theatre (Barbican) before moving to The Other Place at Stratford and thence to a national and international tour; *The Winter's Tale* was part of an RSC winter season, opening at the Royal Shakespeare Theatre in Stratford and then moving to the Barbican Theatre in London; *Macbeth*, also part of an RSC winter season, opened at the Swan Theatre in Stratford before a national and international tour, a season at the Young Vic in London, and a video; *King Lear*, which opened at the Saitama Arts Theatre, Tokyo, before moving to the Barbican Theatre and thence to the Royal Shakespeare Theatre in Stratford, was a joint production of the RSC and Thelma Holt Ltd, with the Sainokuni Shakespeare Company.

The Tempest
Pit Theatre (Barbican), 20 October 2000
Director: James MacDonald
Designer (set and video): Jeremy Herbert
Costumes: Kandis Cook
Lighting: Nigel Edwards
Music: Orlando Gough
Choreography: Peter Darling
Sound: Rebecca Watts

The Comedy of Errors
RST, 11 April 2000
Director: Lynne Parker
Designer: Blaithin Sheerin
Lighting: Tina MacHugh
Music and Sound: Bell Helicopter
Fights: Terry King

A Midsummer Night's Dream
RST, 19 March 1999
Director: Michael Boyd
Designer: Tom Piper
Lighting: Chris Davey
Music: John Woolf
Movement: Liz Ranken
Fights: Terry King
Sound: Mic Pool

Twelfth Night
RST, 13 April 2001
Director: Lindsay Posner
Designer: Ashley Martin-Davies
Lighting: Pat Collins
Music: Gary Yershon
Movement: Jane Gibson
Fights: Renny Krupinski
Sound: Mic Pool

The Winter's Tale
RST, 10 December 1998
Director: Gregory Doran
Designer: Robert Jones
Lighting: Tim Mitchell
Music: Ilona Sekacz
Movement: Siân Williams
Sound: Andrea J. Cox

Macbeth
Swan Theatre, 2 November 1999
Director: Gregory Doran
Designer: Stephen Brimson Lewis
Lighting: Tim Mitchell

Music: Adrian Lee
Movement: Siân Williams
Fights: Terry King
Sound: John A. Leonard

Romeo and Juliet
RST, 23 June 2000
Director: Michael Boyd
Designer: Tom Piper
Lighting: Chris Davey
Music: Stephen Warbeck
Movement: Liz Ranken
Fights: Terry King
Sound: Mic Pool

Timon of Athens
RST, 7 August 1999
Director: Gregory Doran
Designer: Stephen Brimson Lewis
Lighting: Howard Harrison
Music: Duke Ellington
Movement: Siân Williams
Fights: Terry King
Sound: Tim Oliver

Hamlet
Lyttleton Theatre (National Theatre), 15 July 2000
Director: John Caird
Designer: Tim Hatley
Lighting: Paul Pyant
Music: John Cameron
Fights: Terry King
Sound: Christopher Shutt

King Lear
Saitama Arts Theatre, Tokyo, 22 September 1999
Director: Yukio Ninagawa
Designer: Yukio Horio
Costumes: Lily Komine
Lighting: Tamotsu Harada
Associate Director: David Hunt
Music: Ryudo Uzaki

Movement: Suketaro Hanayagi
Fights: Masahiro Kunii
Sound: Masahiro Inoue

Othello
RST, 9 April 1999
Director: Michael Attenborough
Designer: Robert Jones
Lighting: Peter Mumford
Music: George Fenton
Fights: Terry King
Sound: Charles Horne

Antony and Cleopatra
RST, 11 June 1999
Director: Steven Pimlott
Designer: Yolanda Sonnabend
Lighting: Hugh Vanstone
Music: Jason Carr
Movement: Sue Lefton
Fights: Malcolm Ranson
Sound: Andrea J. Cox